The Wings of Change

The Army Air Force Experience in Texas
During World War II

Military History of Texas Series: Number Two

The Military History of Texas Series tells the colorful, dynamic, and heroic stories of the state's soldiers, battles, and battlefields from Spanish times to the present. The series promotes the larger mission of the McWhiney Foundation Press: to encourage traditional narratives and make history accessible to the broadest audience possible.

Donald S. Frazier
General Editor

The Military History of Texas Series is funded in part by grants from the Carl B. and Florence E. King Foundation and the Summerfield G. Roberts Foundation.

Cover: A neatly aligned flight of training planes heads toward the Gulf of Mexico from Houston's Ellington Field.
Courtesy Texas Military Forces Museum, Austin, Texas.

The Wings of Change

The Army Air Force Experience in Texas
During World War II

Thomas E. Alexander

MCWHINEY FOUNDATION PRESS
MCMURRY UNIVERSITY
ABILENE, TEXAS

Library of Congress Cataloging-in-Publication Data

Alexander, Thomas E., 1931-
    The wings of change : the Army Air Force experience during World War
II / Thomas E. Alexander.
       p. cm. -- (Military history of Texas series ; no. 2)
Includes bibliographical references and index.
    ISBN 1-893114-35-X (hardcover)
1. World War, 1939-1945--Texas. 2. United States. Army Air
Forces--History--World War, 1939-1945. 3. Texas--History--1846-1950.
I. Title. II. Series.
    D769.85.T4A44 2003
    976.4'062--dc21

                                              2003000904

McMurry Station, Box 637
Abilene, TX 79697-0637

Printed in the United States of America

ISBN 1-893114-35-X
10 9 8 7 6 5 4 3 2 1

Book Designed by Rosenbohm Graphic Design

All inquiries regarding volume purchases of this book should be addressed to
McWhiney Foundation Press, McMurry Station, Box 637,
Abilene, TX 79697-0637.
Telephone inquiries may be made by calling (915) 793-4682

C O N T E N T S

LIST OF MAPS AND PHOTOGRAPHS

Maps

M-1   The State of Texas including locations of all World War II Army airfields

M-2   The East including San Antonio (Kelly and Randolph Fields), Hondo, Greenville (Majors Field), Austin (Bergstrom Field), and Houston (Ellington Field)

M-3   North Texas including Dallas (Love Field) and Fort Worth

M-4   On the Border including Harlingen, Laredo, Del Rio (Laughlin Army Airfield), and El Paso (Biggs Army Airfield)

M-5   The West including Fort Stockton (Gibbs Field), Marfa, Midland/Odessa, and Pyote

M-6   Panhandle/Plains including Sweetwater (Avenger Field), Lubbock, Amarillo, Pampa, and Dalhart

Photographs

Section A   Kelly Field, Randolph Field, Hondo Army Airfield, Majors Field, Bergstrom Field, Ellington Field, Love Field, Fort Worth Army Airfield, Harlingen Army Airfield, Laredo Army Airfield, Laughlin Army Airfield, and Biggs Army Airfield

Section B   Gibbs Field, Marfa Army Airfield, Midland Army Airfield, Pyote Army Airfield, Avenger Field, Lubbock Army Airfield, Amarillo Army Airfield, Pampa Army Airfield, and Dalhart Army Airfield

FOREWORD

During my tenure as commander of the United States Air Force Education and Training Command at Randolph Field, I regularly reminded the members of the command that "Change is inevitable, growth is optional." When considering the history of the U. S. Air Force and its predecessors, one quickly concludes that both the Air Force and Texas changed rapidly and grew as a result of the number of training bases established in the state before and during World War II.

Tom Alexander has done a masterful job of researching and capturing the lasting impacts of establishing and operating training bases which frequently doubled the population of the cities, towns, and communities in which the bases were built. Such rapid growth in most Texas cities created massive economic challenges and opportunities for the entire region. The ensuing influx of people from all sections of the United States also resulted in rapid social and cultural change within the communities as the military personnel and the local populace worked together to defeat common enemies.

Even in those days the Pentagon didn't simply decide that a particular town was the perfect location for a training base—there were hundreds of ideal locations in the state. Towns were most frequently selected because the townspeople and their congressional delegation, spurred on by one or more local business leaders, convinced Army leaders that "this is the place you need to be."

As one may expect, such rapid expansion always created problems for both the community and the military that were "shoe-horned" in on short notice. In this book, those problems, the solutions, and the resulting impact on all parties are presented from the views of people who were there and who were directly impacted. All speak in a positive manner of the compromises made by all parties involved.

Texas, and the Air Force, changed and grew as a direct result of the bases in the state. In that same vein, hundreds of thousands and perhaps millions of men and women from across this great nation have lasting, and mostly pleasant, memories of the sacrifices made by the great patriots in this state who opened their communities and their homes to the fly-boys (and fly-girls) the war had brought to their doorsteps.

The Air Force of today owes much of its success to the values and attitudes set in place half a century ago by the aviation pioneers who came to Texas and by the Texans who were determined that there should be growth with this change. To the extent of my knowledge, *The Wings of Change* is the first book to fully underscore the immense importance of this critical yet colorful chapter in our history.

Gen. Billy J. Boles
USAF (Ret.)

A C K N O W L E D G M E N T S

There is absolutely no way to properly acknowledge each of the many lovers of history who helped make this work possible. With sincere apologies to those not included in this necessarily short list, here are the major contributors:

• Bruce Ashcroft, of the Air Education and Training Command History Office at Randolph Field, who once again used his magical computer to discover all but forgotten links to the past

• Betty and Bill Hargus, of Fort Stockton, who preserve and nourish the legacy of that city's wartime airfield

• Elizabeth Heath, archivist and guardian angel of the history of Ward County and its legendary Rattlesnake Bomber Base

• Rick Doehne and Dave Campbell, of the University of Texas Lands System, who took time to conduct a memorable tour of what was once upon a time Pyote Army Airfield

• Joe Moreno, of the Laredo Public Library's History Department, who scoured his collection to find long-hidden nuggets about the city's little-known World War II airbase

• Former WASPs Rosa Lea (Fullwood) Meeks Dickerson and Florene (Miller) Watson, who shared their very clear memories of what it was like to fly the most challenging Army airplanes in what had traditionally been solely a man's sky

• Paul O. Russell, a veteran of Del Rio's Laughlin Field, who apparently has kept every single one of his Air Force notes and logs so that he can share their lore with others

• A.C. Greene, the late "Dean of Texas Letters," whose kind words of praise made this lesser author's spirits soar higher than any Army airplane ever could

• Stanley Marcus, the sorely missed Texas icon, who for over thirty years was a friend and mentor, and who contributed to this book even though his own pen is now forever stilled

• Finally, a special toast to my wife Capy, who as key researcher, fierce editor, and best friend ever, makes a valiant and loving effort to guide me through the swamp of egregious error. That I flounder there with distressing regularity, however, is totally my own doing, but I am so glad she keeps trying. For that and countless other reasons, this book is dedicated to her.

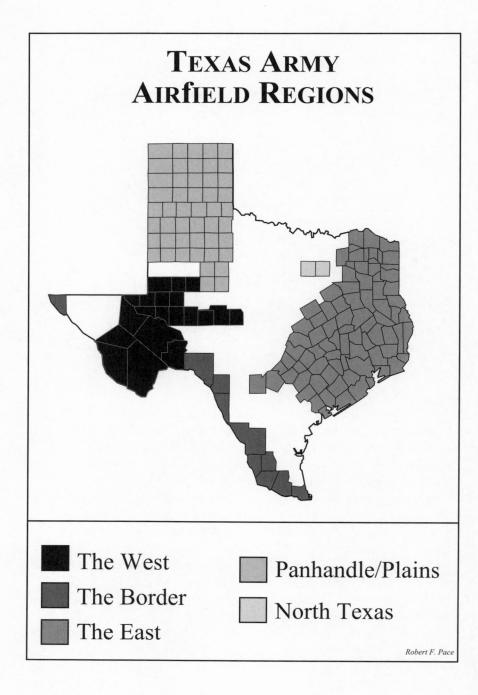

TEXAS ARMY
AIRFIELD REGIONS

The West

The Border

The East

Panhandle/Plains

North Texas

Robert F. Pace

CHAPTER ONE

THE PASSING PARADE

No matter how far we may wander, Texas lingers with us,
coloring our perceptions of the world.

Elmer Kelton
San Angelo, Texas

Throughout its long and colorful history, the destiny of Texas has been almost constantly altered by various and powerful military influences. The consequences of those influences have sometimes been dire but more often positive and long enduring in terms of social, economic, cultural, and political significance. While each visiting military force has in its own way left a collective footprint on the soul of Texas, the changes brought about by the United States Army Air Force during World War II were arguably the most profound in the modern history of the state.

In the sixteenth century, Spain sent her legions of conquistadors to what would eventually become the Lone Star State in a sometimes ruthless search for new converts to Christianity, great quantities of gold, and martial glory for her soldiers. As the years passed, French and, later, Mexican troopers arrived to either explore or defend their respective nations' interests in this new world of opportunity. When Texas became one of the United States in 1845 following its brief period as a Republic, U. S. Army forces marched down her roads to do battle with Mexico, ostensibly to ensure the permanence of the newest American state, all the while not so subtly laying another cornerstone for U. S. President James A. Polk's policy of Manifest Destiny.

During America's great Civil War that soon came about at least in part because of Mr. Polk's policy, gray clad Confederate troopers replaced soldiers in Union blue at frontier outposts across Texas. When victorious Federal forces returned from the Civil War in 1865, a framework of military socioeconomic influence was put in place that would alternately expand and contract over the next century and a half, before reaching its zenith during the tumultuous years of World War II.

In his outstanding study of the historic beginning of this enduring framework, Thomas T. Smith meticulously traces the bonding created between federal forts along the Texas frontier and nearby civilian communities that looked to the Army for both military protection and economic survival if not economic wealth and expansion.[1] The emerging pattern so well identified in Smith's work became even more apparent in Texas during World War II, as towns and cities again turned to the Army to provide fiscal well being — this time, however, in the form of military airfields rather than frontier outposts.

The broad scope of the socioeconomic impact that stemmed directly from such airfields is the subject of this book. Not only did the many wartime Army air bases bring a sudden and highly welcome end to a smothering financial stagnation that had plagued the state for nearly a decade, they also brought about a social awakening and infusion of fresh thought that served to thrust much of Texas, particularly the more isolated rural parts of it, into the twentieth century. Because that century was already 41 percent complete when the war began, the immediate impact of the newly arrived military presence on the long established way of life becomes even more starkly dramatic in retrospect.

Here, then, is the story of Texas in the early 1940s and its fateful yet fascinating relationship with the United States Army Air Force, a relationship that rapidly proved to be a primary factor in changing the face of the Lone Star State.

Texas 1940

*The people of Texas look back to a remarkable past; they look
forward to a promising future.*

> Ralph W. Steen
> *Twentieth Century Texas*
> July 4, 1942

Such great military captains as Francisco Vasquez de Coronado,
René Robert Cavelier, Sieur de La Salle, Zachary Taylor, and Antonio
Lopez de Santa Anna painfully came to realize during their careers
that Texas was, is, and will likely always be a very large place indeed.
By 1940, although somewhat diminished from its glory days as a
Republic, the state still encompassed over 263,000 square miles,
measuring roughly 820 miles from east to west and 875 miles from
its northernmost border to its southern tip. It was, as any true Texan
loved to observe at the time, the largest of the forty-eight states.

Although not quite a century had elapsed since the gigantic
state had been admitted to the Union, Texas, on the brink of World
War II in 1940, was still relatively sparsely populated. According to
the national census conducted that year, just over 6.4 million people called themselves Texans. There were well over a million more
people living in New York City at the time than in all of the Lone
Star State. More than half of the Texans were found by census tak-
ers to be at rural or small town addresses, with only one-sixth of
the total population residing in such major urban centers as Houston, Dallas, San Antonio, Fort Worth, or El Paso, the state's larger
cities at the time. With fewer than 28 people for each of its 263,000
square miles, even including the far more densely populated urban
centers, Texans could rightly boast of their legendary wide-open
spaces.[2]

The sheer vastness of the state and its low density of population
created something of a natural condition of isolation. Relatively
limited transportation and communication amenities only tended
to exacerbate the almost palatable feeling of remoteness. In 1940,
only one of every five Texans owned an automobile, one out of six
owned a radio, and one of every ten had access to a telephone. Over
half of the state's 693,000 phones were located in the larger urban
centers, further illustrating the paucity of direct communication
throughout the vast rural area.[3]

More men were engaged in agriculture-related occupations than in any other vocation, while most women were simply classified as being "housewives." The harsh demands of the highly labor-intensive farm and ranch industry made it virtually mandatory that most males and nearly all females in the average rural family stay home to share the burdens of plowing, sowing, reaping, cooking, and washing. As a predictable result, almost 60 percent of all rural Texans over age twenty-five had not completed high school when the 1940 census was taken. As might also be expected, a college education for sons and daughters of Texas farmers and ranchers was an even rarer accomplishment.[4]

Both compelled and literally bound by family economic necessity, rural Texans of the late 1930s tended to remain close to their birthplace throughout their lives. The children of the farmers and ranchers were likely to raise their own children in much the same way they themselves had been raised. Each new generation of rural parents demanded and indeed sorely needed the same total dedication of labor from their offspring as their own parents had demanded of them.

Out of this lingering frontier culture had developed a common but strong personal sense of self-reliance and a rugged individualism that formed the very foundation of Texan culture. Although part of a closely knit society, these sons and daughters of the pioneers were also keenly competitive and eager to prove that their ability to deal with the often harsh Texas environment was every bit as well developed as that of their parents, their neighbors, and their pioneer ancestors as well.

At the core of traditional Texas life stood the churches. Nearly half of all families claimed affiliation to a specific religious denomination, with 750,000 Baptists being by far the most prevalent, followed by some 500,000 adherents to Roman Catholicism. From these and other denominations came the basic tenets that shaped rural living, and from the pulpits flowed strict moral guidelines for temperance, frugality, tolerance, fidelity, and moderation. These solid standards had been in place for generations, and without newcomers or strangers to challenge any of them there was no reason to question that they would remain sacrosanct for at least another century or two. This adherence to frontier-like morality, although perhaps less essential to basic survival than the harsh demands of the agrarian economy, was for the most part no less binding.[5]

As oppressive or at least inflexible as these traditional lifestyle cycles might seem to today's far less fettered society, it should be considered that many rural youth had little if any reason to break the chain, at least publicly. By sustaining the age-old frontier traditions, existence could be fairly predictable and relatively safe, involving as it did a likely marriage to a neighbor's son or daughter, the raising of a large family, and a lifetime of work within a few miles of the place of birth. Few if any surprises, for better or for worse, could be imagined.

While cultural activities, entertainment, and social opportunities in the large urban centers in Texas were at least comparable to those found in other southern cities, the rural areas offered few such refinements. An occasional dance, a church function, or perhaps Saturday nights at the movies were the principal ways of relaxing after a hard week in the fields or in the kitchen. Such stars as Clark Gable, Shirley Temple, Hopalong Cassidy, and Mickey Mouse were listed as the favorites among moviegoers. What were billed as added attractions also filled the screens of the many movie theaters located throughout the state. Among these additional features were such newsreels as *Movietone News* and the always-dramatic *March of Time*, narrated in memorably stentorian tones by one Westbrook Von Voorhees. It was from these heavily edited and often theatrically contrived news programs that most Texans got much of their information, such as it was, about the world-shattering international events that were taking place in the years and months prior to America's entry into World War II.

It is impossible to gauge just how much the edited news of an exploding Europe and a ravaged Asia might have meant to those Texans who watched in darkened, popcorn-scented theaters throughout the late 1930s and on until late 1941. Though fiercely patriotic to state and nation, many of them likely felt that such news from a world so far away was of little direct concern to them. Most were shackled by either circumstance or choice to a way of life identical to that which had been experienced by their parents and grandparents and so on for nearly a century. Except for the few mavericks among them, they thought themselves likely to be forever safely enfolded within the blissfully sheltering remoteness of rural Texas.

It is, however, by no means accurate to assume that this isolation born of vast distances and economic necessity, compounded by a minimal degree of effective communication, produced only generation after generation of country bumpkins. Though for the most part not highly educated in the formal sense, these certainly were not stupid people. Rather, they were simply content to lead their lives in a manner they well-understood in a relatively closed society that was comfortable for them. Few chose to leave that clannish society through the invisible but nonetheless very real gate that protected it, and, perhaps just as important, even fewer outsiders ever found any reason to attempt to enter through that same gate. As we shall soon see, however, all this was about to change.

In addition to the more traditional elements of Texas life in the pre-war years, another and perhaps even more restrictive and onerous aspect had arisen in the early 1930s. The Great Depression that had begun in the east in 1929 did not reach the Lone Star State in full force until several years later. When it finally hit, however, it hit hard.

Economic conditions in Texas prior to the Depression had never looked brighter. Lumber, cotton, cattle, and other agricultural products enjoyed a booming nationwide market, while newly discovered oil fields promised even greater riches. In 1940, the state was producing over 35 percent of the nation's oil, nearly 40 percent of its natural gas, and led the country in the marketing of such diverse agricultural commodities as cotton, onions, spinach, pecans, and sorghum. For the first time in its history, pre-Depression Texans had voted for a Republican president in 1928, but when President Herbert Hoover's fiscal policies began to unravel, it soon became all too apparent that the boom was over and an inevitable bust was well on its way.

For a time, the state's political leaders and its newspapers tried gamely to reassure Texans that they had nothing to fear because the problem was clearly an "Eastern" one and limited only to those who owned stock certificates, thus holding few if any ramifications to many residents of the Lone Star State. Unfortunately, dire economic facts soon overran the puffery fiction espoused by the politicians and the press.[6]

To make matters even worse, a prolonged drought continued to wreak havoc with the state's agricultural production. As crop and livestock output all but ceased in many parts of the state, mortgages on farms could not be met and banks foreclosed on the properties. Tenant farmers, sharecroppers, and landowners alike found themselves both out of work and out of funds. In time, many of the very banks that had foreclosed on the farms and ranches also found themselves to be insolvent and were forced to close, denying their panic-stricken patrons access to their own money.

Free bread and soup lines operated in the larger cities, while charitable organizations provided food and clothing for the unemployed and the homeless throughout the entire state. A lessening demand for petroleum products further depleted first corporate and then individual incomes, often to nearly non-existent levels. The situation was dire, but politicians seemed too stunned to find or even seek a potential remedy. As *The New Handbook of Texas* so aptly summarized the situation, "The Depression had, indeed, overwhelmed them."[7]

In time, national and statewide leaders were finally able to piece together plans to at least stanch the flow of red ink and set the nation and the state on the course to economic recovery. The supreme leader on what would prove to be a difficult road back to financial health was Franklin Delano Roosevelt, elected in 1932 to replace Mr. Hoover. Texans, it should be noted, returned to the Democratic Party en masse to help elect Mr. Roosevelt, and their disappointment in Hoover was not soon forgotten.

If one were to create a timeline to trace the significance of the impact of the U. S. Army Air Force on Texas during World War II, the election of FDR at the peak of the Great Depression would be the pivotal point at which the two lines of economic recovery and military necessity would begin to merge. As the case studies to follow in this book will illustrate, Roosevelt's remedial economic programs included a series of vast aviation facility construction projects in Texas that in time spawned the massive wartime presence of the Army Air Force throughout the state.

No matter what his many critics might have thought of Mr. Roosevelt's policies in general, his political astuteness in using economic recovery as a lever to build the mightiest Air Force in modern times can only be admired. The president and his advisers clearly recognized that they had not one but two priorities as the Depression held steady while the threat of an international war simultaneously grew ever more ominous. FDR first had to find work for countless thousands of unemployed men while at the same time prepare for a looming war that would, at least based on the success of Adolf Hitler's Nazi *Luftwaffe* over Europe, require an exceptionally strong and well-trained American air arm.

Further, the president also recognized that he had a daunting task ahead of him in convincing many of his "fellow Americans" that another world war was inevitable and that preparing for that war was vital, despite the misgivings of the large number of his countrymen who abhorred the thought of any foreign entanglement. In a series of political masterstrokes, FDR accomplished all of these seemingly impossible tasks more or less simultaneously.

For openers, the president had representatives of the Civil Aeronautics Administration (CAA) begin combing the United States in 1939 to evaluate existing air facilities for expansion programs and to identify new sites for airfields. Once approved, these sites, old and new, would be converged upon by thousands of relief workers now on the government payroll as employees of the Works Progress Administration (WPA) and the Civilian Conservation Corps (CCC). Even though the national airfield project was ostensibly for the purpose of modernizing America's domestic airline infrastructure, few observers doubted that the true purpose of the scheme was military in nature.

At the same time as his CAA survey was being conducted, the president also began to put into effect what was known as Public Law 18. Under this provision, which became law in April 1939, 6,000 new military aircraft were scheduled for production, 3,203 pilots were to be trained to fly them, and 45,000 enlisted men were to be recruited to support the pilots and their airplanes. A staggering $300 million appropriation bill to fund all of this had skyrocketed through Congress in just three months, and Mr. Roosevelt now had both the money and a mandated need for the airfields his CAA officials had been seeking.[8]

Of the 191 potential airfield sites originally investigated by the CAA, 149 were initially chosen as suitable to receive federal funding. A particularly significant point to note along the Texas and Air Force timeline is that nearly half of these sites were located in the Lone Star State. On May 16, 1940, following the almost immediate success of his earlier military airpower initiative, Roosevelt called for an astounding 50,000 additional aircraft and 30,000 more pilots to fly them. As a direct result of that presidential action, the stage was set for the historic World War II Air Force experience in Texas. Mr. Roosevelt offered vast quantities of federal funds to build airfields for military training, construction money that would almost instantly transform a depressed economy into boom times and would soon provide unlimited additional cash for military and civilian payrolls for the personnel to be assigned to each airfield. Further, there was the attractive possibility that many Texas towns and cities might someday have a new airport of their very own after the war, if indeed war came, and have it paid for by the U. S. government.[9]

Here was the answer to a politician's prayer, and Mr. Roosevelt, master politician if ever there was one, must have felt trebly blessed to have had his prayers, or perhaps his schemes, prove to be so fruitful. In a series of bold sweeps, he had reversed the Depression and started his country on its path to a war it would ultimately win because of a highly enhanced degree of military preparedness. Almost as important, he had convinced all but the most ardent of isolationists that it was better for Americans to go to bed at night with a full belly made possible by preparing for war than it was to go hungry hoping for peace.

His popularity soaring, Mr. Roosevelt prevailed in unprecedented third and fourth presidential elections. In the meantime, city fathers throughout Texas vigorously plotted, schemed, competed, lied, and otherwise pulled out all the stops to snare one of FDR's promised fields for their own political backyards. The state's elected representatives in Washington, D.C., wined and dined War Department officials in an almost frantic effort to convince them that towns in their congressional districts held the greatest potential as an airfield site. Lyndon B. Johnson and his wily mentor Sam Rayburn led particularly effective campaigns for their parts of the state, while Senators Tom Connolly and W. Lee "Pappy" O'Daniel kept all of Texas in the forefront of War Department consideration. One source observes that the intensity of the airfield lobbying efforts of the Texas legislative delegation caused the selection of some of the earlier air facilities to be based far more on political clout than on any strategic consideration. At least a cursory glance at the placement of some airfields might well indicate that politicians initially did in fact have more say than generals in putting air bases in certain locations.[10]

There is much evidence that at least some citizens were concerned about what the coming of a military airfield might mean to their community, again largely in rural Texas so long cloistered in frontier-like isolation. However, the troubling visions of uniformed strangers trooping down small town streets, perhaps up to all manner of nefarious and almost unthinkable evil deeds, were soon all but obscured by the reality of federal dollars flowing into citizens' pockets long empty and civic coffers all but bone dry. With the

Japanese attack on Pearl Harbor in December 1941, a surging spirit of patriotism universally overcame any shreds of lingering doubt about the need not only to have the bases close by, but to welcome military personnel to the community with open arms as well.

Those airfields already under construction in Texas went on an accelerated building program after the Pearl Harbor attack, with workmen on the job twenty-four hours a day, seven days a week. Work began on new fields almost daily and by the time the war ended in 1945, there were sixty-five Army airfields located in Texas, more than in any other state.[11]

The purpose of all of these bases was, of course, to train men and, eventually, women in the skills of war. Thousands upon thousands of Air Force personnel — including pilots, navigators, bombardiers, gunners, and engineers — flooded into the state, swarming over little towns, making their presence keenly felt in big cities and, collectively, leaving an indelible impression on a state many casual observers might have thought to be much too large in both attitude and area to be impressed by anything.

Who were these "uniformed strangers" and, for that matter, just exactly what was this United States Army Air Force anyway? As nearly every Texan was to learn during the war, it was the military outfit destined to change Texas. More than the lightly armored men from Spain or General Philip Sheridan's hard-riding "bluebellies," these high-flying Air Force men and women would swiftly challenge, test, and severely bend if not sometimes completely shatter time-honored traditional economic and social values long embraced by many Texans. There was a war to be won and, it was popularly reasoned by the uniformed newcomers, no time could be spared for observing quaint frontier morality or antiquated laws. The Air Force had come to Texas in a big way, and changes, as well as the wings of thousands of airplanes, were in the air.

The United States Army Air Force

Fundamentally, the AAF [Army Air Forces] is a people's Air Force, and its bombs dropping on the enemy represent the work of millions of Americans in and out of uniform.

H.H. Arnold
Commanding General, USAAF
1944

Sticklers for accuracy in all things historical, and other purists, are often quick to point out that there never was an organization called "The United States Army Air Force," even though this erroneous appellation is used throughout many published works, including this one. The fact of the matter is that on June 20, 1941, what had been known as "The U. S. Army Air Corps" officially became "The U. S. Army Air Forces," the plurality of the new name reflecting the newly-created multiple-numbered air forces such as the Second Air Force, the Eighth Air Force, etc., that made up the whole of the Army's modern air branch.[12]

Despite this official change in nomenclature authorized by President Roosevelt himself, personnel serving in the newly named branch persisted in calling it by its former "Corps" title. It is easy to find many veterans today who will swear with great heat that they proudly served in the Army Air Corps throughout the entire war, even though the record shows that what had been "the Corps" became "the Forces" six months before World War II got underway.

The matter of the inadvertent or even intentional use of the inaccurate singular "Force" rather than the plural "Forces" in the service's title is altogether different. Many writers of air history understandably soon grew weary of wrestling with the plural possessive punctuation required when using "Forces," to say nothing of the resulting grammar machinations required. For example, it is obviously correct to write, "the Army was," or "the Navy is," but to make the awkward statement that the "Air Forces was" or "the Air Forces is" puts too much of an undue strain on both reader and author, or at least so this writer believes. That said, the singular and convenient "Air Force" title will be used throughout this book, with sincere apologies to all those who know better.

Actually, the air branch of the Army has had a long history of name changes dating back to its inception as the Aeronautical Division of the U. S. Army Signal Corps in August 1907 just two years after the first manned flight by the Wright Brothers. In 1914, the air branch became known as the Aviation Section of the Army's Signal Corps, with an authorized strength of 60 officers and 260 enlisted men. In 1920, just six years later, the name was changed again to the U. S. Army Air Service, reflecting the growing military importance of a branch that had just been successfully tested in the skies over embattled France during World War I. In July 1926, the Air Service became the U. S. Army Air Corps as further indication that the War

Department had almost fully accepted the airplane as a viable and highly flexible combat weapon. The Air Corps title would remain in place for another fifteen years before changing once again, as noted above.[13]

By any of its many names, the Army's air arm and its totally independent successor, the U.S. Air Force, have played a pivotal role for nearly a century's worth of Texas military history. In 1909, the two-year-old Aeronautical Division of the Signal Corps was ordered to move the Army's only flight training center from College Park, Maryland, to Fort Sam Houston in San Antonio, Texas. According to an account in *Aviation In Texas*, the decision was based on three significant factors, namely the flat terrain, the mild (if occasionally windy) weather, and the sobering fact that "unrest in Mexico merited an aviation observation unit in the area."[14]

In what proved to be either an all too rare brilliant use of its personnel or just plain luck, the War Department selected one Lt. Benjamin Foulois to open the new flight training center as the Army's sole aviator, flying the service's solitary airplane known as the Wright S.C. (for Signal Corps) No. 1. Foulois, a small but evidently fierce officer and an ex-plumber, had distinguished himself during the Philippine insurrection a few years earlier by killing six of the enemy in hand to hand combat. He had in the meantime learned the principles of flight from no less than Orville and Wilbur Wright themselves in a ground school of a reported one-hour's duration.[15]

Equipped with only his ground school knowledge of aviation, Foulois packed his aeroplane into several crates, supervised the loading of said crates on railroad flat cars, and set out from Maryland for Texas. Once safely in San Antonio, the lieutenant proceeded to apply what he had learned during his brief ground school session toward actual flight. Apparently, he was able to get his flimsy little airplane off Fort Sam Houston's drill field without too much difficulty and what became routine flights of nearly nine minutes duration did not seem to present the fledgling aviator with much of a problem. Unfortunately, however, landing the craft seemed to be a daunting challenge for him. Rather than glide his plane in for a smooth return to earth, Foulois frequently tended to come down with something resembling a barely controlled crash. When repairs to his even-slightly damaged aircraft exceeded the ability of his overtaxed maintenance crew to fix it, Foulois would write his mentors, the Wright Brothers, seeking their guidance, presumably about how to softly land as well as how to repair the Army's only airplane. The final result of these early flight operations was that the tiny plane reportedly averaged three weeks of repair time for each week it was able to fly.[16]

Despite these annoying start-up difficulties, the daring and perseverance of the diminutive plumber-turned-pilot gave Texas the distinction of becoming the first military aviation-training center in the United States. Due at least in part to Foulois's insistence and obvious dedication to the future of military airpower, a second aircraft was approved for the War Department. Imaginatively dubbed S.C. No. 2, the new plane was crated and shipped to San Antonio to complement S.C. No. 1, or at least what was left of it following Foulois's repeated extremely hard landings.

More airplanes meant more pilots, of course, and after a year of being the Army's only aviator, Foulois welcomed three other fledgling fliers to his tiny air force. One of these, Lt. George E.M. Kelly, was to lend his name to one of the nation's most important air facilities but only through tragic circumstances that also brought a temporary but abrupt halt to the Army's initial interest in Texas as its primary, and only, flight training center.

On May 10, 1911, Kelly was attempting to land S.C. No. 2 on Fort Sam Houston's parade ground when the aircraft suddenly swerved toward an infantry tent city near the intended landing site. To avoid flying into the congested troop area, Kelly banked too steeply and crashed, fatally fracturing his skull on impact. The accident, with its tragic loss of the pilot's life and the barely avoided crash into the crowded infantry camp, caused the fort's commander to ban all further flight operations from his suddenly ill-fated parade ground. War Department officials, correctly sensing that flight training and the simultaneous close order drilling of foot soldiers are not at all compatible on the same field, ordered Foulois and his remaining squadron of two pilots back to Maryland. It appeared for the moment that the role of Texas in military aviation had died along with George Kelly on Fort Sam's parade ground.[17]

Lieutenant Foulois himself was given an infantry assignment, but a flare-up of the political unrest in Mexico that had originally been partly responsible for his coming to Texas a few years earlier caused him to return to San Antonio, now as commanding officer of the Army's just-recently formed First Aero Squadron. In time, Foulois led his tiny eight-plane squadron into the skies over northern Mexico and along the Rio Grande in support of Brig. Gen. John J. Pershing's futile attempts to locate the notorious Francisco "Pancho" Villa, the Mexican revolutionary leader who had dared cross the United States border on a killing raid against Columbus, New Mexico, on March 8, 1916.

Despite heroic efforts by Foulois and his men, the performance of the First Aero Squadron was no better than Pershing's embarrassing ground campaign. The mocking Villa easily evaded the American force while Foulois's JN-2 aircraft suffered major maintenance problems and were seldom able to become airborne. Of the original eight aircraft deployed in Pershing's so-called Punitive Expedition, only two were still in flying condition after just one month of air operation. At the conclusion of the campaign, even those two were found to be unfit for further duty and were promptly returned to Fort Sam and somewhat petulantly set afire by Foulois himself.[18]

The failure of the First Aero Squadron to even find Pancho Villa, let alone cause him any punitive damage, eventually proved to be a blessing, albeit deeply disguised, for the future of Texas military aviation. A mortified War Department realized that in effect it had no military air branch even remotely worthy of the name. By 1917, as a direct consequence of the Mexican fiasco, the government had become convinced that drastic remedial action had to be taken and taken swiftly in view of the significant air action taking place over Europe as World War I entered its third year. The rapid and massive build-up of American airpower following the debacle in the skies above northern Mexico brought the United States and particularly Texas into the forefront of modern military aviation. It can perhaps also give rise to a facetious but not totally unfounded speculation that Generalissimo Francisco Villa might arguably be considered the godfather of today's American air force.

Reeling from the inability of its aircraft to get off the ground let alone find Villa in the Mexican mountains, the government attempted to rapidly remedy its heretofore general indifference to military airpower. Even as Foulois's last two remaining aircraft were being reduced to ashes in Texas, Congress approved a military aviation appropriation of over $13 million. This was more or less the same Congress that only five years earlier had grudgingly passed a military flying bill amounting to a mere $125,000. Clearly, the government had been shocked into wakefulness by the Mexican air charade.[19]

As a result of its congressionally bestowed newfound riches, the Army's air branch grew rapidly, with Texas being among the greater beneficiaries. Just as had been the case in 1910, weather and terrain became the deciding factors in making San Antonio once again the nation's primary air training center. The old and ill-fated flight school at Fort Sam Houston was, however, finally deemed inadequate for the Army's new and greatly enlarged air service. As a consequence, another site for the flight school was found in what was then a sparsely populated area just a few miles from downtown San Antonio. Period photographs of the site and its all but vacant environs can, of course, give no hint of the urban sprawl that would in a few short years all but engulf the newly selected flying field location.

Named Kelly Field in honor of the early heroic aviator who had lost his life while unintentionally demonstrating that foot soldiers had no business being encamped dangerously close to an airfield's landing site, the new flight school began operation on August 11, 1917. By December of that same year, over 32,000 officers and men were on duty and undergoing air training at the field. Within less than a year, the Kelly primary and advanced flight schools had produced nearly two thousand pilots. This somewhat startling statistic graphically reflects the early growth and importance of military aviation in Texas, where seven years previously the total pilot census of the U. S. Army had listed only one fearless aviator. San Antonio's Kelly Field was, at the end of the First World War on November 11, 1918, the largest flying school in the world.[20]

When the demands made on Kelly Field proved to be too great for the nearly four thousand acre facility to absorb, a second training center was opened south of San Antonio on December 8, 1917. Named Brooks Field in honor of Sidney J. Brooks, who had died in a training plane crash just before he was to receive his aviator's wings, the new installation became a primary training facility. Six months of successful work at the new field led to six more months of advanced flight training at Kelly and the ceremonial awarding of the coveted wings to the freshly minted Army pilots.

Even though San Antonio held the distinction of being the first Army flight-training center in the nation, other Texas cities had air facilities during the First World War. Dallas, Fort Worth, Houston, Waco, and Wichita Falls each had either training or logistical missions. When the First World War ended, however, only Kelly Field in San Antonio could boast of being what the Army termed a "permanent air facility." For nearly eighty-five years, that term proved to be valid. Unfortunately, history would eventually show that the use of the words "permanent" and "military air facility" in the same sentence is frequently oxymoronic.

Throughout the 1920s and into the early 1930s, military aviation continued in Texas but at a much lower level of activity than that of the First World War years. However, those aviators who managed to stay on active duty following the Armistice in 1918 kept the general public titillated by their air races, barnstorming, balloon ascensions, and speed-record setting. All of these apparently frivolous but dangerous antics were in fact part of a public relations campaign orchestrated by the Army to both keep alive and enhance the public's awareness of the great potential inherent in aviation. Those who flew in Texas during the barnstorming years between the two world wars include such famous names from the Air Force's pantheon of heroes as Billy Mitchell, James Doolittle, Charles Lindbergh, Carl Spaatz, Ira C. Eaker, and Henry H. Arnold.[21]

As the late 1930s moved rapidly toward the next decade, Texas stood poised, unknowingly for the most part, on the threshold of the most exciting period in its military aviation history. It was a widely-held conviction that the state's unlimited skies and generally pleasant weather offered near perfect conditions for flight training. In addition, vast quantities of flat and inexpensive land more densely inhabited by jackrabbits and rattlesnakes than by people soon provided the ideal arena for a unique demonstration of just how an unlimited flow of federal money, fueled by a national emergency and sparked by an urgently growing need for thousands of pilots and crew members, could transform nearly all of Texas and the skies over it into the world's greatest military flight school.

As World War II swiftly approached, the curtain was ready to go up on a scene that had been building for decades. To prepare for what was now an inevitable war, the U. S. Army Air Force was on its way back to Texas in all but unimaginable force, and six and a half million Texans were in for an experience they would not soon forget.

[1] Thomas T. Smith, *The U. S. Army & the Texas Frontier Economy, 1845-1900.*

[2] *Texas Almanac and State Industrial Guide, 1943-1944,* 62.

[3] *Texas Almanac and State Industrial Guide, 1939-1940,* 265.

[4] "State Superintendent of Public Instruction Annual Report, 1940," 82, 117, 221.

[5] *Texas Almanac, 1939-1940*, 334.

[6] Ron Tyler, ed., *The New Handbook of Texas*, vol. 3, 301.

[7] Ibid., 303

[8] Jerold E. Brown, *Where Eagles Land: Planning and Development of U. S. Army Airfields, 1910-1941*, 115.

[9] Walter J. Boyne, *Beyond the Wild Blue Yonder: A History of the U. S. Air Force*, 364.

[10] Brown, 94.

[11] A. Ray Stephens and William M. Holmes, *Historical Atlas of Texas*, 48.

[12] Roger Bilstein and Jay Miller, *Aviation in Texas*, 271.

[13] Ibid., 271.

[14] Ibid., 17.

[15] Eldon Cagle, Jr., *Quadrangle: The History of Fort Sam Houston*, 30.

[16] Ibid., 68.

[17] Ann Krueger Hussey and Robert Browning, III, *A History of Military Aviation in San Antonio*, 5.

[18] Cagle, 93.

[19] Bilstein, 50.

[20] Ibid., 51.

[21] *The Flying Times*, February 5, 1944, 13.

THE EAST

ARMY AIR FORCES STATIONS

① Hondo Army Airfield, Hondo

② Kelly Field, San Antonio

③ Randolph Field, San Antonio

④ Bergstrom Field, Austin

⑤ Ellington Field, Houston

⑥ Majors Field, Greenville

AREA DETAILED

Robert F. Pace

CHAPTER TWO

THE EAST

*I must say as to what I have seen of Texas, it is the garden spot
of the world.*

> David Crockett
> Upon entering East Texas
> 1836

One way to present at least something of a true perspective of
the scale of the Army Air Force experience in Texas during World
War II is to arbitrarily divide the huge state into five rather loosely
defined regions — the East, North Texas, the Border, the West, and
Panhandle/Plains. A study of some of the airfields and their host
cities located in each region affords an opportunity to compare not
only the impact the Air Force had on both urban and rural Texas,
but also to gain a composite view of the various social, economic,
and cultural changes brought about in the state by the war.

While the review of the Eastern region focuses on such major
metropolitan localities as San Antonio, Austin, and Houston, the
smaller communities of Greenville and Hondo are also included.
Although even the most casual of Texas geographers should rightly
blanch at the mere suggestion that the town of Hondo be placed in

anything even vaguely construed as an Eastern setting, it is included in this section of the book only because of the Army's reason for placing an airfield there sixty years ago.

The rapidly accelerating growth of San Antonio as the nation's military air capital from the early 1930s through the early 1940s made it imperative that additional flight training facilities be constructed relatively close to the big city yet far enough away to provide an abundance of uncrowded and thus hopefully safer skies. The increasing number of day and night training flights originating at Kelly Field had already made it necessary for the Army to begin construction on Randolph Field in 1930, on the opposite side of San Antonio. However, the combined aerial operations of these two major fields soon filled the skies over the immediate vicinity of the Alamo City to even more hazardous levels, and as a direct result, construction was begun on another regional training facility at Hondo, located some forty miles west of Kelly Field. Although in an admittedly curious geographical arrangement, Hondo's airfield is herewith temporarily thumbtacked onto San Antonio and placed in the Eastern section of this study.

San Antonio

Bejar is in a class by itself. There is not another like it in the Western Hemisphere.

> Gen. Antonio Lopez de Santa Anna
> Mexico City
> 1834

As previously noted, San Antonio had laid claim to the title of America's military air capital for three decades by the time World War II began in 1941. The successful growth of Kelly Field, along with such other flying facilities as Brooks, Duncan, and Stinson, had led to the opening of Randolph Field in early November 1931. The sheer magnitude of the combined aerial operations of the Army's many flying fields in the San Antonio area clearly gave the city more than ample reason to boast of its importance to the nation's military airpower program.

Long before Benjamin Foulois brought the Army's first and only aeroplane to the Alamo City, San Antonio was enjoying a well-deserved reputation as a first-rate Army town. Since its founding late in the eighteenth century, the city had frequently been the scene of various skirmishes, raids, and fully pitched battles including, of course, the legendary siege of the Alamo in March 1836. During America's Civil War, San Antonio played a vital role as a supply center for Confederate forces. When the victorious federal army opened Fort Sam Houston on a ridge overlooking downtown soon after the Civil War ended, San Antonio took on new importance as one of the nation's premier military centers. The later arrival of Lieutenant Foulois and his solitary airplane, however, truly served to provide the Alamo City with the vital key to its future as the Army's most important aviation hub.

Kelly Field

The fact is that the "Kelly Katies" proved they were equal to any challenge. They helped open doors for successors who desired to excel beyond the rivet gun and the typewriter.

Councilwoman Debra Guerrero
San Antonio, Texas
October 4, 1990

The move from Fort Sam Houston to the newly-built Kelly Field in late 1916 gave the Army's air force its first major installation in San Antonio. By the time World War II ended twenty-nine years later, the field had grown to become the largest military aviation and servicing center in the world. Encompassing 4,660 acres in 1945, the facility employed more than twenty thousand workers, many of whom were females, the legendary "Kelly Katies."[1]

The initial growth of the facility stemmed directly from the Roosevelt administration's pre-war aircraft building program that earmarked $170 million for new military planes. In addition to this planned expenditure, another $130 million had been appropriated to provide recruiting, training, and salaries for thousands of new pilots and aircrew members. As a result of Roosevelt's farsighted military aviation initiative, the strength of the Air Force grew from 24,724 officers and enlisted men to over 354,000 from July 1939 to December 1941. Pilots were being trained at the rate of seven thousand per year during this same time period, well exceeding the originally foreseen twelve hundred trainees. These figures, stunning as they were at the time, were to grow to even more astounding levels when America became directly involved in the war following the Japanese attack on Pearl Harbor in December 1941.[2]

This accelerated growth of the Air Force directly translated into growth for Kelly Field's advanced pilot training program and eventually its logistical mission. As the Army's oldest flight school, Kelly had been routinely turning out aviators since 1917. Nearly every Air Force officer who would play a significant role in the winning of World War II had been stationed at Kelly Field, as did the first ten men who would serve as the chief of staff of the United States Air Force after it became an independent service in 1947. Generals Carl Spaatz, Hoyt S. Vandenberg, Curtis E. LeMay, John P. McConnell, John D. Ryan, Nathan G. Twining, Thomas D. White, George S. Brown, and David C. Jones were all Kelly pilots who eventually rose to the top of the Air Force chain of command. Another of the historic field's aviators, Capt. Colin P. Kelly, was America's first heroic fatality in the air war in the Pacific.[3]

The crop of Kelly Field's pre-World War II flying cadets faced many of the same challenges that their predecessors had in the years before them. The heat of the Texas summers still withered the aeronautical ambitions of many of those who had been sent south to learn to fly. Although little could be done about the heat, all cadets arriving after 1939 were at least spared the additional discomfort caused by the wearing of the archaic Sam Browne belts and ceremonial sabers that earlier trainees had been required to wear. At one early point in the field's history, General John J. Pershing had expressed his great disappointment that the cadets did not wear regulation spurs while flying their aircraft. Only the cool and rational arguments of senior air officers kept cavalry spurs from becoming a mandatory item of Kelly Field's flying outfits.[4]

In 1940, as the prospect of war grew more ominous, some of FDR's newly-ordered aircraft finally began to appear on Kelly's flight line. Although the school was at least officially listed as a twin-engine facility, few such aircraft were actually available until after the war had started. However, the easy-to-fly AT-6 "Texan" single engine training planes began to arrive in something approaching adequate numbers in mid-1940, much to the delight of the student pilots. By late 1942, with the war not quite one year old, the first of the multi-engine training aircraft began to arrive at Kelly Field. Unfortunately, the first class to train in the newly arrived planes proved to be the last flying class scheduled to graduate from the field.[5]

Even though the advanced pilot training program was being phased out at Kelly, other fliers found themselves with orders to travel to San Antonio. Although the daunting goal of training seventy thousand new pilots had initially occupied the full attention of Air Force officials, it soon became apparent that other aircrew members were also going to be needed. Accordingly, Kelly Field took on the additional task of training navigators.

While it was difficult at first to find enough pilots to fly the aircraft required by the navigation school, it proved even more difficult to find men willing to become navigator cadets. There was little that seemed particularly romantic about becoming a navigator, at least when contrasted with the popular movie-hero perception associated with being a pilot. Initially, the principal source for navigator trainees was from those individuals who had washed out of pilot school, but in time it developed that it was wiser to seek qualified candidates from civilian life who simply wanted to fly, despite having minor physical disqualifications such as less than perfect vision. Just as effective testing procedures were being introduced to identify and evaluate candidates for training at Kelly, the entire navigation school was relocated to the new base just being completed at nearby Hondo.

With the departure from Kelly of Class 42-K in September 1942, and the transfer of the navigator cadets to Hondo a few weeks earlier, the field's long history of aviator training came to an end. There was, however, a vital new mission for what had become the Army's oldest continuously operating airfield. On February 1, 1943, the primary function of Kelly Field became the supply, service, and maintenance of aircraft. It was in this capacity that the giant installation would flourish for over a half-century. As the Army Air Force's largest logistical center, Kelly Field brought a large degree of social and economic change to San Antonio.

Lt. Col. Clements McMullen (later General McMullen, with a San Antonio expressway to honor his name) orchestrated Kelly Field's change in course that would assure it of a long, and some thought permanent, existence. In July 1941, then-Colonel McMullen had written to his superior officer suggesting that Kelly be made a part of adjoining Duncan Field, with the combined facility being dedicated solely to aircraft maintenance and supply. Unless a new purpose could be found for it, McMullen pointed out that "within six months, Kelly Field will be just another advanced training

school." Showing an unusual degree of concern for the field's civilian neighbors, McMullen went on to note that "Kelly is so close to
the city that continuous flying, as now carried on there, is certainly
an annoyance to the populace of San Antonio."[6]

While the immediate response to Colonel McMullen's plea is not
known, he obviously felt obliged to try again in another letter to
headquarters dated October 25, 1941. "A site for an advanced training school can much more readily be obtained than can the site for
a depot," he wrote, claiming that such a maintenance facility had to
be proximate to a major population center to provide an adequate
supply of employees. McMullen concluded rather pointedly that a
flying field, on the other hand, "could be established in the middle
of a desert if water is available."[7]

Although his superiors finally took the colonel's advice, things
did not turn out exactly as he had asked. The consolidation of Duncan and Kelly did take place in early 1943, but it was Duncan Field
that became part of Kelly, not the other way around as McMullen
had envisioned. According to the official history of the base, the sentiment and nostalgia which senior air officers held for the old airfield where they had earned their wings, led to the decision to
preserve the name Kelly and to erase the name Duncan Field from
the list of Texas military air facilities.

By any name, Kelly Field was immense in both size and importance. It rapidly grew to be the central core of anything and everything to do with re-supplying the massive air armada mandated by
President Roosevelt just a few years earlier. In all likelihood, almost
every aircraft in that armada had either actually been serviced at
Kelly at one time or contained parts supplied by the huge depot.

Much of the challenge of keeping Kelly Field's newly created San
Antonio Air Service Depot running smoothly fell in large measure to
its many civilian workers. By offering meaningful employment to a
great number of San Antonians without undue regard to long-
standing attitudes toward either gender or ethnicity, the field became
a significant agent of change within the entire community. When the
war ended in 1945, Kelly had 22,117 civilian employees on its payroll,
including ten thousand women. Meanwhile, the Army had reduced its
military personnel on the base to a relatively low level of six thousand
officers and men, down 25 percent from the previous year.[8]

Known collectively as "Kelly Katies," the women workers were
the Texas counterparts of the better-known "Rosie the Riveters"

then at work in war plants across the nation. They came from all levels of San Antonio's richly diverse society to take the place of men who had been called to active military duty. From Junior Leaguers living in the prestigious Alamo Heights section of town to Hispanic housewives from the city's barrios, San Antonio's women answered repeated calls for employment out of a sense of patriotic duty, or financial need, or both. They learned to work with lathes and welding torches as well as rivet guns. Classroom and on-the-job training gave the women workers new skills to master in place of the traditional housekeeping chores they had learned from their mothers who in turn had learned to cook and sew from their own mothers and grandmothers. The war-caused emergence of women from out of their kitchens or out of their bridge games into the regional workforce put in place a social and economic phenomenon that continues to this day.

Despite the obvious and almost desperate need for the skills of the "Kelly Katies" during the war, their acceptance in what had been a totally male-dominated society did not come easily. In September 1941, Major Isaac Ott, who later became an Air Force major general, first broached the idea of hiring women to do what had always been assumed to be man's work. The major wrote to his commanding officer at Kelly Field not only to identify the various tasks he felt women could accomplish but also to assign the ratios to which they should be employed within each task. An overview of Major Ott's analysis indicates that, while he was clearly a pioneer in opening employment doors to females, he was still harboring some rather traditional male viewpoints. According to Ott, women could be employed at a 100 percent ratio in available positions as clerks and janitors, an 85 percent ratio in jobs in the fabric department, and 75 percent in fuselage assembly, but only 20 percent in dismantling and 30 percent in the propeller and minor repair departments. For some obscure reason, Ott believed no women were to be hired as spark-plug workers. While perhaps narrow in its concept, Ott's plan was at the very least a significant breakthrough, albeit one that was not universally endorsed by his fellow officers. Although he pointed out that his suggested hiring ratios were to be phased in only gradually, an all-male advisory board that had been convened to address the female worker issue concluded that " . . . it was not desirable to place any other female employees in the shops for training until such a time as it was absolutely necessary."[9]

Once they finally gained the opportunity to work at the facility, the vanguard of the "Kelly Katies" proved to be highly efficient and reliable employees. When their abilities came to be recognized by all but the most chauvinistic of male officials, Kelly's personnel department launched a coordinated recruiting drive for more female workers. One senior officer wrote a recruiting letter to every young woman scheduled to graduate from the University of New Mexico and the Arizona College of Mines with the class of 1942, asking that they consider becoming a "Katie." The field's public affairs office came up with the idea of having an all-woman crew overhaul a giant C-39 all by itself for newspaper publicity purposes. As the end of the war statistics clearly indicate, women more than adequately performed their vital tasks. It has been suggested that the nearly 50 percent women ratio of the total workforce at Kelly would have been far greater if more of the men who were classified as essential civilian workers by their draft boards had been called into the armed services during the war.[10]

The "Kelly Katies" proved themselves to be as dedicated to their work as they were professional in doing it. Many had husbands, sons, or brothers on active duty, but concerns about the safety of their loved ones failed to dampen the enthusiasm that the "Katies" displayed toward their tasks at the field. Julia Macha came to her job in the maintenance shops only hours after learning that her son was missing in action. Hazel Hughes was presented with the Medal of Honor posthumously given her husband Lloyd for his heroism as a B-24 pilot, while Leona Spielman learned that her son had escaped from a Japanese prison camp only by reading an account of his adventures in a magazine when she returned home from work at the field. No matter how difficult the war made their own personal lives, the "Kelly Katies" worked long shifts at the logistical center, each helping to ensure a victory for America.[11]

In addition to its policy for the hiring of women, Kelly Field also brought about another important change in San Antonio's traditional employment practices when it led the way in placing Hispanics on the payroll. Although apparently no records were kept indicating how many workers with Hispanic family names were hired from 1940 through 1945, it is evident from general articles about employees appearing in the field's newspaper that a large number of Hispanics worked at Kelly throughout the war years.

Even though there is positive proof that Kelly Field offered San Antonio's large Hispanic community employment opportunities in the early 1940s, it is interesting to note how important the Hispanic workers continued to be to the field's mission after the war was over. According to a 1975 study conducted by what had evolved into the San Antonio Air Logistics Center at Kelly, nearly 55 percent of all employees at the facility were of Hispanic ethnicity, and fifteen years later, that ratio had risen to over 61 percent. Nationally, only 6.4 percent of the entire workforce was shown to be Hispanic at the time of the study.[12]

Clearly, the unusually high percentage of Hispanic workers at the Kelly Field facility in later years could not have come about in a short period of time. The immense demand for wartime employees at the field must surely have overcome any lingering traditional repression of opportunities for workers of races other than white. Based solely on what took place during the war in other principally Hispanic communities such as El Paso, jobs at federal facilities gave workers from those communities a golden opportunity to become upwardly mobile for the first time in their lives. Better jobs led to more spending power, a higher level of education, and, in general, an improved standard of living. The testimonies of Kelly workers interviewed in the late 1990s often refer to a family's immense pride in being a third and even fourth-generation "Kelly Family." Without the needs of wartime Kelly Field for workers of other races, it is easy to assume that the emergence of many of San Antonio's citizens from the barrios would have been long delayed if not all but impossible.

Henrietta Lopez Rivas, for example, found that the war gave her more than just a greatly increased level of income. In an oral history interview conducted in 1999, Mrs. Rivas recalled that in 1942 she found herself able to attain a level of employment that had been denied her prior to the war. As a result, she experienced a new found sense of equality. She eventually became the assistant supervisor in her department at Kelly, ". . . because of my ability," she noted. Her interviewer summarized Mrs. Rivas' story in one succinct phrase, "The war had given her belief in herself."[13]

Other members of San Antonio's society found new employment opportunities at Kelly. At least four of the field's security guards were retired Texas Rangers, for example. As had many others who enjoyed after-retirement jobs at the base, these men brought years of training and experience into the workforce. John Gillon had joined the elite Texas Rangers in 1916, where he eventually became a close personal friend of Governor Coke Stevenson. According to the field newspaper *The Flying Times,* Gillon "had pursued rum-runners, cattle thieves, and dope peddlers" during his long career before retiring and later becoming a guard at the base. Two other former Rangers soon joined Gillon on the Kelly security detail. John J. Edds had served as a deputy sheriff just before coming to the base, while fellow guard Robert Burrell had given up his career as a Ranger who "specialized in chasing Mexican bandits West of the Pecos" to move to his new job at Kelly.[14]

The base newspaper also told of another Kelly employee who had a colorful past. Hugo Villa had been the right hand man to sculptor Gutzon Borglum for over twenty years. A sculptor himself, Villa had taken a leave of absence from Borglum's Mount Rushmore project to come to Kelly as a die-maker. Even though he was glad to be involved in war work, the Italian-born Villa was eager to get back to Borglum's South Dakota mountainside where only the busts of George Washington and Thomas Jefferson had been completed. "When it is over," he said, "I hope to go back and finish the other two [presidential busts]. It's a fine thing."[15]

When the war ended, Kelly Field continued to be the most important logistical center in the Air Force. Enhanced by its diverse labor pool, the supply and maintenance function of the one time flying field continued to flourish through the Cold War years. By 1993, however, it became evident that the future of Kelly's Air Logistics Center was bleak if not black. A prolonged and spirited show of support staged by the citizens of San Antonio initially convinced members of the federal government's Base Realignment and Closure Commission (BRAC) that the field should remain fully operational, but two short years later, another BRAC recommendation called for the field to close and its logistical operations to be transferred to Tinker Air Force Base in Oklahoma.

Although the efforts by the community to reverse the BRAC ruling were even more vigorous than before, the ruling became final when July 13, 2001, was given as the date of closure of the nation's oldest Air Force base and its realignment with the adjacent Lackland AFB. Privatization of many of Kelly Field's functions preserved the jobs of a number of the civilian employees, while others were transferred to Tinker AFB, but as difficult as it was for many longtime San Antonians to accept, the city's first

Army airfield and the original center of military aviation had faded into history.

Randolph Field

There can be no doubt about it whatsoever. San Antonio is now the crowning glory of the Army Air Corps, and Randolph Field is the brightest star in that crown.
            The San Antonio Light
            April 9, 1938

Randolph Field, which enjoys the positive distinction of being the first Army airfield to be designed by an actual pilot, was opened in San Antonio in November 1931. Located across town and twenty-five miles east of the Kelly site, the Randolph facility was created to provide relief to the congested air traffic conditions caused by the ever-increasing flight activity both at Kelly Field and its neighbor, Brooks Field.

Despite San Antonio's nearly twenty-year love affair with Army aviation, the effort to create a new primary and basic flight school at Randolph became a curious study in public apathy, legal wrangling, and military heavy-handedness. When it became apparent that the combination of crowded skies and encroaching urban growth around Kelly and Brooks mandated another flight training center, Army officials announced the beginning of a nationwide search for an appropriate site.

Although cities located in Louisiana, California, Florida, and elsewhere in Texas made presentations to the board of officers charged with selecting the new site, Maj. Gen. Mason Patrick, chief of the Army Air Corps, privately let it be known that he preferred another training airfield be built in the San Antonio vicinity. The general, who had visited the Alamo City frequently, based his recommendation on the simple facts that the flying conditions there were ideal and that San Antonio loved aviators just as much as aviators loved San Antonio. As proof of his first reason, Patrick released a study that indicated that flying conditions in the immediate vicinity of San Antonio were nearly perfect at least 95 percent of the time.[16]

While the Army was apparently willing to award the new field to its long established historic air capital, San Antonio's city fathers appear to have been strangely apathetic about the prospect of getting an additional air base. In 1927, however, the city finally advised the commander of Air Corps Training Center, Brig. Gen. Frank P. Lahm, that it would make land available for a new training facility. Even though Army officials were ultimately able to find a site that was acceptable to the demanding General Lahm, the city had encountered considerable difficulty in raising enough money to actually purchase the approved site. In very short order, Lahm ran out of his reportedly small reserve of patience, letting it be known that unless the whole deal was closed by New Year's Day, 1928, he would assume that San Antonio not only did not want the new base but also did not care to keep Kelly and Brooks either. After the announced date, if money to buy the land for a new field had not been given to him, the general implied that he would immediately begin looking elsewhere for a site while simultaneously recommending the closing of both Kelly and Brooks.[17]

Although it now had a scant eight months to come up with the cash, San Antonio's leaders realized that General Lahm apparently held the key to the city's economic future and there was no time to lose in meeting his demands. In a series of behind the scenes machinations that included the city council's total disregard of a legal opinion from its own city attorney that the procedure being followed to raise the money was illegal, the New Year's deadline for finalizing the transaction was met by only a few hours. As a result, the impressive sum of $546,460 was made available to General Lahm, the site was acquired, and construction on what would eventually become Randolph Field was soon underway.[18]

Just over two years later, the $11 million airfield was dedicated and named for Capt. William M. Randolph, a Kelly Field pilot who had died in a plane crash at Gorman, Texas, on February 16, 1928. At the field's dedication ceremony, Governor Dan Moody delivered what turned out to be a particularly prescient speech. "It occurs to me," declared the governor, "that the future of our whole country may depend on a well-trained Air Corps. All that we are to become may depend on the men who are trained on this field." As the audience of almost twenty thousand pondered those weighty words, Governor Moody delivered a punch line that would become historic fact in just over a decade. "It may be that we must depend on the heroes of the air," Moody concluded, "for the defense of the future."[19]

Later that evening, the city sponsored a post-dedication celebratory event at the Gunter Hotel. Military officers, including a triumphant General Lahm, mingled with civic dignitaries and social leaders as if to underscore the momentous significance of what had taken place earlier in the day. In its coverage of the dedication and the banquet that celebrated it, the *San Antonio Express* wrote, "This is our night. Our city will forever be in the forefront of military aviation, and all San Antonio should rejoice in that confidence."[20]

Work on the new facility continued the very next day, and by October 1931 the headquarters of both the basic and the primary flight schools had been transferred to the nearly completed Randolph Field. Thirty days later, the first cadet class was in session. From its stunning administration building, dubbed the Taj Mahal, to its highly unique and often confusing vehicular traffic layout, Randolph Field was in business at last.

Lt. Harold Clark, the pilot who created the basic layout of the airfield, was also responsible for developing the challenging street design that has confused motorists for over seventy years. When asked about his unusual wheel-like roadway plan many years later, the retired brigadier general could only smile somewhat wanly and say, "I love this place, you know, but every time I come out here, I get lost."[21]

Life for Randolph's new cadets was anything but glamorous or elegant, at least while they were in class on the field or in their training aircraft flying over it. A lengthy period of ground school gave way to in-air instruction and the long-awaited first solo flight without an instructor. After logging sixty-five hours of solo time, the basic student pilot moved on to the primary phase of his training on the field. Upon successful completion of the primary curriculum, the young pilots-to-be were transferred across town to Kelly Field for the final, advanced aspect of their training, after which they received the coveted silver wings and gold bars of an Army Air Corps second lieutenant.

The exciting prospect of meeting and getting to know these future Army aviators appears to have been highly attractive to the eligible young ladies of San Antonio society. To prepare the cadets for the social life they could expect to enjoy in the city, each was presented with an official handbook upon his arrival at Randolph. To put the incoming cadet's mind at ease about his chances for social success while at the field, the handbook rather optimistically observed that:

> By virtue of his flying cadetship, the Randolph field
> newcomer is recognized without further test as
> being personally and socially eligible, and during
> his stay in the San Antonio neighborhood, he will
> have no difficulty in securing reasonable dates.[22]

Presumably filled with self-confidence gained from reading this
welcome bit of social advice, the new cadet must have looked forward to his first sortie into "the San Antonio neighborhood" to
secure his initial "reasonable" date. One can only wonder what
might have been considered an unreasonable date. At any rate, by
way of mild caveat, the handbook went on to further advise the
newcomer, "If a cadet does not have a date [presumably reasonable
or otherwise] it is usually his own fault."[23]

As an attractive venue at which a cadet might try his wings in
San Antonio society, the city's elegant Gunter Hotel sponsored the
Flying Cadet Club. Open to student pilots and young women only,
the club was the center of the social activity of cadets from throughout the immediate area. On the second Saturday following his
arrival at Randolph Field, the new cadet was invited to attend what
was billed as a tea dance at the Gunter's club. Graduating upper-
classmen from the airfield were asked to introduce the newcomers
to the many young ladies who apparently attended the events on a
regular basis, perhaps to determine if the new crop of student pilots
contained any more interesting prospects than had the soon-to-
depart upper cadet classes. Following this introduction to the Flying
Cadet Club, the aviator-to-be could return as often as he liked to
dance and socialize with the belles of San Antonio. According to the
official history of the Gunter Hotel, "The Flying Cadets were celebrated as an elite corps. Cadets were treated with deference even in
entertainment."[24]

Sunday afternoons seemed to be more or less reserved for the
cadets and what the Gunter book refers to as "select young ladies."
The groups dined from extraordinarily lavish buffets and danced to
the music of a full orchestra. According to its history book, "All during the war, tea-dances at the Gunter were part of the social scene in
San Antonio."[25] It is clear that from the early days of the war and
continuing into the twenty-first century, the men of the Air Force
found much to admire among the ladies of the Alamo City. In 1942,
the *Cadet Handbook* proudly announced that "so many officers have

married local girls, San Antonio is called the 'mother-in-law' of the Army."[26] One Air Force widow recalls that she met her first husband at a Gunter tea dance in 1943 while he was still a cadet. When he was killed in action soon after their wedding, she waited an appropriate period of time before returning to the Flying Cadet Club to try again. "The same magic worked for a second time," she remembers many years later, "and I married another lieutenant I had met at the Gunter. He made it through the war in good shape and I had this one with me for over fifty years."[27]

The elite reputation enjoyed by Randolph Field and its cadets soon earned for it the prestigious title of "The West Point of the Air." Nearly all of Class 42-K at the field was in fact made up of former cadets from the United States Military Academy at West Point in New York. To distinguish this particularly elite contingent, they were allowed to wear black shoes instead of the customary brown ones, as well as black ties and a specially designed cadet insignia. Among those who were permitted to wear this distinguishing uniform was B.D. Randolph, the son of the man for whom the field had been named only twelve years earlier.[28]

When the cadets gathered at formations on base or perhaps at a Gunter tea dance, it is possible they felt inspired to sing what some old-timers contend was the forerunner of an unofficial and somewhat bawdy Air Force song perhaps better known as "Into the Air, Junior Birdmen." Written by Maj. William J. Clinch in 1941, the lyrics somehow manage to convey the rustic, yet rousing esprit d' corps that has characterized the nation's aviators from the earliest days.

"Spirit of the Air Corps"

Into the air, Army Air Corps
Give her the gun, pilots true.
Into the air, Army Air Corps,
Hold her nose up to the blue.
When you hear our motors singin',
And our steel props start to whine,
You can bet the Army Air Corps
Is along the fightin' line.
Then when our last flight is over
And we meet our flyin' boss,
You can bet the air is clear, men,
From Orion to the Cross.[29]

Perhaps motivated if not amused by such colorful lyrics, Randolph Field's aviators played a vital role in World War II. Over sixteen thousand U.S. pilots trained there along with aviators from numerous other countries. The contribution the field made toward changing the face of the venerable old city that was then and continues to be its hostess was also immense. During the war years, the population of San Antonio grew by an astounding 61 percent, and in the five year period immediately following World War II, Bexar County overall experienced a nearly 50 percent increase in population. It is clear that many of the thousands upon thousands of instructors, pilots, and cadets who had been temporarily assigned to the San Antonio area during the war found ample reason to return as permanent Texans when they again became civilians.

Just as military construction and payroll spared the Alamo City much of the economic despair visited upon many other Texas cities during the bleak days of the Great Depression, so did the economic influence of the military aviation experience in San Antonio continue years later to contribute to the city's growth and fiscal well being. In 1997, for example, the federal government reported that the combined civil and military payroll for all of its bases in San Antonio exceeded $1 billion.[30]

From Kelly Field, founded in 1916, to Brooks that came into being one year later, and on to Randolph, which opened in 1931 to be followed by Lackland in 1942, the United States Air Force, by all of its many historic names, has been an immensely important partner in San Antonio's growth. In addition to its continuing positive impact on the community's economy, the many contributions the Air Force has made toward gender and racial equality are now a significant and permanent part of the intricate fabric of life in the Alamo City.

Hondo

I think that the most miserable day of my entire life was spent taking an eight-hour, fourth-week navigational exam in a tarpaper shack in the middle of August in Hondo, Texas.
Donald E. Collins
Hondo AAF Class 42-17

When contrasted with the lasting influence that military aviation has had on San Antonio, the impact the Army's air force had on nearby Hondo during World War II might seem, at least on the surface, to have been initially dramatic but relatively short-lived. However, in the memories of those who actually experienced the coming of the Air Force to the much smaller city in 1942, such is not the case.

One longtime resident, the late John Wentz, was ten years old when the war started and he remembered clearly how much his hometown was forever changed when Hondo Army Airfield opened in August 1942. "Nobody here had ever seen anything like it," he recalled in 1998. "All of a sudden, there were new faces everywhere and Hondo just wasn't the same little shut-in country town anymore." Because his mother worked at the airfield, young John was allowed to ride his bicycle through the base's main gate each afternoon to watch the cadets stand retreat for the lowering of the flag. "All the time I stood there during those ceremonies, at attention and saluting just like the cadets, I kept thinking how much better off we all were because these fellas had come here to live with us for awhile. I guess it was pretty much of a high water mark for Hondo, and we've been trying to get back up there ever since."[31]

As noted earlier, Air Force officials in San Antonio had long been thinking about Hondo as a possible safety valve training site to take some of the pressure off the dangerously overcrowded skies around Kelly and Brooks fields. Six months before the attack on Pearl Harbor, Hondo's name appeared as a suggested location of an alternate airfield in a memorandum urging that a new site be found away from the immediate vicinity of San Antonio. Located some forty miles west, Hondo, then an unincorporated village with a population of twenty-five hundred, had an excellent highway link to the very front gate of Kelly Field, a major east-west rail line, and more than adequate quantities of inexpensive and, save for one unfortunately prominent hillock, relatively flat land.

Taking these positive factors into consideration, and urgently motivated to find a new home for its recently opened navigation school at Kelly, Air Force officials launched a site-selection study of the Hondo area. Every effort to keep the study a secret to minimize real estate speculation proved to be totally futile. As any secrets are difficult to hide in small communities, reports that Army men had been seen in the vicinity promptly found their way into the local newspaper and on January 23, 1942, the *Hondo Anvil Herald* tattled that, "Several Army officials were here today, scouting for a location for an air training field." So much for military secrecy![32]

By March, the paper was able to report to its excited readers not only that the air-training field was to be a navigation school, but also how big the site was to be and exactly where it was located. One month later, on April 3, 1942, the proud *Anvil Herald* put all specu-lation about its airfield predictions to rest by reprinting a telegram from U. S. Senator W. Lee "Pappy" O'Daniel that officially announced the approval for a $5 million airfield for Hondo, with construction to commence at once.[33]

It would appear that the phrase "at once" was taken to heart quite literally by both the town fathers and the firm of H.B. Zachry, which already had obtained the contract to build the base. While it took Hondo a short three weeks to vote to become an incorporated city, it required the Zachry men just one week to unceremoniously and a bit ruthlessly evict the few families that had occupied homes on the site, destroy their houses and often their personal posses-sions, uproot trees and fences, and level the ground so that the mas-sive construction project could get under way.

Mr. Zachry obviously believed in speed. His firm had been given just a hundred days to transform the four thousand acre tract into an airfield designed to accommodate up to eight thousand personnel in over six hundred buildings served by a complete infrastructure of roads, utilities, and a network of runways and taxiways requiring 650,000 square yards of concrete. As the *Anvil Herald* understated, "This is a big job and the government wants it done in a hurry."[34]

The Zachry Company had accomplished other big jobs in a hurry for the War Department in other parts of the United States. Occasionally, specifications for building such things as barracks needed a bit of local modification. The universal governmental template for such buildings called for a roof that could withstand the weight of at least eight inches of snow. According to John Wentz, in order to accomplish this requirement within budget for the Hondo facility, Zachry had to eliminate any kind of flooring within the barracks. In a country that experienced little if any snow but endless days of scorching heat, the barrack huts were planned to have extra sturdy roofs but only floors of dirt. A pru-dent last minute realignment of construction priorities fortunately provided the barracks with wooden floors rather than snowdrift-resistant roofs.[35]

As work on the base continued at a feverish pace and military cadre personnel began to arrive, the little city was faced with a serious housing problem. Workers and soldiers alike found living quarters in what just days before had been chicken houses, cattle barns, and tents. Any civilians who felt tempted to complain about all of this sudden chaos, however, were admonished by the *Anvil Herald* to grin and bear it. "You best do your part by accepting conditions as they are," proclaimed the newspaper, "and keep smiling."[36]

John Wentz recalled that for the most part, Hondoans followed the periodical's advice. "Almost everyone I ever heard about seemed proud to be a part of something bigger than how the high school football team was likely to do on Friday night. Everybody thought they were suddenly on a team that was much more important than the Hondo Owls."[37]

In a stunningly short span of time, the construction workers finished their tasks, moved out of their chicken houses, and left town. Zachry had built his airfield in eighty-nine days rather than the one hundred he had been allotted. As might be expected, however, he had spent a few million dollars more than the original budget had specified, but there was a war on after all, and the exceeding of airfield construction budgets was already well on its way to becoming a national art form unto itself.[38]

On July 4, 1942, with construction complete, the Kelly Field Navigation School was packed up in toto and moved west on U.S. Highway 90 to the new facility on the edge of Hondo. Classes that were already in session at the old school made the transition in such an efficient manner that reportedly not one hour of scheduled training time was lost in the move. In less than three months time, Hondo had gone from being a relatively isolated unincorporated village to become a bustling small city and host to what would soon become the world's largest navigation school.

The townspeople loved it, according to John Wentz and others who remember the wartime experience in Hondo as the city's glory years. The local paper that had brought its readers the first rumors that a massive change in their way of life was about to take place now took pains to welcome the newly arrived uniformed guests to the city. In an apparently heartfelt greeting, the *Anvil Herald* printed a poem that advised any cadet who happened to read it just what he might expect in Hondo, and what Hondo in turn expected of him. Two verses from that poem of welcome say much:

> We are just a peaceful village small,
> With nothing much to offer at all!
> Just friendship true, good water and air,
> And we trust that you will treat us fair.
> You're Uncle Sam's best, so we've been told,
> Gentlemen true, not rude nor too bold,
> So we're glad to have you come our way,
> To protect us from harm — night and day.[39]

Not every airman found the friendship, good water, and air promised in the welcoming poem compelling enough reasons to grow fond of his new duty station. One young soldier named William H. Rehnquist, who would later gain fame as a chief justice of the United States Supreme Court, writes that his "memories of Hondo are not particularly favorable, though I could say the same for some of the other places I was stationed." Other than going to high school football games, the very pinnacle of social activity in many Texas towns, then as now, the chief justice recalls, "There wasn't much to do in Hondo." As a result, the young Rehnquist often hitchhiked to such cities as Houston and Corpus Christi on weekends to seek a diversion from his chores as a weather specialist at the airfield.[40]

During its three and a half year existence during World War II, the Hondo facility produced 14,185 navigators who saw action in every combat theatre, and later some 3,000 flight engineers who flew on the Air Force's giant B-29s at the end of the war.[41] Clearly, Hondo would never be quite the same as it had been before H.B. Zachry's giant earthmovers set to work transforming a Texas prairie into a mighty military installation. The town's population that had soared from twenty-five hundred in 1942 to nearly thirteen thousand by 1945 plummeted to forty-three hundred in less than a year. An economy that had flourished, buoyed by a six-fold increase in population, swiftly reverted to pre-war levels. Although the field was reactivated during the Korean-Cold War years, little now remains of the once vast array of buildings except for a few dilapidated hangars and rows of thick foundations.

There are still, however, a number of old timers who remember how Hondo was abuzz with activity and excitement when the giant field first came to town in 1942. According to some of them, the next three years were Hondo's days of glory and an exciting time not likely to be repeated.

Greenville

We wuz hongry!

W. A. Caplinger
Greenville, Texas
October 14, 1998

W.A. "Cap" Caplinger grew up with Greenville's Majors Field. As a nine-year-old youngster in 1942, he watched from his family's farmhouse yard as construction crews swiftly converted neighboring cotton fields into a sprawling Army airfield. By the time he was just a few months older, the constant sounds of BT-13A aircraft roaring aloft from the field's four newly constructed mile-long runways frequently kept him awake at night.[42]

As vivid as the now-retired Hunt County rancher's memories might be of destroyed cotton crops and the noise of ear-splitting aircraft engines, his lingering recollections of the dire effects of the Great Depression are even clearer. That it took the coming of Majors Field to end the economic nightmare still strikes Caplinger as being somewhat ironic. "Nobody was buying our cattle or our cotton," he recalls, "because nobody anywhere had any money to buy anything. When the construction companies started handing out the biggest paychecks any of us in Hunt County had seen in years, however, things began to turn around in a hurry." "Then," as Caplinger tells it, "the Army men came, drew their pay and put it all right back into Greenville's cash registers. We wuz [sic] hongry [sic] before all this building and flying business started, but money soon took care of that."[43]

Statistics indicate that Mr. Caplinger's version of what Greenville and Hunt County's economic scene was like before the war is right on target. Seventy percent of the county's population lived on 5,891 farms in 1940, even though over fifteen hundred other farms had been abandoned since the Depression had begun some ten years earlier. Only 685 individuals living in the entire town could be classified as steady, non-agrarian wage earners. Even more telling, perhaps, was the fact that 2,259 of the county's residents were shown to be on the relief rolls.[44]

As the number of people on relief increased and more and more desperate rural families left their farms and moved to larger cities seeking employment, Greenville's city leaders continued to seek answers to the region's economic woes. The Rotary Club, for example, adopted as its principal project in 1938 the obtaining of an airport, hopefully to be built with federal government funds and thus creating a much needed infusion of cash generated by such a construction project. Further, the Rotarians reasoned, the day might come when Love Field at nearby Dallas would be overcrowded to such a degree an alternate air facility relatively close by would flourish.

When one agency of the federal government quickly expressed at least a degree of interest in the Rotarians' airport scheme, the Greenville Chamber of Commerce took over the project and proceeded to convince the CAA that the city was indeed a worthy candidate to receive federal funding to construct a new field. The chamber had two very strong allies in its corner, the first being the influential Congressman Sam Rayburn, speaker of the United States House of Representatives. The second powerful ally on Greenville's side was timing itself. The chamber's request for CAA funds just happened to coincide with the Roosevelt administration's call for a massive enhancement of the Army's air force and an airfield-construction program to support that enhancement. This fortuitous coming together of historical need giving rise to the potential for federal spending gave Speaker Rayburn all the ammunition he needed to get his Greenville constituents the money as well as the administration's approval to begin building what was now to be an Army airfield rather than a municipal airport. The new facility would indeed someday become the property of the city, as the Rotarians had hoped, but the Army would pay for the $5 million in construction costs in order to use the field for "national defense purposes as long as deemed necessary."[45]

Although the United States involvement in World War II was still almost six months in the future when these negotiations were taking place, the actual coming of the war greatly accelerated the entire process. By early February 1942, the deal was finalized and two months later Speaker Rayburn was able to announce formal approval to start construction. Within weeks of that announcement, the young Caplinger became one of the first civilians to watch giant earthmovers and gangs of workers begin to clear the site five miles south of Greenville to make way for hangars, runways, and squadrons of training aircraft. The hometown newspaper perhaps best summed up what was foremost in the minds of the local citizenry. "Greenville," proclaimed the *Evening Banner*, "eagerly anticipated the wealth that comes from huge construction contracts."[46]

By existing East Texas standards, the word "huge" could not adequately convey the magnitude of the Majors Field construction project or the contract to build it. In total, the military city that was erected in a few short months was almost one half as large as Greenville itself. Over two hundred buildings were built, including shops, barracks, hangars, a hospital, two churches, and over five miles of runways, each half a football field in width.

By early August 1942, the first class of cadets had arrived on the vast new field to begin their primary flight training. At any given time during its peak years of operation, Majors was home to at least five thousand officers, cadets, enlisted men, and civilian workers. Construction work on the base was ongoing as the need for pilots accelerated throughout the war's early years.[47]

While many of Greenville's long-running economic woes were greatly diminished by the construction of Majors Field and the relatively well-paid personnel assigned to it, certain age-old social problems underscored by the arrival of those same personnel were not as easily resolved. As was true in much of deep East Texas at the time, the relationship between the black and white races was strained. The fundamental problem had originated late in the Civil War when cotton planters located in some other Confederate states sought to protect their human chattel property by moving slaves from Mississippi and Louisiana to East Texas plantations. As a result of this forced migration, the black slave population in Hunt County grew rapidly, doubling in two short years. When the Civil War ended in 1865, the slaves were freed and simultaneously given the right to vote, at least technically. During the dark days of Reconstruction following the Civil War, the sudden insertion of the former slaves into what had been an all-white society helped set the stage for the racial unrest and conflict that raged throughout East Texas and the rest of the former Confederate states for years to come. The written history of those troubled times indicates that the commonly perceived way to avoid an out-and-out shooting war was a rigid segregation between the two races.[48]

When men of both black and white ethnicity came to Greenville's Majors Field with the U. S. Army Air Force (which was itself segregated), they found an East Texas city that had in time come to accept and live within the clearly defined and rarely challenged guidelines that separated the black community from the white. Unfortunately, history also showed that when those lines appeared to have been crossed, the result was often brutal and tragic. Greenville, not unlike many other so-called "Southern" communities in East Texas, had witnessed its share of burnings and lynchings of blacks in the decades following the Civil War.[49]

Although the city was not alone in having serious racial problems, it was unique in having a very public sign that many believed reflected a definite attitude. "Greenville - Welcome," read the sign that for years stretched across Lee Street downtown, "The Blackest Land – The Whitest People." The *Texas Almanac and State Industrial Guide, 1939-1940*, obviously taking its cue from the then eighteen-year-old sign and apparently finding nothing irregular about its implied message, noted editorially that "Greenville is known nationally as the city of the blackest land and the whitest people."[50]

The easily misinterpreted sign is still controversial, even though it was removed over thirty years ago. To some, it had no negative racial implications whatever, while to others it was both repugnant and divisive. Regardless of how the message on the sign was perceived by the thousands of military personnel, both white and black, who saw it during the war years, the simple fact remains that it was there and easily seen by anyone who passed through town on the Katy Railroad or drove down Lee Street.

W.A. Caplinger and Vincent Leibowitz, a former director of a local museum, agree with others that with or without any influence drawn from the sign, Greenville was very much a segregated city when the first Army Air Force troops arrived in 1942. For the most part, incoming black soldiers found it prudent to comply with Greenville's racial restrictions. They sat in the balcony of the one theater in town that would admit them at all, and only ate in restaurants located in the black section of town.[51]

To their credit, base authorities attempted to make it possible for black soldiers to participate in local events, at least in a token manner. When city officials refused admission to black personnel attempting to attend an event at the municipal auditorium, Capt. Lyle V. Kleinjan, the base adjutant, protested in writing. He then proposed that twenty-five balcony seats be reserved for black soldiers at the next event scheduled in the auditorium. Apparently in an effort to minimize the potential for any unpleasantness, the captain promised city officials that those who wished to attend would come from the field by truck to be marched in formation to their assigned seats where they were to remain throughout the show and until all white attendees had left the auditorium. Only then would the black soldiers again be marched back to the trucks and immediately returned to Majors Field.[52]

While all of this regulated black and white segregation was taking place, the Army saw fit, perhaps inadvertently, to introduce a third element into the racial mix of Greenville, Texas. Whether the Army's curious decision to bring an entire squadron of Mexican airmen to the city late in the war was an innocent act based solely on military necessity or a deliberate attempt to break down the traditional walls of racial discord will likely never be known, but in all probability the War Department was far too busy with other more pressing military matters to come up with this unlikely liberal sociological experiment.

When the government of President Avilla Camacho sent its elite 201st Fighter Squadron of the Mexican Expeditionary Force across the Rio Grande on July 21, 1944, there could have been no earthly reason to believe the unit would train anywhere but in South Texas, where most of the Army's flight training centers were located. Indeed, the so-called *Aguilas Aztecas* were first assigned to San Antonio's Randolph Field where they were quickly assimilated into the growing contingent of Latin American units learning to fly in the United States. After only a short time, the Mexican unit was transferred to Foster Field near Victoria, Texas. Here, too, the large Hispanic community welcomed the officers and men as warmly as they had been in the Alamo City. This welcome was particularly pleasing to the enlisted men, many of whom did not speak English.[53]

After a pleasant ten-week stay in South Texas, the 201st was abruptly transferred to Pocatello, Idaho, where an unusually severe winter forced them back to Texas and a climate more suitable for flight training. At their new post at Majors Field, they encountered a different social environment than that which they had enjoyed in San Antonio, Victoria, and even Pocatello. The enlisted men in particular felt that the people of Greenville "were more suspicious" of them than residents of other cities had been.[54]

For the flying officers of the 201st, who were by Air Force regulations all proficient in the English language, life at Majors was pleasant enough, although the Spanish-speaking enlisted men encountered many obstacles. Several of the officers met local girls whom they later married, and while some may have felt that as foreigners they were held in suspicion, other accounts suggest that such was not always the case. One historian and observer of life in Greenville during the war years believes the local citizens were more confused about how to treat this group of newcomers than actually suspicious of them. Since the post-Civil War period, it has been suggested, there had never been any doubt about the rigid lines of division that separated the black and white societies in East Texas. The Army's sudden insertion of a third and heretofore unknown racial element into the long-established social pattern touched off a whole new set of questions about where the lines of segregation should be drawn. As a result, it seems likely that many of the long-standing and stereotypical racial parameters then began to blur and, at least in part, began to weaken. A growing post-World War II civic sense of racial tolerance born of an exposure to people from a different land and culture, perhaps owed its origin to a still-curious Army Air Force decision to bring the foreign squadron to East Texas.[55]

When the war was finally over in mid-1945, and the Mexican 201st Fighter Squadron had performed with valor in the South Pacific, Majors Field was closed. Its legacy, however, lives on. As Vincent Leibowitz puts it, "Majors [Field] was one of the most important things in Greenville's history." Hunt County's historian W. Walworth Harrison noted a few years after the gates at the old airfield had swung shut that, "The building of Majors Field airport proved to be the threshold for Greenville's long-dreamed of industrial growth and payroll."[56]

Indeed, what was once Majors Field has evolved over the years into a gigantic industrial complex, affording strong employment opportunities to many, including some who might well be the grandchildren of the cotton farmers who were forced off their family farms by the Great Depression in the late 1930s or of the black citizens long ago compelled to sit in theater balconies. As "Cap" Caplinger puts it, "I saw things go on in Greenville when the airfield was open for business that I never dreamed I'd see here, but I'll tell you what, Majors saved our bacon for sure."[57]

Austin

Mr. Speaker, I ask unanimous consent for an indefinite leave of absence.

Lyndon B. Johnson
Washington, D. C.
December 11, 1941

Mrs. Johnson wasn't the only congressman's wife who took over the office when her husband was gone, but she was the only one who considered it a full time job and did it.

J.J. Pickle
U. S. Congressman
1973

It should come as no great surprise that political persuasion and military capital expenditures in the United States have long been very closely knit. When it came to getting governmental approval for and the constructing of Army airfields in the early 1940s, one historian contends, as previously noted, that political interests were quite often the main determinant in the locating of military airfields. Not unexpectedly, the honorable members of the Texas delegation to Congress from 1936 through 1942 clearly did not shy away from using all of the formidable political clout at their disposal to attempt to gain a major military airfield for their district and their state, more or less regardless of any strategic implications inherent in placing the facility at any given site.[58]

There was nothing illegal or particularly unethical about the lobbying and pressuring tactics directed by senators and representatives toward the site-selection officials within the War Department hierarchy. This was, after all, what these individuals sent to the nation's capital by the electorate were supposed to do, and the Texas players on the national legislative team were masters at twisting arms or bending elbows or whatever else it took to put a Greenville, an Amarillo, an Austin, or any other Texas city first in line for consideration as an airfield site.

As previously mentioned, Sam Rayburn, speaker of the U.S. House of Representatives and congressman from Texas, was the key player in obtaining Majors Field for his constituency in Greenville, while the office of his protégé, Lyndon B. Johnson, was instrumental in bringing Bergstrom Field to Austin in 1942. Although the mayor of Austin at the time, the powerful Tom Miller, had been in eager pursuit of some kind of major military or defense project for his city long before Pearl Harbor, it took Congressman Johnson and later his politically savvy wife Lady Bird to finally bring such a project to fruition.

Records indicate that Mayor Miller first wrote to Johnson on April 9, 1941, to tell him of the city's "fervent desire" to get the approval for some kind of defense installation, "preferably an air base." Miller apparently recognized both the short-term importance of creating huge construction and military payrolls to aid his Depression-ridden city, and the long-term benefit of letting the federal government pay for an Army air facility that could quite possibly become Austin's premier civilian airport after the war. Clearly eager to convince Washington of the city's sincerity in the matter, Miller offered to buy the land necessary for such an undertaking and then lease it back to the War Department for a mere one dollar per year once an airfield had been built. Just over five months later, and only eight days before the Pearl Harbor attack, an Army site survey team arrived in Austin, reportedly persuaded both by Miller's offer to provide land for an air base and by Johnson's already renowned ability to get what he wanted in Washington, D.C.[59]

After due deliberation, the survey team decided that a three thousand acre site southeast of Austin would be the ideal location for the training field it was now considering. The entire issue moved into high gear in just a matter of days when the United States was suddenly thrust into the war. The Army Air Force, now eager to get underway with building the new field, asked the city of Austin to proceed urgently with its previously announced intention to buy the agreed-upon site. A special bond issue election held on March 4, 1942, guaranteed the availability of the $466,600 that would be required to buy the acreage.[60] Although it now seemed the airfield project was guaranteed, a problem soon arose over who would hold title to the land. The city contended it should have the right until the war was over while the War Department insisted on holding a clear title indefinitely.

Once again, it fell to Johnson to come to the rescue. The undeniable hitch to this rescue effort was the fact that Congressman Johnson was now Lieutenant Commander Johnson, United States Naval Reserve, and on duty in the South Pacific. As it developed, however, his wife was most effectively handling Johnson's governmental duties during his absence. In an oral history interview conducted long after the war, Lady Bird Johnson recalled the importance of the airfield issue. "One of the most pressing things, one of the things we hoped the most for," she stated, "was to get some unit of the armed forces stationed in Austin, *because it would build the city then and later* [italics added]." She went on to recollect that, "The best chance for getting the unit was through the Army Air Support Command,"

and by extension, it can be assumed, an airfield to accommodate that command, which "later developed into Bergstrom Field."[61]

Mrs. Johnson went to the office of Robert Lovett, assistant secretary of war for air, to talk "on Lyndon's behalf" about the proposed field and the problems that were being encountered in finalizing the title negotiations. Ever the politician's wife and with an eye on future elections, she asked Secretary Lovett to let her "know a few hours ahead of time when they reached their decision, very especially if their decision was yes, so that we could notify the papers." In this way, Mrs. Johnson felt her husband's constituents "would know that he was on the job, his deputy [herself, of course] was still on the job, still working for them."[62]

While she was working the bureaucratic network in Washington, Mrs. Johnson also stayed in almost constant contact with Tom Miller back in Austin. On March 14, 1942, the *Austin Statesman* reported that she had earlier that day notified the mayor that the new base had been officially approved. Miller, quite understandably elated at this long-sought and highly-welcome news, publicly thanked Lyndon Johnson in the same edition of the newspaper, and praised him for obtaining the airfield for Austin. Unfortunately, the mayor failed to mention the tireless efforts of the congressman's wife who had done so much on behalf of the whole project at the national level.[63]

Work on the airfield finally got under way just weeks after the War Department approved it. A construction crew of over fifteen hundred men set about razing homes that had been on the site for decades, then leveling the land, and beginning to build at the rate of from ten to fifteen buildings per day. Runways, ramps, and taxiways were also hurriedly put in place and on September 18, 1942, less than four months after the work had begun, the partially finished base was officially activated as Del Valle Army Airfield. The urgent wartime need for the Air Transport Command that Mrs. Johnson had so vigorously sought had accelerated the construction project, but had allowed little time or money for anything resembling decorative touches. Most exterior walls were covered in black tarpaper and some buildings had only floors of dirt. To many early visitors, the field took on an outward appearance of the "early-Depression" era.[64]

In spring 1943, Congressman Johnson's office again took an active role in airfield affairs. When a close personal friend who was vice president of the Austin National Bank asked to have the name of Del Valle Airfield changed to honor a bank employee who had been killed in the war, Johnson, back from active duty, weighed in with full force. He relentlessly wore down the Army's then-standard reluctance to name a military facility after a local hero and as a result, the base was re-named Bergstrom Field on November 11, 1943, in honor of John August Earl Bergstrom, the fallen former employee of the bank.[65]

Bergstrom Field admirably performed its mission as the Troop Carrier Command's operations center throughout the war. When that war had been won, however, the Army began to evaluate the need for many of the bases located in Texas and elsewhere. Once again Lyndon Johnson threw his inestimable support behind Bergstrom Field, finally causing military officials to accept the fact that it was far easier to allow the Austin facility to remain open than it was to deal with Johnson's boundlessly energetic and forceful campaign against closing it.[66]

The field remained active as a military air base until 1993, well past the lifetime of the man who, along with considerable help from his wife, had helped create it, re-name it, and protect it. In his years as president in the mid-1960s, Johnson often flew into Bergstrom Air Force Base from Washington enroute to his Texas White House near Johnson City. During one winter trip from the nation's capital, President Johnson commented on how much he always looked forward to the green grass of Texas after seeing only the dry and brown lawns in the east. Much to his dismay, he was shocked upon landing to find the grass at Bergstrom had also turned brown following an unusual Texas cold snap. The base commander immediately heard of the president's considerable displeasure over the totally unacceptable color of Bergstrom's grass. To spare himself any further wrathful comments from the often volcanic Johnson, the commander ordered that, henceforth, in advance of any Johnsonian arrival and departure, the grass along the route always taken by the presidential motorcade was to be dyed a natural-looking green. There is no record to indicate if Johnson ever questioned why on many occasions only the lawns along his path of travel at the airbase were green when all other grasses within his range of vision were sometimes a dull and wintry brown.[67]

Before it was closed as a military base to begin its transformation into a modern international airport for the city of Austin,

Bergstrom was again called upon to be of service to Lyndon Johnson, its principal advocate and benefactor. After the ex-president
died at his ranch on January 22, 1973, his body was flown from
Bergstrom Field to Washington D.C. for a national service and then
back to Austin for burial on the ranch. It was an appropriate place
to mark the end of his final flight.

The enormous impact of the World War II Army Air Force on
Austin can best be realized by measuring the importance of the
modern civil air center that emerged from the old military base in
1999. A vital element in Austin's potential as an increasingly important national and international city, the new facility bears the proud
and symbolic name Austin-Bergstrom International Airport, reflecting both its historic military past and its rising hopes for a prosper-
ous future.

Houston

*It was kind of funny, I guess, come to think of it. My father was
stationed at Ellington about twenty-five years before I was. I
canstill remember him telling me about how he saw the first
airplane land at the field after Thanksgiving Day, 1917.*

Felix B. Neale, Jr.
Houston, Texas

Eighty-five years following its founding as a First World War
flight training center, Ellington Field could offer precious little tangible evidence of its rich military legacy. The installation had, in
fact, played a key role in both world wars, even though the federal
government found it necessary to demolish the original airfield not
long after the first war had ended.

The government's initial decision to build the airfield some fifteen miles from downtown Houston in 1917 was, as might be
expected, strongly influenced by the intensive lobbying efforts of
local politicians and the city's chamber of commerce. One of the
major advantages in locating an airfield near Houston, according to
the well-orchestrated lobbying campaign, was the excellent flying
weather to be found in the immediate vicinity of the proposed site.

As the aviators in the Army's fledgling flying service discovered
to their dismay as soon as the field became operational, the claims
of good flying conditions were totally without merit. The occur-

rence of frequent and violent thunderstorms, as well as the occasional hurricane in the region, made the scheduling and execution
of training flights a highly problematical matter. Further, the presence of thick fog banks often reduced visibility to inches and created
dangerous situations for trainees and instructors.

George Sessions Perry, an astute chronicler of the Lone Star
State, wrote some years later about the lack of governmental wis-
dom in placing Ellington Field in what was then little more than a
gigantic thirteen hundred acre tangle of swamp grass. "There it now
sits," snapped the acerbic Perry, "be-fogged, be-rained, be-mired,
wasting precious hours of precious personnel and precious bi-
motored training planes." "Houston," Perry concluded sharply, "has
a jack-ass killing climate."[68]

Whether any of the mules used in clearing the airfield site were,
in fact, killed by the climate was not recorded. Despite mosquitoes,
weather, and the boggy terrain, the huge Army airfield was in operation near Houston just seventy-three days after work began on it in
mid-September 1917.[69]

As the construction work was nearing completion, the Army
announced that the new facility would be named Ellington Field in
honor of Lt. Eric Lamar Ellington, a native of Illinois who was a
graduate of the United States Naval Academy rather than West Point.
The lieutenant had served in the U.S. Cavalry after graduation from
Annapolis, which seems unusual enough, before earning his wings as
an Army pilot. Although he had no recorded connection with either
Houston or the state of Texas, the sad fact that Ellington had lost his
life in an aeroplane crash in 1913 apparently was reason enough to
make his name a suitable choice for the new field.

The Ellington Field of the First World War was, even by later Air
Force standards, a very large installation. It consisted of twenty-four
hangars, twelve barracks, four warehouses, and two school buildings. It also had a full service hospital, an officers' club, two post
exchanges, several service clubs, and four motion picture theaters.
The field's main runway was over eight thousand feet long and a
generous eight hundred feet wide. Most stateside military runways
in use during World War II were less than one-quarter as wide.[70]

When the First World War ended on November 11, 1918, over
twenty thousand Army personnel reportedly were assigned to the
year-old field. By way of contrast, nearby Houston showed a population in the 1920 Federal Census of slightly more than 150,000.[71]

Within two years of its 1918 operational peak, the field was deactivated and by 1926 the Army had demolished nearly all the buildings so recently constructed. The razing efforts were greatly abetted by a major fire that spared only a concrete water tank as the sole reminder that a great military city had once flourished on what had again become a thirteen hundred acre bramble patch.[72]

In less than fifteen years, however, the brambles and coastal grass again gave way to the ground-clearing efforts of the Army's Corps of Engineers, this time working without mule teams. Mounting fears about a possible enemy attempt to invade Texas from the Gulf of Mexico had compelled the War Department to seek a strong defensive military installation in the Houston area in order to protect the region's many industrial and petrochemical facilities located along the city's ship channel. Since the government had retained ownership of the Ellington site, it was duly decided that the burned-out and abandoned old airfield should arise, phoenix-like, from its own ashes in the swamp. A new Ellington Field was born.[73]

The herds of cattle that had been grazing on the site were trucked away, and by June 1940 all utilities for the resurrected base were in place and the construction of new runways was nearing completion. The field's aircraft parking apron alone required nearly 3.5 million cubic feet of concrete, making it at the time the world's largest one-piece slab of cement, according to the *Houston Chronicle*.[74]

By the time the overall building project was nearly finished, the original construction estimate of $3 million had been more than doubled and six hundred thousand man-hours of labor had been expended. In return, the Army had acquired 301 new buildings, two one-mile-long runways, and the record-breaking concrete apron that was itself a mile and a half long and 740 feet wide.[75]

By late 1941 the base was almost fully operational with over five thousand military personnel assigned to it. As one of the nation's major flight training centers, Ellington was reportedly projected to produce fully one-third of the Army's new pilots each year. As reported in the *Houston Chronicle* of October 26, 1941, this meant that exactly 7,280 aviators would be receiving their silver wings at the field.[76]

The first commander of the new Ellington Field was, ironically, the same man who had been the last commander of the old Ellington. Lt. Col. W.H. Reid had served at the installation in 1918, had been an instructor pilot with the field's Texas Air National Guard unit in the years immediately following the First World War, and was in command of the original base when fire ravaged it in 1927.[77]

As an active participant in much of the field's history, Colonel Reid was keenly interested in preserving at least some of its heritage. As a result, he arranged to commission a local Houston painter to render a portrait of Lt. Eric Ellington to be prominently displayed in the field headquarters as an enduring symbol of the historic linkage between the earlier First World War airfield and the new one that was now poised on the threshold of yet another international conflict. Presumably following at least a suitable period of consideration, the colonel announced that he had chosen Mrs. E. Richardson Cherry, a Houston artist, to create the oil painting of the late Lieutenant Ellington from a photograph he had located. In reporting the colonel's choice in its May 28, 1941, edition, the *Houston Press* perhaps tactfully made no mention of the fact that the chosen artist was also Colonel Reid's mother-in-law.[78]

No one apparently found reason to question how closely Mrs. Cherry's painting resembled the actual Lieutenant Ellington until 1958 when the aviator's sister visited the base to view her brother's portrait for the first time. After only a few quick moments of cursory study, she rather brusquely dismissed the work as being "not a very good likeness" and strode away.[79]

When he was not commissioning his relatives to paint portraits, Colonel Reid was kept busy running a very active flight-training center. Student pilots were required to undergo a strenuous ten weeks of ground and flight instruction that took place both night and day. During the first two years of World War II, it was reported that one of every ten active duty pilots had been trained at Ellington Field. Although this was substantially less than the three-of-every-ten ratio originally projected, the field was nonetheless an important flight training facility.[80]

Later in the war, the instruction of pilots was transferred to other airfields and Ellington became the location of the Army Air Forces' Advanced Navigator Training School. From 1943 through the end of the war in mid-1945, more than four thousand navigators graduated from the field.[81]

On the day the war ended, well over five thousand officers and men were assigned to the field, including navigator trainees from several foreign countries, including China and France. Following the surrender of Japan in September 1945, the foreign trainees were allowed to complete their training at Ellington, but the American students were either assigned to non-flying duties at other airfields or simply discharged.[82]

Despite the efforts of Congressman Albert Thomas and other political leaders, the base was ordered to be closed by March 15, 1946. The federal government continued to retain ownership of the deactivated base although the actual operation of the facility became the responsibility of the Texas Air National Guard. From 1946 through July 1948, Ellington Field was the weekend home of aviators assigned to the 111th Air National Guard squadron, a unit that had served with distinction during the war.[83]

In the summer of 1948, the increasing heat of the Cold War compelled the Air Force to once again bring Ellington Field back into full federal operation. With only limited usage by the Texas Air Guard, many of the field's six hundred buildings had fallen into disrepair and the runways had deteriorated. Following a sizeable expenditure for its rehabilitation, the thrice-born Ellington Field again became a major Air Force installation.[84]

The primary mission of the revitalized base was once again the training of navigators. From 1949 through 1958, the 3605th Navigator Training Wing produced thousands of highly qualified fliers who were as well versed in the new and rapidly developing electronic technologies as they were in the old, if tedious, techniques of night celestial, pressure pattern, Loran, and polar grid navigation. Ellington's navigation school graduates saw active service in all of the unheralded, secretive, often dangerous, and generally unappreciated aspects of America's long Cold War.

In 1960, the Air Force deactivated the base for the third time in its history, only to reopen it again in 1963. Finally, in 1976, the federal government turned the facility over to the Texas Air National Guard and then withdrew its aircraft from Ellington, probably for the last time.

At the outset of the twenty-first century, Ellington was still home to the Texas Air Guard's 147th Fighter Group, successor to the 111th Squadron. The field's runways were also being shared with planes of the National Aeronautics and Space Administration, general aviation, and commercial air freighters. The City of Houston, owner of most of the former military facility, also was using it as a third municipal airport.

The story of Ellington Field is unique in that it so clearly demonstrates both the recurring strategic value of an historic airfield and the powerful impact upon such a facility created by the explosive encroachment of residential and commercial real estate development. In the years between the many openings and closings of the field, the once vacant land that surrounded it grew and wildly flourished into a confusing and often towering maze of houses, schools, shopping malls, and office buildings that greatly restricted flight-training operations. Its traditional mission thwarted by the ever-tightening circle of civilian progress, the old military field was destined to dwindle and slip into obsolescence.

No historical marker can be found on the site to afford even a hint of the vital importance that this now largely vacant field could once so proudly claim. Born and re-born more times than any other Texas air base, historic Ellington Field is not likely to be born again. What was once a thriving military city is now largely a vacant, park-like expanse of grass. Ironically, the vast open space provides both a welcome oasis and an effective buffer against the tide of development that has served, at least in part, to throttle Ellington's future and all but erase its glorious past.

[1] Kelly Field Vertical File, UT Institute of Texan Cultures, San Antonio, Texas.

[2] *The Official World War II Guide to the Army Air Forces: A Directory, Almanac and Chronicle of Achievement*, 39.

[3] Kelly Field Vertical File.

[4] Ibid.

[5] Ann Hussey and Robert Browning, *A History of Military Aviation in San Antonio*, 29-30.

[6] Ann Krueger Hussey and Dr. Robert S. Browning III, *A Heritage of Service: Seventy-Five Years of Military Aviation at Kelly Air Force Base*, 1916-1991, 18.

[7] Ibid., 18.

[8] *A Pictorial History of Kelly Air Force Base*, 93.

[9] Hussey and Browning, *A Heritage of Service*, 96-98.

[10] Ibid., 98.

[11] Dave Stokes, *Air Force News*, October 6, 1999, 2.

[12] Napoleon B. Byars, "Kelly Air Force Base and the Hispanic Contribution," 1.

[13] Sherri Fauver, "Henrietta Lopez Rivas – "Kelly Air Force Base Her Proving Ground," 2.

[14] *The Flying Times*, March 18, 1944, Kelly Field Public Information Office, 4.

[15] Ibid., 11.

[16] Rossi L. Selvaggi, "A History of Randolph Air Force Base," (master's thesis, University of Texas, 1958), 11.

[17] Ibid., 13.

[18] Thomas Manning, Pat Parrish and Dick Emmons, "Randolph Field," *A History of Military Aviation in San Antonio*, 17.

[19] *San Antonio Light*, June 20, 1930.

[20] *San Antonio Express*, June 20, 1930.

[21] "Randolph Field," 80.

[22] J. Frank Davis, *Randolph Field: A History and Guide*, 84.

[23] Ibid., 85.

[24] Mary Ann Noonan Guerra, *The Gunter Hotel In San Antonio's History*, 30.

[25] Ibid., 31.

[26] Davis, 85.

[27] Marie Tanner Welles, interview with author, San Antonio, Texas, July 13, 2000.

[28] Selvaggi, 108.

[29] Davis, 88.

[30] "USAF Almanac, 1998," *Air Force Magazine*, vol. 81, no. 5, May 1998, 123.

[31] John Wentz, interview with author, Hondo, Texas, September 12, 1999.

[32] *Hondo Anvil Herald*, January 23, 1942.

[33] *Hondo Anvil Herald*, April 3, 1942.

[34] *Hondo Anvil Herald*, April 19, 1942.

[35] Wentz interview.

[36] *Hondo Anvil Herald*, April 19, 1942.

[37] Wentz interview.

[38] Ron Tyler, ed., *The New Handbook of Texas*, vol. 3, 681.

[39] *Hondo Anvil Herald*, August 14, 1942.

[40] Chief Justice William H. Rehnquist, letter to author, June 11, 1999

[41] Robert D. Thompson, *We'll Find the Way: The History of Hondo Army Air Field During World War II*, 160.

[42] W. A. Caplinger, interview with author, Greenville, Texas, October 15, 1998.

[43] Ibid.

[44] Tyler, ed., 785.

[45] W. Walworth Harrison, *History of Greenville and Hunt County*, 345.

[46] *Greenville Evening Banner*, January 6, 1942.

[47] W. A. Caplinger and Jim Conrad, "A History of Majors Airfield, Greenville, Texas," 7.

[48] Tyler, ed., 785.

[49] Harrison, 387.

[50] *Texas Almanac and State Industrial Guide, 1939-1940,* 426.

[51] Vincent Leibowitz, interview with author, Greenville, Texas, October 15, 1998.

[52] Caplinger and Conrad, "History of Majors Field," 8.

[53] William G. Tudor, "Flight of Eagles: The Mexican Expeditionary Air Force 'Escuadron' 201 in World War II." (PhD. diss., Texas Christian University, 1997), 2.

[54] Fred H. Allison, "The Fighting Eagles: Mexico's Squadron 201 in World War II Texas." (Paper presented at the annual meeting of the Texas State Historical Association, Austin, Texas, March 3, 1998), 4.

[55] Ibid., 4.

[56] Harrison, 387.

[57] Caplinger interview.

[58] Jerold E. Brown, *Where Eagles Land: Planning and Development of U.S. Army Airfields, 1910-1941*, 93.

[59] Tom Miller to Lyndon Johnson, letter dated April 9, 1941, Letter Box 27, Lyndon B. Johnson Library, Austin, Texas.

[60] *The Austin Statesman*, May 27, 1941.

[61] Mrs. Lyndon B. Johnson, oral history interview XVI, February 1, 1980.

[62] Ibid.

[63] *The American Statesman*, March 14, 1942.

[64] Robert Sligh, *Bergstrom AFB: A History*, 2.

[65] "Bergstrom Field History," 1.

[66] Sligh, 18.

[67] Ibid., 19.

[68] George Sessions Perry, *Texas: A World In Itself*, 247.

[69] *Houston Chronicle,* December 3, 1917.

[70] *The Houston Post,* December 31, 1942.

[71] *Texas Almanac and State Industrial Guide, 1943-1944,* 77.

[72] *Ellington Field Yearbook*, 1943, 28.

[73] Erik Carlson, *Ellington Field: A Short History, 1917-1963*, 16.

[74] *Houston Chronicle*, June 6, 1940.

[75] *The Houston Post*, December 31, 1942.

[76] *Houston Chronicle,* October 26, 1941.

[77] *Ellington Field Yearbook*, 27.

[78] *Houston Press,* May 28, 1941.

[79] Carlson, 45.

[80] *Houston Chronicle,* March 18, 1945.

[81] Ibid.

[82] *Houston Chronicle,* March 19, 1946.

[83] Ibid, July 27, 1948.

[84] Ibid, July 28, 1948.

NORTH TEXAS

AREA DETAILED

Tarrant
①

Dallas
②

ARMY AIR FORCES STATIONS

① Fort Worth Army Airfield, Fort Worth

② Love Field, Dallas

Robert F. Pace

North Texas

The war made such an enormous impact on our North Texas culture it's almost like talking about two different planets separated by only four years!

> Knox Bishop
> Col. USAF (Ret.)
> Frontiers of Flight Museum
> Dallas, Texas

Both Dallas and Fort Worth gained important and lasting benefits from the wartime Army airfields that were located on what in the early 1940s were the outskirts of these two North Texas cities. Perhaps their comparatively large size made the impact of the air bases less immediately apparent than was often the case in much smaller towns across the state, but history clearly indicates that both Dallas Love Field and Fort Worth Army Airfield were vital factors in the future economic development of their respective host cities.

Military aviation had been important in North Texas long before the coming of World War II. Fort Worth had been home to no less than three training fields during the First World War, while Love Field had opened as an Army facility on October 19, 1917. By the

end of the First World War, Hicks, Carruthers, and Barron Fields in
the Fort Worth area had ceased military operations, while Love
Field, which had served double duty as an advanced pilot training
center and an aircraft repair facility, was briefly closed before
becoming the city's municipal airport in 1923. The subsequent
re-mergence of Dallas and Fort Worth as major wartime military air
centers would prove to be a significant milestone for each city and
the entire metropolitan area.

Dallas

*War preparations brought new industry to Dallas and new
customers to Neiman-Marcus. War workers, like wildcatters,
wanted the best as soon as their incomes rose sufficiently to
enable them to buy the best.*

> Stanley Marcus
> *Minding the Store*
> ©1974

The war workers who helped ready Dallas's Love Field for its
return to military operations might have wondered how the airport
came to have such a decidedly unmilitary sounding name. According to Army records, Love Field was named to honor the memory of
a fledgling military flyer who apparently never so much as passed
through the city. Lt. Moss Lee Love was a native of Virginia and an
officer in the 11th U.S. Cavalry who had been in the Lone Star State
in 1913 just long enough to join the newly formed Aeronautical Service at its temporary headquarters in Texas City. Love had taken
only a few flight lessons before dying in a plane crash a few months
later in San Diego, California.[1]

During the First World War, the facility that had been named
for the late Lieutenant Love turned out on average fifty Army
pilots each month. There were twelve hangars on the field, each of
which could accommodate eleven Curtiss biplanes. The government had originally promised to buy the land on which the
hangars and runways had been built by the War Department at a
cost of approximately $1 million, but after the war in Europe
ended on November 11, 1918, the Army no longer had any need
for the field. Accordingly, it stopped paying the $20 per acre
annual lease fee on the land, auctioned off the buildings, and

NORTH TEXAS   7 3

abandoned all flight operations on the site for what would prove to be a twenty-three year hiatus.[2]

A group of Dallas entrepreneurs doing business as the Love Field Industrial District Trust then took up the option to buy the property. The several farming families who had been raising cotton on the site prior to the war had already voted to relinquish their rights to the land for cash, primarily because the recently-built airfield runways and remaining concrete foundations made cotton farming all but impossible. A unique large chalk and gravel square that the Army had placed on the exact center of the field as a directional guide for its aviators was also considered by the farmers to be particularly detrimental to the growing of cotton.[3]

By 1923, the city of Dallas was the new lessee of the old Army airfield, and three years later, the first scheduled airmail flight to leave the city departed for Chicago from what had become the municipal airport. The next year, Dallas bought Love Field for $43,000. Four years later, the city acquired additional land surrounding the airport for $325,000 with the money being raised through sales of airport bonds.[4]

Dallas's unique geographical location at the center of the nation virtually ensured that its new air facility would be a success. Soon the airport boasted a modern terminal that accommodated not only domestic travelers but passengers bound for Central and South American destinations as well.

The same fortuitous geographical location that had made Love Field so attractive to commercial airline companies also became of major interest to the Army Air Force in 1942. Suddenly faced with fighting a war in both the European and Pacific Theaters of Operation, the Army urgently needed a prime central location for the headquarters of its 5th Ferrying Group. It was the mission of this group to handle the movement of men and war materiél to both coasts and beyond. To more efficiently accomplish its mission, the Ferrying Group preferred to be situated close to the nation's geographical heart, and Love Field was located almost exactly at that point.

In mid-1942, the Army began moving back to its old World War I airfield located just a few miles north of downtown Dallas. Official permission for the airport's partial return to military usage had been given to federal officials by the city on June 24, 1942, following a series of meetings between Dallas Mayor Woodall Rodgers and the Army's regional chief real estate supervisor, Lt. Col. Leonard Cowley.

As the *Dallas Times-Herald* noted in reporting on the meetings in its April 19, 1942, edition, "The local airport has been used to service an increasing number of [military] planes which are en route to coastal areas and to war fronts." Colonel Cowley was recorded as saying that the meetings were "a preliminary way" to ascertain if the airport might be used by the Army Air Force. Mayor Rodgers quickly responded, "If the Army feels that Army use of Love Field is essential to the prosecution of the war, we gladly tender that use." Mr. Rodgers said his city hoped to retain management control of the airport, but he went on to say that Dallas "will give this to the Army also, if the Army feels this is necessary."[5]

Just two months after Mayor Rodgers's statement, the War Department did indeed feel it was necessary to begin transferring the 5th Ferrying Group Headquarters and all of its operations to Love Field from its temporary location at Hensley Field west of Dallas. The final move was delayed, however, until enough buildings at the headquarters site could be constructed to accommodate the incoming men and aircraft of the Ferrying Group. While the construction work at the airfield was being completed, the Group's personnel were billeted at an old Civilian Conservation Corps camp located on Dallas's White Rock Lake.[6]

On September 28, 1942, the 5th was in full-scale operation at Love Field. Over the next three wartime years, the unit posted an impressive service record that featured forty million miles of air transport missions in one fifteen-month time period. Some of the regularly scheduled flights of the Group were over Central and South American routes, although trips to other worldwide destinations were not uncommon. In addition to ferrying aircraft to combat units bound for Europe, the Group also participated in evacuating military personnel who had been wounded in action to hospitals closer to their homes, as well as flying regularly scheduled air routes to domestic and foreign destinations.[7]

The pilots of the Ferrying Group crews included the Women's Auxiliary Ferrying Squadron (WAFS), civilians, and members of the Women Airforce Service Pilots (WASP) organization as well as the Army aviators. Although the WASPs were on civil service and not military status, they regularly flew aircraft directly to combat zones with the same dedication to duty as that shown by their male Army counterparts.

Even though the WASPs were denied most of the benefits afforded military personnel, they were allowed to have their uniforms fitted by tailors from Neiman-Marcus. The already famous Dallas store regularly sent its fitters to the airfield to ensure the female pilots looked smart in their newly purchased uniforms.[8]

Florene (Miller) Watson was one of the original group of pilots to volunteer for the WAFS. She remembers that male applicants for positions as ferrying pilots were required to have at least 250 hours of flying time plus a commercial license to be considered for acceptance, while she and the other female applicants had to have 500 hours and a commercial license. Looking back on what at the time might have appeared to be discrimination, Mrs. Watson laughs that the women had "already done all the dumb stuff new pilots always seem to do while the men candidates had not flown enough yet" to avoid the inevitable pitfalls of rookie flyers.[9]

When she entered the Ferrying Auxiliary in 1943, Mrs. Watson already had over one thousand hours of flying time. During her career at Love Field as a WAF, and later the WASP squadron commander, she flew more than twenty different types of aircraft, ranging from the early P-40s through the B-17 and the B-25. "The war," she believes, "gave me an insight on life other than the kitchen sink." Without that war, Mrs. Watson is convinced, many opportunities that were afforded women would only have come their way years later, if at all. In her opinion, one of the most important of the opportunities provided to her by wartime service was to become the pilot of "bigger, better, faster airplanes."[10]

WASP Rosa Lea (Fullwood) Meek Dickerson, who had made her first solo flight at age twelve, also loved flying faster airplanes. On several occasions during the war, she flew from her Love Field base to the East Coast to climb into the cockpit of a newly-built Bell P-63 King Cobra fighter plane and ferry it to an air base at Great Falls, Montana. From there, Russian women pilots, known as the "Night Witches," would fly the lend-lease planes back to their home fields in the Soviet Union. When American men stationed at Great Falls would speak admiringly of the Russian women's ability to handle such a spirited aircraft, WASP Fullwood delighted in softly reminding them just who had flown the plane to Montana.[11]

There were other females assigned to Love Field besides the WAFS and WASPs. Over two hundred members of the Women's

Army Corps (WAC) served as mechanics, mess sergeants, motor pool drivers, and technicians. Private Helen Wilkey, who was a stock clerk, was named "the most typical WAC" on the base after her husband, a fellow soldier, wrote an essay that won for her the coveted title and for both of them a three-day pass.[12]

For the thousands of modern day travelers to and from Dallas who might tend to think of Love Field only in terms of hectic traffic, crowded parking garages, and long lines of commuting passengers, it may be difficult to envision the bustling airport as a wartime airfield. There were no parking garages then, of course, little automobile traffic, and only uniformed military personnel who were either coming back from the war or traveling out to the battle zones as passengers on aircraft of the 5th Ferrying Group.

By all accounts, Love Field was a visually attractive base, providing an excellent environment for those assigned to it. Both male and female off-duty personnel, for example, were provided with leisure facilities that were apparently among the best in the Army Air Force. A post gymnasium offered organized sports activities that reflected the mix of servicemen and servicewomen assigned to the field. There were male and female volleyball, softball, tennis, and bowling leagues, as well as reportedly well-attended co-ed night activities that featured mixed athletic events. The gym even had its own seemingly minutiae-oriented clerk, who duly recorded for posterity that in its first nine months of operation, the handball court had been used 6,920 times, 17,200 men and women had visited the barbell room, 12,000 had played squash, another 10,200 had taken steam baths, and a lucky 6,800 individuals had been treated to massages.[13]

Such vigorous physical activity called for a nourishing diet, and while modern day nutritionists might cringe at what the Love Field enlisted men's mess offered in 1944, the fare was considered extraordinary at the time. For example, the men and women were regularly served huge T-bone steaks, and during the heat of the summer, diners were offered bacon and tomato and toasted cheese sandwiches on a twenty-four-hour basis. To make these popular culinary items perhaps even more pleasant to consume, live dinner music was provided nightly by Love Field's own 691st Army Band. According to a poll among soldiers taken two years after the dining facility had opened, the most popular of all its amenities was the permission to smoke cigarettes or cigars at any time of the day. In the mess hall the combination of music and smoking, as well as the quality of the food, was apparently appealing to the enlisted personnel, with over two million meals being served in a two-year period.[14]

When it was not providing background dinner music for the GIs, the airfield's 691st Army Band was busy elsewhere. It played at the daily retreat ceremony as well as a formal parade held every Saturday. Each Friday night, various ensembles from the band played for dances at the enlisted men's mess, the non-commissioned officers' club, and the officers' club on a regular weekly basis. The full band also gave concerts for Dallas area citizens and traveled to other Army posts to perform. In addition to all of this activity, the group's trumpet players served as buglers each day on the field, starting with reveille at sunup and concluding with taps late at night.[15]

The maintenance of a high level of morale was obviously a top priority at Love Field during the war. Good food, music, and an active health and fitness program, give or take a tobacco-smoke filled mess hall, all contributed to the physical and mental well-being of airfield personnel. Overseeing all components of the ongoing effort was the base special services office, which offered educational, social, and recreational activities to all servicemen and women. Included on the special service schedules were parties, motion pictures, dramatic performances, art classes, dances, city tours, foreign language instruction, and lectures. The office also operated a library with 4,500 volumes that attracted nearly a thousand weekly visitors. Over 2,000 individuals attended movies at least once each week, and an average of 1,250 soldiers were present each Friday for a regular lecture series.[16]

Despite all of the activities available to them on the field, a large number of the personnel preferred to make the short trip to downtown Dallas on weekends. According to a report in the *Dallas Morning News*, an average of six thousand servicemen came into the city each weekend. On one typical Saturday night in June 1945, only one hundred soldiers were arrested by military police on charges that included drunkenness, fighting, and disturbing the peace. Even though Dallas was identified by the newspaper as being one of the largest concentration centers for soldiers on leave in the Southwest, a mere one out of sixty, or 1.67 percent as calculated by the *News*, were apprehended by the police each week.

When asked their opinion as to why the soldiers seemed to be so relatively well behaved, local authorities expressed several theories.

One police officer, noting that "the percentage of soldier-drunken-ness in this war is far below that of the last war," believed the reason was that the 1940s soldier had to train much harder than had his 1917 counterpart. Another factor behind the good behavior was, according to another officer, that "the average soldier in World War II is more serious-minded." Dallas County Sheriff Smoot Smith believed that the fact that most of the men in uniform "are far away from home" compelled them to "act particularly well" or at least better than "a group of civilians [might act] under similar circum-stances." The sheriff did not publicly elaborate further on his rather unique explanation, which might seem to run counter to most pop-ularly held theories.[17]

By the time the war ended, the Love Field-based 5th Ferrying Group had broadened its area of responsibility to include other facil-ities in five states, including major stations in Tulsa, Albuquerque, Wichita, and Brownsville. Its C-47s and C-54s continued to carry supplies and personnel to units overseas long after the conclusion of actual fighting. By 1947, however, military flight operations had ceased and the Army had once again departed the historic base.

Soon after the war, additional land was acquired for Love Field by the city, which saw an opportunity to make good use of the many improvements the government had made to the facility. The long runways and large hangars built by the Army Air Force proved to be additional incentives to such major companies as Braniff Airways and American Airlines that had continued to operate out of Love Field on a limited basis throughout most of the war years. By 1962, when these and eventually seven additional commercial carriers began to expand their operations on the former Army airbase, the $45 million Love Field had become the most active airport in the entire Southwest, boasting 274 arrivals and departures each day.[18]

The explosive growth of air travel following the introduction of jet aircraft to the commercial airline industry in the late 1960s gave even greater importance to Dallas's enviable position at the aerial crossroads of the nation. When a 1970s independent study showed that Love Field, by then landlocked by residential and commercial development, would soon be inadequate to handle the ever-expand-ing demands of the air travel industry, the planning began for a huge new world-class air facility to replace the city's old airport. In 1975, with the opening of Dallas Fort Worth International Airport, it was mandated that the one-time military airfield so near downtown Dallas be closed to all but general aviation. Historic Love Field, it seemed, was soon to be nothing but a memory. However, when the maverick Southwest Airlines flatly refused a federal order to move its flight operations to the newly opened international airport and defiantly expanded its schedules out of Love Field, the old military installation survived and, in time, managed to flourish once again as a vital interregional airport.

Although no tangible material evidence remains of the field's military origins, its continued prominence as a vital center for modern air transportation undoubtedly stems directly from its historic importance as an Army airfield. Love Field, in two wars and in peacetime, has served Dallas and the nation well.

Fort Worth

West Texas is bound on the north by Colorado and Oklahoma,
on the west by New Mexico and on the east by Amon Carter.
                    Amarillo Globe
                    April 18, 1936

In most instances, the successful lobbying for and acquiring of Army airfields in Texas during World War II was a joint effort between local politicians and their powerful national counterparts in Washington, D.C. The big bomber base that opened in Fort Worth in 1942, however, was almost solely the handiwork of a colorful one-man gang named Amon G. Carter, Sr.

As publisher of the influential *Fort Worth Star-Telegram*, Carter was a tireless advocate and promoter of his city, and as such, he made it his business to become a close personal friend of anyone who might help make Fort Worth every bit as great as Carter thought it should be. Included on his long list of powerful acquaintances were President Franklin D. Roosevelt, Generals Douglas MacArthur and Henry H. Arnold, and virtually every member of the Texas congressional delegation in Washington.

According to one of his biographers, Carter had spoken with his friend the president as early as 1939 about the grim prospect of America becoming involved in the war that was threatening to engulf much of the world. As the Roosevelt administration had already begun its massive buildup of the nation's military air armada being assembled in aircraft manufacturing plants all across

America, it is highly likely that Carter urged the president to help obtain such a plant for Fort Worth.[19]

The administration's plan for enlarging the Army's fleet of airplanes a thousand-fold involved a unique government and private industry alliance. Under this scheme, the War Department would build the aircraft manufacturing facilities, which in turn would be operated by a civilian corporation. Further, the Army had also determined that a flight training base should be located adjacent to each manufacturing plant on the logical theory that "complete flight crews could be produced" at the same rate as the airplanes rolled off the assembly line to become instantly available for Army service.[20]

To a highly motivated entrepreneur such as Amon Carter, this arrangement was doubly ideal, because if he were to be successful in his efforts to get a war plant for his city, he would also snare an Army airfield to complement it. Both entities would clearly be enormously beneficial to the future of Fort Worth, and that was, after all, Carter's lifelong preoccupation.

It did not take the publisher long to get his defense plant campaign underway. In May 1940, Brig. Gen. Jacob E. Fickel arrived in Fort Worth to inspect potential sites large enough to accommodate both an aircraft plant and an adjoining flight-training base. The general's visit was the result of promises the city's leaders had made to Maj. R.H. Fleet, who was president of Consolidated Aircraft Corporation and another close friend of Carter. In cooperation with the Fort Worth Chamber of Commerce, the publisher had put together a proposal that offered Consolidated generous tax-abatement offers, city-furnished utility and transportation upgrading projects, and an unlimited pool of skilled workers. Impressed by the Fort Worth proposal, Fleet had suggested the Army send someone to the city to evaluate the site's potential. General Fickel was that someone.

Carter had been successful in convincing Consolidated Aircraft's management team that a site on Lake Worth, on the western edge of town, was ideal as the location for the plant and airfield combination package. Initially, however, the visiting General Fickel and the Army were not at all impressed with the Fort Worth site, preferring instead another location near Tulsa, Oklahoma.

Maj. Gen. George H. Brett, the Army's chief negotiator on site selection, was soon embroiled in an exchange of telegrams with Consolidated's president, R.H. Fleet. "We think Fort Worth site is ideal," Fleet wired the general, clearly impressed by Carter's generous proposal. Brett, apparently not at all swayed by offers of reduced taxes and low cost utilities, bluntly countered with, "Fort Worth not under consideration in present project." In an effort to persuade the obviously still unconvinced Brett with a bit of levity, Fleet sent another wire, dated December 19, 1940, that read, "Your telegram reminds me of Henry Ford statement that customer could choose any color he desired just so he chose black." Brett, obviously not amused and still firmly set on building the new facility in Tulsa, fired back, "Choose any color you wish but you are still going to get black."[21]

There could have been no question to either Fleet or Carter that when Brett said black he really meant Tulsa. If Fleet became even temporarily resigned to operating one of his corporation's aircraft plants in Oklahoma in view of Brett's intransigence, Carter steadfastly refused to admit defeat. He quickly entered the telegram wars by sending a wire of his own directly to Franklin Roosevelt himself, in which he denounced Brett's decision to build in Tulsa rather than Fort Worth as being "un-American and a crime against national defense."[22] In an uncharacteristically meek reply, Roosevelt told Carter that the decision favoring Tulsa "was strictly an Army matter," and as such, his presidential hands were tied.[23]

Even rejection from the White House could not cause the publisher to admit defeat. He immediately launched a letter and telegram barrage aimed at congressmen, military leaders, and personal friends of Roosevelt, imploring them to join in his crusade to convince the president that Fort Worth was without doubt far better suited than Tulsa to nourish both a Consolidated Aircraft plant and its attendant military airfield. Within fourteen days of the opening of Carter's counterattack on the U. S. Army, Roosevelt realized it was useless to deny his friend's relentless quest for the defense facility. Apparently in an effort to satisfy all sides in the issue, however, the government announced on January 4, 1941, that *both* Fort Worth and Tulsa would soon be getting Consolidated plants.[24]

Within three days of the announcement, a group of suddenly enthusiastic Army Air Force officers came to the Texas city to officially endorse the site for the twin aviation facilities that Carter had been so vigorously advocating for over six months. Within two years of this early 1941 visit, the Consolidated Aircraft Corporation would be turning out B-24 "Liberator" bombers from its new plant on the shores of Lake Worth, and Fort Worth Army Airfield, located just across the runway from the plant, would soon be fully operational.

Even with his victory, however, Carter was not yet quite finished with Roosevelt. For a start, he sent the president a folksy telegram that read, "Bless your heart, and thanks for your timely and friendly help."[25] Next, the ever-resourceful publisher asked Morris Sheppard, the United States senator from Texas and chairman of the Senate's powerful Military Affairs Committee, to have Roosevelt's son, a mere Air Force captain at the time, appointed the "Military Overseer" of construction at the Consolidated plant site. Even though he was the president's son, the younger Roosevelt did not have enough military rank to gain this important assignment.

Finally, Carter again went back to the president with a request that he believed vital to the pride of Fort Worth and, for that matter, to the pride of all Texans. Upon learning that the Tulsa plant and the one in his city were to be identical in size, a shocked Carter advised Roosevelt that by tradition everything in Texas simply had to be bigger and, by his reasoning, this included Consolidated aircraft plants. Apparently growing weary of being the constant target of the publisher's aggressive determination, Roosevelt obligingly ordered the plant being built in Fort Worth to be extended by twenty-nine feet to satisfy Mr. Carter's Lone Star patriotism. When the Consolidated facility was completed, it was over a mile in length, and much to Amon Carter's delight, the largest aircraft manufacturing facility in the world.[26]

As construction on the huge plant continued, the Army completed its negotiations for the adjacent land that would become the training base for flight crews manning their newly built Consolidated B-24 bombers. Naming the Army field for some reason proved to be a difficult task. At first, while it was still under construction, the facility was quaintly referred to as simply "the airstrip next to the bomber plant." When this descriptive if bland title did not seem to be impressive enough for such an important installation, the name was briefly changed to "the Lake Worth Industrial Airport." When military officials argued that the newest name was much too civilian sounding, the field was re-titled "the Army Air Force Combat Crew School." This soon gave way to "Tarrant Field," then "Tarrant Aerodrome," and finally to "Fort Worth Army Airfield."[27]

By February 1942, with the United States now officially at war, the aircraft plant was producing B-24s even though the manufacturing facility was still not fully completed. Five months later, the Army activated its crew training school adjacent to the plant. As the planes came off the civilian production line, they were taken directly across the runway where the Army Air Force would accept them and then assign a training crew to each aircraft. The transition from being a just-completed product to a weapon of war was thus drastically reduced, as ferrying time from plant to field became a matter of minutes rather than the several days that had previously been the case.

Several additional months were required to get the base functioning at fully operational standards after it opened. Nearly two hundred buildings had been constructed on short concrete piers on what had just months earlier been an open field sloping down to the boggy shores of Lake Worth. The initially published cost of the hangars, barracks and classrooms that comprised the new field was $6.5 million, but construction on the base never really stopped throughout the war. It had required some 3,200 workers to get the base ready for occupancy, but additional living quarters were required shortly after the field opened. Original plans had called for approximately four thousand personnel to be stationed on the facility, but that number grew by over 30 percent in a matter of months.[28]

On October 14, 1942, the first group of officers arrived at the airfield to begin crew transition training in the Liberators being built next door. The aircraft was authorized a complement of eight airmen, consisting of a pilot, co-pilot, navigator, and bombardier, all of whom were usually officers, plus an engineer and three gunners, who were enlisted men. All of the flight personnel who came to the Fort Worth airfield had already graduated from their respective specialty schools and had arrived at the field to be assigned to combat crews.

According to an article in the *Fort Worth Star-Telegram* on October 12, 1942, each transition team was scheduled to "eat, sleep, study, and train together twenty-four hours a day and even learn each others' minds and reactions."[29] After completing this intensive course of training, the crews and the Fort Worth-made B-24s were given orders directing them to proceed to a combat zone.

Some published reports indicate that the eating-together part of the crew training regimen could also be a twenty-four-hour-per-day activity. The field's mess hall was open all day long seven days a week. Breakfast was served from 5:00 A.M. to 10:00 A.M., lunch from 10 A.M. until 3:00 P.M., supper from 3:00 P.M. until 8:00 P.M., with sandwiches, soup, and coffee available all night. Ann Perlman, a reporter for the *Star-Telegram*, discovered that the food service was as plentiful as it was endless. Believing herself to be the first female to eat lunch in what she termed "the strictly stag" mess hall on a December day in 1942, Miss Perlman wrote that the place was so new she could still smell the paint. Apparently, any lingering paint odors did not diminish the appetites of the airmen who joined her in the chow line. As she usually preferred eating only cottage cheese with pineapple for her luncheon, Miss Perlman was astounded at the portions placed on her tray by the mess hall stewards. The first KP slapped a one-inch-thick slab of roast beef on her metal plate, and surrounded it with "at least a thousand calories worth of mashed potatoes." The next server ladled out what she termed "a small mountain of peas," only to then douse the entire mass with "a thick sea of gravy." Although she was by her own admission ready to "wave the white flag" in surrendering to this caloric onslaught, Miss Perlman could only watch in dismay as "salad, bread and butter, and punch" were added to finish what she called a "gastronomical orgy."[30]

As was usually the case in smaller Texas communities, the larger city of Fort Worth also warmly embraced and supported the airmen assigned to its airfield. The ladies of the University Place Music Club, for example, joined with the members of the Optimists Club, the Utopian Club, and the Harmony Club in a drive to collect pianos for the field's various service clubs. Other groups also staged musical instrument collection drives to benefit the base. An 1813 violin, a complete set of drums, a flute, and a mandolin to be donated to Army musicians were received at the field.[31]

Music was evidently an important pastime for base personnel. In addition to having access to the instruments donated by the citizens of Fort Worth, the field also took pride in its full-size Army band that had been transferred as a group from Majors Field. The band's musical director, M/Sgt. Harry Bluestone, had been the concertmaster for Paramount Pictures in Hollywood before enlisting in the Army, while Pvt. Homer Mensch had played string bass under the baton of Arturo Toscanini, Leopold Stokowski, and Serge Koussevitzky. Many other pre-war professional musicians performed with the airfield band when it gave frequent concerts throughout the community.[32]

Those personnel who were not particularly musically inclined found many other things on the base to occupy their off-duty hours. A theater, several service clubs, day rooms, and a fully equipped gymnasium were available to the airmen, with lessons in various athletic activities, including golf, proving to be a favorite pastime. One of the instructors on the golf course was a rising young professional named Ben Hogan. His almost miraculous ability to transform a hopeless duffer into something at least approaching a par golfer eventually led to his being transferred to the Army Air Force Training Command (ATC) headquarters located in downtown Fort Worth. It was reported that the soon-to-be world famous Hogan was encouraged to work his already legendary golfing-improvement magic on the colonels and generals who had offices there.[33]

While at ATC headquarters, Hogan was serving as the unofficial golf pro at what in 1944 was being called the largest single educational institution in the world. Under the command of Lt. Gen. Barton K. Yount, a staff of over seven hundred officers, enlisted personnel, and civilians directed every aspect of Air Force education and instruction. During its peak year of operation, over twenty-five thousand planes were in use as training aircraft. According to the *Fort Worth Star-Telegram*, General Yount had more airplanes at his disposal in 1944 than Germany's Adolf Hitler had in his entire *Luftwaffe*. An astounding eighty thousand Army pilots were graduated from the ATC flight schools each year. In addition to pilots, the ATC also supervised the training of navigators, bombardiers, engineers, armorers, weather observers, and photographers as well as parachute riggers and clerks. Students from many Allied countries joined their American counterparts in training at ATC facilities located in every state except, for some curious reason, Wyoming. According to contemporary reports, the various training programs undertaken by the ATC increased at least a hundredfold from 1939 to 1944, and each of those programs was supervised by the staff located in the Texas and Pacific Railway building in downtown Fort Worth.[34]

The residents of the city were understandably proud of the important role their community was taking in the overall war effort. While the ATC was clearly a key factor in attaining victory over the Axis powers, the thousands of Liberators being turned out by the Consolidated plant and the crews who trained to fly them into combat from the hometown Army airfield were certainly no less vital.

Largely due to the persistent efforts of Amon Carter, the wartime economy was flying as high as the B-24s from Consolidated's assem-

bly line. The aircraft maker employed nearly thirty thousand workers, while the on-going construction projects at the Army airfield
created payrolls that augmented the checks regularly issued by both
the flight training school and the ATC. During the war years and
immediately beyond, Fort Worth banks reported a 300 percent
increase in earnings while countywide payrolls jumped by more
than 700 percent. According to one historian, "Fort Worth's Army
Airfield was the driving force behind that growth."[35]

As the war entered its final year, production of the Consolidated
B-24 Liberator bombers began to slacken. Since 1939, 18,482 of the
large planes had been built at plants all across the nation, with over
three thousand of them coming off the Fort Worth assembly lines.
Records show that more B-24s were manufactured in the United
States during the war years than any other bomber type made anywhere else in the world. The planes had dropped an impressive
634,831 tons of bombs on Axis targets in the course of 312,734 sor-
ties, while gunners on board the big warbirds had downed 4,189
enemy aircraft.[36]

Despite the Liberators' illustrious battle record, changing aerial
warfare strategies caused it to become obsolescent by 1944 and the
production of the plane was soon halted. When the Boeing Company's B-29 Superfortress eventually became the Air Force's prime
weapon, the Fort Worth Consolidated plant turned its attention to
the production of the newly-designed B-32 Dominator bomber, an
aircraft designed to be the back-up for the Superfortress. More than
1,200 of the B-32s were ordered to be built in Fort Worth, and deliv-
ery of the first of the new aircraft began in September 1944. By that
time, however, the progress of the war had already rendered the
Dominator obsolete, even though 114 of them had been built. The
short and unhappy career of the B-32 was marked by two curious
events. In August 1944, its nickname was changed from Dominator
to Terminator because of what one reliable source cryptically refers
to as "political reasons." With its new name intact, one B-32 managed to gain the dubious distinction of shooting down the last
Japanese warplane to be lost in the war. Regrettably, Japan had formally surrendered one day earlier.[37]

With the surrender of Japan, the future of Fort Worth Army Airfield was very much in doubt. However, just a month after the fighting had stopped, the War Department announced that while three
hundred Army installations located across the country were soon to

be closed, the Fort Worth facility would remain open, at least on an interim basis. As if to prove its sincerity in the matter, the government simultaneously announced that it would soon spend $2 million to improve the airfield's runways.[38]

Two months later, on December 8, 1945, the War Department gave Fort Worth the welcome news that the 7th Bombardment Operational Training Wing would shortly be coming to the Army's field. The arrival of six thousand men and their B-29s was made even more exciting to the Fort Worth community when it was further announced that the coming of the 7th Wing meant that Fort Worth Army Airfield was to become a permanent peacetime military installation. Although the statement of permanency would eventually prove to be false, it must in all fairness be noted that Fort Worth's military aviation installation proved to be more permanent than most. From the end of World War II until the base was officially closed in 1992, the big airfield continued to be a vital cog in the nation's defense machine.[39]

In 1948, the facility was renamed Carswell Air Force Base in honor of Maj. Horace S. Carswell, a Fort Worth native who as a Liberator pilot had posthumously received the Medal of Honor for his heroism in action in the South Pacific in 1944. As Carswell AFB, the air base continued what had been a long and close relationship with the aircraft manufacturing plant located across the runway from it since the early days of World War II. The General Dynamics Corporation, successor to Consolidated and Convair, held contracts to build many of the aircraft used on the neighboring field, including the B-36, the B-58, and the FB-11. By 1980 it was estimated that Carswell AFB, as an important facility of the Strategic Air Command, created an economic impact on the city of Fort Worth that exceeded $260 million annually. The payroll for the 5,400 military personnel assigned to the field alone averaged $61 million per year, and more than $1 million in federal aid went to area schools on behalf of the 1,751 children from the base who attended classes in the city. Any thoughts that the so-called permanent base might go the way of other military installations that had also once been so designated were put at ease when the Defense Department soon announced that $9 million in further improvements to the field had been approved.[40]

Despite reassuring official statements issued throughout the 1980s as to the permanency of Carswell, it was announced on April 12, 1991, that the long-lived facility would be deactivated by the end of 1993. On June 1, 1992, the proud flag of the Strategic Air Command was lowered for the last time at Carswell Air Force Base, and the sole remaining B-52 roared off the twelve thousand foot long runway to climb over Lake Worth before banking toward the east and its new home field at Barksdale, Louisiana. Though no longer an active Air Force facility, the old wartime field continues to function as a joint Navy and Air Force Reserve installation, while across the runway the Lockheed Martin Corporation now builds sleek jet fighters where Consolidated once mass-produced the gallant Liberators.

To be sure, Amon Carter's Fort Worth has changed immensely since the time over sixty years ago when he successfully pushed his city into the forefront of military aviation. Out of his tireless efforts, however, stemmed massive and continuing economic benefits that first came to town long ago with the builders of mighty warbirds and with the men who came to Fort Worth to fly them into combat.

[1] "Love Field Overview," Dallas Municipal Archives and Records Center, (File #87-3931), 1.

[2] *The Dallas Morning News*, September 30, 1962.

[3] Ibid.

[4] "Love Field Overview," 1.

[5] *The Dallas Times-Herald*, April 19, 1942.

[6] *The Flying "V"*, September 15, 1944.

[7] *The Flying "V"*, September 22, 1944.

[8] Rosa Lea (Fullwood) Meek Dickerson, interview with author, Kerrville, Texas, March 18, 2002.

[9] Florene (Miller) Watson, telephone interview with author, March 8, 2002.

[10] Ibid.

[11] Dickerson interview.

[12] *The Flying "V"*, September 22, 1944, 4.

[13] *The Flying "V"*, September 29, 1944, 6.

[14] Ibid., 8.

[15] *The Flying "V"*, September 15, 1944.

[16] *The Flying "V"*, May 7, 1946.

[17] *The Dallas Morning News*, June 20, 1943.

[18] *The Dallas Morning News*, September 30, 1962.

[19] Jerry Flemmons, *Amon: The Life of Amon Carter, Sr. of Texas*, 433.

[20] "History of Fort Worth Army Airfield," *Lone Star Scanner*, February 16, 1946, 6.

[21] Flemmons, 434-435.

[22] Ibid., 436.

[23] Ibid., 436.

[24] *Fort Worth Star-Telegram*, January 4, 1941.

[25] Flemmons, 436.

[26] J'Nell Pate, "Impact of the Military Base Called Carswell," 2.

[27] Ibid., 3.

[28] *Star-Telegram*, June 8, 1991.

[29] *Star-Telegram*, October 12, 1942.

[30] *Star-Telegram*, December 10, 1942.

[31] *Star-Telegram*, October 25, 1942.

[32] *Star-Telegram*, October 3, 1943.

[33] *Star-Telegram*, February 8, 1943

[34] *Star-Telegram*, February 20, 1944.

[35] Oliver Knight, *Fort Worth: Outpost on the Trinity*, 216-226.

[36] Ray Wagner, *American Combat Planes*, 213.

[37] Ibid., 404.

[38] *Star-Telegram*, October 14, 1945.

[39] *Star-Telegram*, December 8, 1945.

[40] *Socioeconomic Impact Analysis Study of Disposal and Reuse of Carswell AFB*, 8.

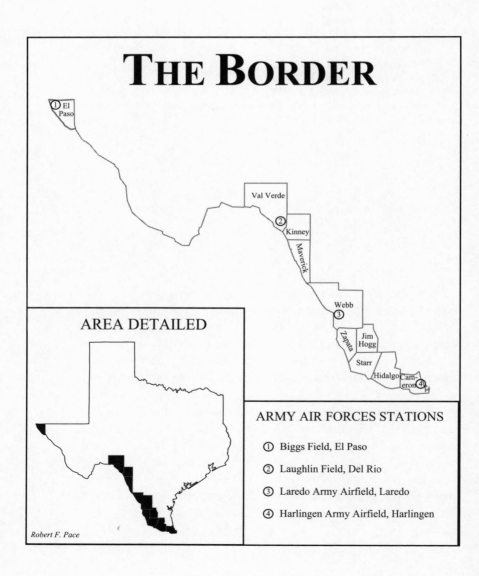

THE BORDER

① El Paso

Val Verde

② Kinney

Maverick

Webb
③

Zapata

Jim Hogg

Starr

Hidalgo Cameron ④

AREA DETAILED

Robert F. Pace

ARMY AIR FORCES STATIONS

① Biggs Field, El Paso

② Laughlin Field, Del Rio

③ Laredo Army Airfield, Laredo

④ Harlingen Army Airfield, Harlingen

CHAPTER FOUR

ON THE BORDER

*Just across the border in Mexico, the city of Juarez offers varied
and unusual entertainment facilities.*
                                        The Air Officer's Guide
                                        April 1948

For well over a century, the long international boundary between Texas and Mexico was cause for varying degrees of concern by United States military authorities. From 1845 through the first year of World War II, the fear of an armed assault launched from the Mexican side of the Rio Grande had ebbed and flowed with much the same lack of consistency as that displayed by the river itself.

Since the earliest days of Army aviation, surveillance of the border region had been given high priority, and when World War II seemed imminent, the number of air bases along the Rio Grande was increased dramatically. By the end of the war, six of the Army's airfields in Texas were located on the border. In addition to the bases proper, almost a million acres of unpopulated land on the United States side of the river were used for gunnery and bombing range purposes.

Only one of America's borderland airfields had existed prior to the war. Biggs Field, located at Fort Bliss near El Paso, had been a modestly important military aviation center since 1919, even though flying activity had been carried on at the fort at least three years earlier. All of the other border fields, however, were part of the network of new training bases created by the Air Force during World War II.

The positioning of the military airfields along the Rio Grande proved to be of particular economic and social importance to the border communities on both sides of the river. The effect of the Great Depression on the total region's agricultural industry had been appalling, and unemployment was at record levels before construction on the airfields began.

The demand for both skilled and unskilled construction workers created job opportunities that brought a much-needed flow of federal dollars into an economy that had long languished. Later, when the airfields were declared operational, civilian jobs on the bases continued the rapid improvement in the general economic well being of the region.

As was the case in San Antonio, Hispanic workers found it easier to get better jobs because of the war when positions previously held by Anglos became vacant due to enlistments in the armed services and the military draft. Since most of the newly vacated positions required job applicants to show proof of American citizenship, many Hispanics in the border towns suddenly became eager to learn to speak English and become citizens of the United States.

While the civilian payroll in the region was greatly enhanced by wartime construction projects, the arrival of thousands of American servicemen to the newly constructed airfields was even more significant. The unrationed and virtually unlimited availability of food, fuel, and other products across the Rio Grande, even though usually at higher prices, did much to spur the border economy in general. Too, as the excerpt from an early *Air Officer's Guide* might suggest, military men have long crossed the Rio Grande with pockets full of American dollars to invest in the "varied and unusual entertainment facilities" offered on the opposite side of the river. From Harlingen to El Paso, and points in between, the war brought a vastly improved economy to both sides of the Rio Grande and, as we shall see, it brought lasting social changes as well.

Harlingen

The terrain around Harlingen is totally unsuitable for organized military activity of any kind. There are no hills for suitable maneuvers by the Cavalry and it is much too marshy for the Infantry to march over.

Col. Edmund A. Pearce
Valley Morning Star
April 12, 1938

Colonel Pearce had been sent to Harlingen by the War Department to assess the locality's potential as a site for a military installation. Judging by the report sent back to his headquarters in Washington, the colonel was neither impressed by what he had seen nor apparently aware of a relatively new form of "organized military activity" which thrived on the absence of hills and was usually unaffected by the presence of marshy turf. The eventual success of Harlingen Army Airfield that was announced just three years after Colonel Pearce's negative report must have been gratifying to the community's leaders who had long sought the blessing of the War Department.

Ignoring the decidedly negative tone of the Pearce Report, Harlingen's Mayor Hugh Ramsey had taken an option on a thousand-acre tract of land on the north edge of his town in June 1940. The mayor was clearly convinced that the property was an ideal site for a military air training facility that would prove useful to the Army even though it did not indeed have any hills but it did indeed have marshes. To make his proposal more attractive, Mayor Ramsey arranged to have an additional sixty thousand acres on the nearby King Ranch made available to the Air Force as a bombing range should the Army accept the city's generous invitation to build an airbase on the proffered site.[1]

Eventually, the War Department accepted Ramsey's view of the efficacy of Harlingen as a location for military activity over that of its own investigating colonel. On February 1, 1941, the *Valley Morning Star* declared that an Army airfield for Harlingen was reportedly in the final stages of approval. One month later, the formal announcement was made to the public.[2]

Plans called for $4 million in construction costs to build the airfield on the city's thousand-acre site, which the government had

agreed to lease at the traditional rate of one dollar per year for a
twenty-four year period. In an unusual codicil to such lease agree-
ments, however, the city gave the War Department the additional
option of buying the land at any time for $75 per acre.[3]

With 1,900 men laboring on the project, the field was declared to
be over 30 percent complete on September 15, 1941, after six
months of building time. It is interesting to note that airfields built
after the war had begun were often completed within as few as
ninety days, but since the Harlingen facility was being constructed
under unrushed pre-war conditions, building time was understandably much longer. By October 1941 the base was still considered to
be only half-finished, although all the runways and roads were completed as were a chapel, a hospital, most of the barracks, and the
headquarters building.[4]

The mission of the new base, once all construction work was
completed, would be as an aerial gunnery school. Appropriately
enough, the airfield was at first known as "Harlingen Aerial Gunnery School," resulting in the obvious acronym of "HAGS." When
female personnel were assigned to the base later in the war, however,
the acronym took on a different and supposedly humorous conno-
tation and as a result, the name of the base was officially changed to
Harlingen Army Airfield in June 1943.[5]

Long before the gunnery school opened, however, training
flights began in the region. In January 1941, the Army rather casu-
ally advised the Texas Gamefish and Oyster Commission that
nearby Padre Island, long a center for professional fishing activity,
was now to be off-limits because the island was eventually to
become a gunnery range. Local fishermen mounted a serious
protest to federal and state governmental officials but to no avail.[6]

By Christmas Eve 1941, there was at last some tangible evidence
that the long-awaited base was in full operation although no formal
announcement had as yet appeared in the newspaper. What had
appeared instead in the *Valley Morning News* was a warning to all
residents to stay away from the lagunas and coastal flats along the
Gulf of Mexico throughout the holidays and for the foreseeable
future. The Army, it seemed, did not plan to take a holiday now that
the war had started, intending instead to conduct machine gun firing
operations in the newly closed area immediately. As one newspaper
reporter saw it, the region "was now a place where a warm Gulf
breeze mixed gunpowder smells with the scent of orange blossoms."[7]

Before the student gunners at Harlingen were trusted to fire any machine guns, however, they honed their aiming skills with BB guns and shotguns on ranges located on the field. Once the gunners had advanced to the in-flight phase of their six-week course of instruction, however, they learned to fire live .30 and .50 caliber machine guns from cockpits of fighters and the ball-turrets of Air Force bombers. The aircraft towing the target sleeves in such training exercises were frequently the women of the WASP.[8]

Because the need for combat aerial gunners was so critical, the instruction was highly intensive and continued around the clock. As a result, the trainees seldom had an opportunity to travel even the short three miles to town. On the other hand, the instructors and other personnel assigned to the base often visited Harlingen during their stay at the field, while many others frequently crossed the Rio Grande to enjoy the perhaps more exciting village of Matamoras, Mexico.

Most accounts confirm that the citizens of Harlingen served as excellent hosts to those personnel who came into town. An occasional open house sponsored by public relations-savvy airfield officials allowed the local residents to learn more about what the nearly five thousand soldiers were doing each day on the nearby base.

In some social circles, interest in airfield activities reached a fever pitch when rumors began to circulate that movie idol Clark Gable was on his way to Harlingen to complete his training as a gunner. Despite constant announcements from base officials that Gable was not coming to Texas inasmuch as he was already a combat gunner in the European Theater of Operations, the field's telephone switchboard was flooded by calls seeking the precise time the Hollywood star would be arriving. One now somewhat elderly lady who lived in Harlingen at the time recalls that, "We were just so disappointed to find out he wasn't coming after all. Some girls swore they'd seen him driving out of the base, but I guess they were just daydreaming."[9]

Even though a movie star did not train at Harlingen, other movie stars did come to make a movie about the serious training that was taking place on the field. In mid-1943, Paramount Pictures sent director William Pine and popular actors Richard Arlen, Chester Morris, and Jimmy Lydon to the field to film a motion picture to be appropriately titled "Aerial Gunner." Kate Cameron, a critic for the *New York Daily News*, noted in the June 25, 1943, edition of her paper that the film was "packed with enough action to satisfy any motion picture fan."[10] Another reviewer, however, was disappointed that the script was flawed, but noted that the movie's chief asset was "the fact that most of it was shot on location at the U. S. Army Air Force Aerial Gunnery School at Harlingen, Texas."[11] Almost fifty years after completing his filming on the base, actor Jimmy Lydon recalled how pleasant the experience had been for him and his co-stars. "The Army really took us in as guests," he wrote, "and the people in town made us feel like we were heroes."[12]

When the war ended in 1945, even Harlingen's fame as a motion picture location and an important training facility could not save it from closure. Unlike most other Texas airfields, however, the economic downturn caused by the shuttering of the base was offset by a flood of discharged Army veterans who had been stationed at Harlingen during the war and had liked what they had seen during their tour of duty. Lured back to the region by their memories of the almost perfect year around weather and the hospitality they had enjoyed as soldiers, the former gunners, their instructors, and other veterans returned to South Texas to make Harlingen their permanent postwar home. Only San Antonio's Bexar County surpassed Harlingen's Cameron County in population growth during the decade following the war, with both recording a nearly 50 percent increase in permanent residents.[13]

When the Cold War with the Soviet Union began to turn hot in 1950, the old gunnery base was re-activated as one of the Air Force's principal navigator training centers. After graduating over thirteen thousand navigators, Harlingen AFB closed in 1962, this time touching off an economic slump that was to persist for years. During the twelve years it was open, the Cold War air base had contributed on average nearly one-half of all the dollars annually spent in Harlingen, in addition to the income generated by on-field construction projects that continued until the very day the air base was finally closed.[14]

Despite this crippling financial blow, the city of Harlingen managed to regain clear title to the $18 million facility that had suddenly become what one newspaper article dubbed "the most valuable white elephant in South Texas."[15] Through careful planning, the city was able to eventually convert the valuable white elephant into a far more valuable major international airport, a technical school, a military academy, and a popular museum. In time, what had been a liability was transformed by coordinated civic effort into an extremely valuable asset.

Veterans who earlier had trained at the navigation school had also liked what they had seen and returned in large numbers to join their fellow veterans from the World War II era. As a direct result of its military legacy, Harlingen was named one of America's ten most innovative and progressive cities in 1992. According to one local news source, "The comeback of the area once known as Harlingen Air Force Base has been a major factor in the city's economic success."[16]

Laredo

Water is neutral, and its impartial winding makes the national boundary look like an act of God.

> Paul Theroux
> *The Old Plantation Express*
> Laredo, Texas
> 1979

Although Laredo's active role in military aviation did not reach major proportions until 1942, the border city did have an earlier but very limited involvement with U. S. Army flight activities. When San Antonio's Kelly Field reached the peak of its training operations during the First World War, it became necessary to establish several small auxiliary landing fields throughout South Texas. One of these, located near Laredo, consisted of a single dirt runway with one master sergeant as the only personnel assigned to the tiny facility.[17]

By 1940, Laredo boasted a population of 39,274 and was growing in importance as a port of entry for Mexican-made goods. Anticipating even greater growth for the community, city officials arranged for one-time Laredoan H.B. Zachry to begin the construction of a new airport to replace the old Kelly Field auxiliary dirt landing strip. Zachary, who over the next few years would go on to build several military airfields across Texas, including one in Hondo, named the new Laredo facility in honor of his late father, Col. John Zachry.[18]

It was as Zachry Field that the 320-acre airport came to the attention of Air Force officials who had been invited by the city to visit the nearly completed facility in late October 1940. The Laredo that the visiting officers toured during their inspection visit was clearly a far cry from the bustling modern city that would evolve over the coming decades. A master's thesis written about Webb County in early 1941 describes Laredo as having at the time "an atmosphere that vaguely reminds one of what was once an old Spanish village, . . . but on the whole one breathes the wholesome atmosphere of an American community. It is a peculiar situation which cannot be explained."[19]

Apparently, the reactions of the visiting officers to the wholesome atmospere was positive enough to prompt local political leader Judge John A. Valls to ask his close friend U. S. Senator Morris Sheppard to use his influence to have the still-unfinished Zachry Field be considered as the site for a military air training facility. Sheppard, who was chairman of the powerful Senate Military Affairs Committee, responded by notifying Judge Valls on October 31, 1940, that he had contacted the appropriate authorities about the Laredo Airport and its availability for War Department use. Sheppard concluded his telegram to his friend by assuring him that he would "do everything within my power to secure the prospect's earnest consideration."[20]

Senator Sheppard's sudden death just seven months later apparently caused the Laredo military project to lose much of its momentum, and not until May 13, 1942, could any progress be reported to the public. On that date, the city's mayor, Hugh S. Cluck, received a telegram from an Army official that succinctly stated, "Directive received to acquire airport site Laredo, Texas. Proceed to comply with commitments."[21]

The newspaper story that told of the apparently unexpected but very welcome telegram went on to relate that "It has been known for weeks [that] city, county, civic leaders and many interested citizens have been conferring with Army authorities relative to the building here of an airport." Although details of the negotiations were rather conspicuously absent from its lead story, the paper added "Certain commitments were made in advance by officials complying with requirements." As Frank Hill, Laredo's city attorney, explained, "Full details can not be given now."[22]

In the next edition of *The Times*, the mayor asked the public to be patient and to simply accept the good news with gratitude. "The fact that we have had the airport confirmed should be enough for the time being," admonished the mayor, "and we assure everybody minute details will be given as they develop."[23]

By the end of May 1942, just over two weeks after Mayor Cluck's plea for patience, some less than minute details of the recently confirmed airfield project were released, although much information was still shrouded in secrecy and withheld from the public. It was revealed, however, that the field would be an air training center to cost in excess of $3 million. Perhaps aware of the War Department's well-publicized propensity for overrunning airfield construction budget estimates, the *Laredo Times* saw fit to print the word "EXCESS" in bold face capital letters.[24]

Likely feeling at least somewhat relieved that he could now at last be more definitive, Mayor Cluck publicly divulged that the city had turned over all of Zachry Field to the government and that preliminary work was already under way. The mayor did stop short of saying how the new field would be used. "We are not authorized by the government," said Cluck, "to make public details as to size, character, or scope of the project."[25]

Almost immediately, finding housing for construction workers and the expected eventual influx of military families became the principal concern of the city and its chamber of commerce. The chamber quickly completed a survey of all property, both residential and commercial, that could be readily converted into living accommodations of any kind. Citizens were reminded that although rental rates were to be carefully scrutinized and controlled by the federal government, each property owner was urged to voluntarily place on file any space that would be available for rent to the expected newcomers. As an indication of just how serious the housing situation was, it was also announced that the cost of converting basements, garages, offices, and stores into accommodations would be "at the expense of the government."[26]

By October 27, 1942, the old 320-acre Zachry Field had expanded into the new 2,085 acre Laredo Army Airfield, home of a flexible gunnery school similar to the one located downriver in Harlingen. In addition to the air base near town, the Army Air Force also had the use of a huge 685,000-acre aerial target range tract that began some twenty-five miles north of Laredo and extended to within thirty miles of Eagle Pass farther west up the Rio Grande. An additional 35,000 acres only seven miles north of the city limits was acquired for use by gunnery students as a ground target area. In all, nearly 725,000 acres of South Texas brush country were under the control of the gunnery school.[27]

Experimentation with various types of aerial warfare training ordnance was routine at the Laredo base. Students firing over the huge air-to-air practice range used a type of frangible ammunition that disintegrated upon striking a solid material. Using these newly developed bullets, students fired at specially armored target aircraft equipped with monitoring devices that recorded where each shell fired from the machine guns actually hit. Some of the target aircraft also were equipped with a red light in its nose that lit up like a pinball machine each time a frangible shell hit it. Unlike the cloth sleeves used earlier in the war, the use of actual aircraft as moving targets gave students the exhilarating experience of firing upon real planes with real bullets and with instantly recorded results. Real pilots, however, flying the target aircraft sometimes found all of this realism to be more than a little unnerving when a frangible bullet sharply struck the Plexiglas of the cockpits, creating an eerie frosting pattern only inches from the flyer's head.[28]

Perhaps to help relieve the frequently jangled nerves of the gunnery school's pilots, the city of Laredo leased the Casa Blanca Country Club, which it owned, to the Army for use as an officers' club for one dollar per year. The club encompassed over twelve hundred acres of verdant golf courses, swimming pools, lakes, and tennis courts. Although the club was primarily intended for use of Army officers, the public was still invited to use the nine-hole golf course on a shared basis with the aviators.[29]

In the fall of 1943, the federal government bought all of the airfield property from the city of Laredo and Webb County, paying the two entities a total of $185,000. This amount equaled what the city and county had paid for the land in 1940.[30]

The citizens of Laredo and vicinity proved eager to support the men at the nearby base and indeed just as eager to pitch in wholeheartedly on behalf of servicemen everywhere. War Bond drives in the city regularly exceeded their goals and scrap iron collections usually resulted in countless piles of valuable metal for the war effort.

One unusual campaign might have been exclusive to Laredo. The "Save a Life with a Knife" collection drive seems to have originated in the border city when a Laredo serviceman, Joe Fasnacht, wrote his brother Edward from a combat zone asking him to send a sheath knife to augment his government-issued bayonet. The civilian Fasnacht not only accommodated his brother but also invited other area residents to donate unwanted knives to be sent to the front lines. Dick Misener at the Hamilton Hotel garage was named the official collector for the blades, all of which were to be sent on to

Army service centers for sharpening and refurbishing. Any knife, with or without sheaths, needed only to have at least a four-inch blade to be acceptable for combat duty. Response to the knife drive was reported by Misener as "being more than gratifying."[31]

Other contributions toward winning the war took on many forms in Laredo. Mrs. Luis F. Ochoa, for example, was commended in early 1943 for permitting five of her elder sons to join the nation's armed services. An official emblem of honor was presented to Mrs. Ochoa at a special civic ceremony presided over by Mayor Hugh Cluck. The Ochoa boys included First Lieutenants Louis and Edward, Sergeant Albert, Navy Cadet Fred, and Sailor Peter.[32]

Further evidence of how many Laredoans had joined the military during 1941 and 1942 was offered by Gunner's Mate Sheldon Davenport who came back to town on furlough in 1943 after two years of constant duty. "All my old friends are gone to war," said the sailor, "and the city has certainly filled up with new people." [33]

There is more than adequate evidence to indicate that the city to which Sheldon Davenport had returned had indeed changed during his absence. In a highly unusual action to be taken by a traditional hometown newspaper, the *Laredo Times* placed a stinging open letter to Texas Governor Coke Stevenson on the front page of its February 3, 1943, edition. The letter, reprinted here in its entirety, speaks volumes not only about the politics of Laredo at the time, but also of the conditions in certain sections of the city, all expressed with the obvious frustration of a courageous newspaper evidently more concerned about the welfare of the servicemen who were assigned to the airfield rather than to its own advertising revenue.

An Open Letter

Governor Coke Stevenson
Austin, Texas

Laredo is long overdue in cleaning up a rotten, crooked, gambling red light district.

For the past several months, proper political authorities have been requested repeatedly to cleanup Laredo so that our boys in uniform who are offering their lives in defense of our country can be saved from venereal disease and corruption.

These proper authorities according to printed record have not carried out this duty to our city, our county, our state, our country and our flag.

Some of the finest people in the world live in Laredo. Among these are some of our political leaders. This morning we talked to two of these leaders who are among the highest type men in this community. However, if we were not entirely mistaken, there was nothing come out [sic] of the meeting except to say that they would see what happens and see what you, the governor, does [sic]. In short, they dropped the whole mess in your lap.

In the first place, this situation should have been cleaned up before our armed forces were forced to declare about two dozen joints in Laredo unfit for men in uniform to enter. This political machine has been told repeatedly by the army, and this same political machine has made no denial that some of the worst element [sic] in this community are responsible for this mess. Nothing can be done as long as that element is holding office.

We are not offering you a solution in this open letter because two of our leaders told us this morning frankly that it is all up to you. They said a meeting has been called for this afternoon. Our answer to them was that this meeting will be no different from other meetings. We said there is no more promise of anything coming out of this meeting than previous meetings which have allowed disease and filth to run riot with local approval.

May we suggest that you do something definite about this or do nothing at all? There is no doubt but that some of our politicians have completely antagonized our armed forces. We have told these politicians responsible just that.

Therefore, these [men] have made your position most difficult.

Any dirt laid at your doorstep is not important
from a county which has opposed you with its
handful of votes one time and helped you with its
handful of votes another time.

This political angle is not important to you [,]
Governor, but the welfare of the State of Texas and
the welfare of these thousands of boys here in the
Army is important.

We are going to expect something besides a
whitewash.

The Laredo Times[34]

While it cannot be confirmed if the thousands of airmen stationed at the Laredo Gunnery School appreciated the vigorous
moral crusade mounted on their behalf by *The Times*, the newspaper's outspoken, if somewhat convoluted, position can only be
admired. No matter how successful the reform campaign might
have been, however, there is no compelling reason to believe for
even a moment that any impact from it would have been felt in
Nuevo Laredo just across the bridge in Mexico.

There were many soldiers who might have benefited from *The
Times'* crusade. At the peak of the field's training operations in the
early 1940s, according to a Corps of Engineer review, there were
approximately fourteen thousand personnel stationed at the Laredo
base with some 250 aircraft assigned to it. The first planes to fly
from the field were the North American AT-6s. Later in the war B-
29s and B-32s joined the fleet.[35]

By the end of 1945, all training had ceased at the Laredo facility.
The following year the airfield was declared surplus and promptly
closed by the Army with control of it reverting to the city. An
unusual clause in the original leasing agreement, however, gave the
federal government the right to reclaim the field on a thirty-day
notice should the need arise.[36]

That need arose in mid-1950 with the beginning of the Korean
War, and as a result the newly created United States Air Force prepared to reoccupy what had previously been the Army's aerial gunnery school. Although the old base had been relatively
well-maintained as the city's municipal airport and the location of
various commercial endeavors, the government quickly invested
over $10 million in refurbishing the existing buildings while con-

structing new ones. This extensive federal expenditure was particularly beneficial to the Laredo economy, and local citizens looked forward to welcoming the thirty-five hundred military personnel expected to arrive in early 1952.[37]

The reactivated and reconstructed Laredo Air Force Base served as a basic flight training school for jet pilots for the next twenty-one years, until the facility was once again declared surplus and closed in 1973. Many of the buildings were sold as scrap, moved off the base or occupied by civilian enterprises, leaving the old headquarters building as one of the few recognizable structures from the military days.

One student of Laredo's history found a parallel between the final departure of the Air Force and events that had taken place centuries earlier in the colorful border town. In his doctoral dissertation written in 1979, Gilberto M. Hinojosa observed, "The withdrawal of Spanish garrisons from Laredo caused great economic problems for townspeople in colonial days just as the closing of Laredo Air Force Base did in the 20th century."[38]

In both historic incidences, the venerable city suffered but survived. Today, Laredo is a thriving community that owes much to the military aviation experience that has twice provided it with an economic cornerstone upon which to build a sound future.

Del Rio

It appeared to us immediately that Del Rio would in no way match San Antonio.

S/Sgt. Paul O. Russell
Upon arriving at Laughlin
Field from Randolph Field
February 12, 1943

Del Rio is located 150 miles west of the Alamo and some 180 miles up the Rio Grande from Laredo. Unlike the downstream border town, the wild west city of Del Rio had enjoyed an ongoing relationship with military aviation for over a quarter century by the time World War II commenced in 1941. The very first aircraft to reach the town had made a landing in a nearby pasture in 1911, a scheduled stop in the initial transcontinental air journey across America. Sergio Gonzalez, who had witnessed this memorable event, recalled much later that the noise of the flimsy aircraft's backfiring motor frightened the teams of horses that had been harnessed to carry onlookers to the landing field.[39]

The same rough landing strip was used during 1915 and 1916 by Army flyers who were taking part in the abortive effort mounted by the United States to locate the ever-elusive Mexican revolutionary leader, Francisco "Pancho" Villa. Irene Cardwell, who as a young girl was witness to the comings and goings of the Army planes, remembered that their pilots would often tie the aircraft to her father's fence to keep them from blowing away during the night, and would sleep on the family's porch if a rare rainstorm might occur.[40]

One of the more famous of the early-day Army aviators who often landed their DeHaviland-4B aircraft at Del Rio was James H. "Jimmy" Doolittle. A future Air Force lieutenant general and eventual holder of the Medal of Honor, Doolittle was assigned in 1919 to a surveillance squadron that flew regular patrol flights along the border. In his 1991 autobiography, the legendary aviator recalled that such routine flying could easily become boring and monotonous, and in living up to his widely-known reputation as a daredevil pilot, Doolittle often fashioned ways to make life a bit more exciting. According to his account, one of his most memorable doldrums-breaking feats took place when he flew his DH-4 under the Southern Pacific Railway bridge that spanned the Pecos River Canyon in the beautifully rugged country west of Del Rio. Looking back on the episode many years later, the retired general recalled that he "had to bank the wings nearly vertical to get between the upright piers," but he made the pass-through intact.[41]

Unbeknownst to the young pilot at the time, however, there was someone who was not at all amused by his unauthorized antics. Soon after his flight, Doolittle was officer of the day at his flying field near Dryden, Texas, and in that capacity he found himself confronting what the flyer remembered to be "the biggest, toughest Texan" he had ever seen. The furious visitor galloped up on his horse demanding to see the "SOB who flew under the Southern Pacific Bridge." It was soon made clear to Doolittle that the angry horseman was a telephone lineman who had just strung a line under the bridge only to see it cut in two by a low-flying Army plane. Sensing peril at the hands of the irate lineman, the very rarely meek Doolittle hastily promised to find the reckless pilot who might have committed such a foolish act and then quickly trotted off, out of harm's way.[42]

As concerns for military security along the Rio Grande persisted, Army aircraft, usually piloted by less-mischievous daredevil aviators, continued to fly along the border throughout the 1930s. With the coming of war in 1941, the War Department moved rapidly ahead with plans to build major airfields along the river, both for training and continued surveillance purposes.

At first it appeared that, despite its long association with Army aviation, Del Rio might be omitted from the War Department's building plans. In early 1942, when a military airfield was announced for nearby Eagle Pass, the editor of the *Del Rio News-Herald* became certain that "the Army is not interested in Del Rio or Val Verde County for an Army Air Training School." Noting that the placement of the airfield at Eagle Pass proved that there was no political, economic, or geographical reason why Del Rio should not have a base of its own, the editor could only darkly conclude that "there is something deeper seated than we can ascertain – and the Army doesn't want to even consider Del Rio as a site."[43]

The newspaper became even more agitated a few days later when General Hubert Harmon, commander of the Army's Gulf Coast Training Corps and a major decision-maker in the selection of airfield sites, suddenly arrived in town, looked around for a day, and then announced to city officials that all of the sites he had seen were totally unsatisfactory. Del Rio, it appeared, was not going to get its airfield after all."[44]

On May 15, 1942, however, just three weeks following Harmon's rather terse rejection of the Del Rio sites, the general's San Antonio office reversed its earlier position and announced that an Army Air School was indeed in the city's immediate future. The next day, the chamber of commerce received a telegram from Congressman Charles L. South confirming the approval of an airfield at Del Rio and adding that the estimated cost of the facility would be in the $3 million category. It is interesting to note that the estimated expenditures for the early-war airfields were almost always either $3 million or $6 million. Frequently, the $3 million estimates eventually became at least $6 million outlays of government funds and the $6 million jobs grew to be $12 million federal undertakings. Some things, it seems, never change.[45]

At any rate, a four thousand-acre site located five miles east of town had been found suitable and was quickly acquired by the War Department for what was termed a "non-negotiable" price of

$101,500, or $25 per acre. As other property in the immediate vicinity was being offered at appreciably lower prices, it can only be assumed that the Army had seen exactly what it wanted in the chosen site and had made its owner, a Mr. B.S. Harrison, a take-it-or-leave it offer based on the government's arbitrary evaluation of the land.[46]

Mr. Harrison apparently had no room for negotiation with the government officials, but his tenant, Mr. Gilbert Marshall, proved to be a skilled negotiator. Even though he held only a two-year lease on a section of the huge site, Marshall had for some inexplicable reason been allowed to construct a large house on his leasehold, along with several barns, some corrals, and a windmill. Having gone to this expense, the tenant farmer was understandably reluctant to leave it all behind, war or no war. A curiously benevolent War Department, however, promptly agreed to pay for moving all of Marshall's buildings to another location that he had found and even bore the expense of drilling a new water well to accommodate the windmill that had also been relocated. All of this largesse was by no means customary from a government that was at the time suffering something of a cloudy reputation for simply taking what it needed in the name of wartime necessity and rudely bulldozing out of the way anything that appeared to stand even slightly in the way of eventual victory over the enemy.[47]

By June 1942, Harrison had his money and his former tenant had moved to his brand new place. The Army then wasted no time in building its airfield at Del Rio. In just four and a half months the base was activated but by no means complete. In fact, it could never be termed truly complete as construction work continued on it until the war ended three years later.

Initial plans called for the Del Rio facility to be a bombardier training school, but the desperate need for multi-engine pilots caused the field's mission to be changed before any bombardier cadets arrived. Shortly after its activation, the new airfield was given the ponderous but official title "The United States Army Air Forces Transition Flying School, Medium Bombardment, near Del Rio, Texas." This weighty nomenclature remained in effect until March 12, 1942, when the base was re-christened Laughlin Army Airfield, a name destined to stay largely intact for at least sixty years.[48]

The airfield's final name was chosen to honor Lt. Jack T. Laughlin, Jr. who had been the first serviceman from Del Rio to die in action in the war. The Army had for the most part resisted naming its facilities for local heroes, so its approval of the field's new name was warmly received throughout the region. Maj. Gen. Gerald C. Brant, a regular Army officer who presided at the March 28, 1942, dedication of the field in Laughlin's honor, made note of the fact that the lieutenant's status as a reservist rather than a regular officer made the base-naming an even more unusual honor.[49]

The men who came to Laughlin Field were to be trained as B-26 "Marauder" pilots. While the often-temperamental aircraft initially had a questionable reputation among many aviators, the pilots who flew them in training and in combat had, and still have, a great respect and admiration for the plane. Paul O. Russell, who served as a flight engineer on the planes at Laughlin agrees, noting that "the B-26 Marauder in the proper hands of skilled pilots was a most dependable and rugged aircraft."[50]

At Laughlin, aviators learned to fly the multi-engine Marauders in nine short weeks. By the time they arrived at Del Rio, the men had already completed a nine-week pre-flight school, another nine weeks of basic, and yet another nine weeks of advanced training after which they had been awarded their silver wings. At the Laughlin facility, the mission was essentially to teach the best pilots in the Air Force to become even better. Following their graduation from the Del Rio base, the flyers would go on to operational training units to form combat crews before moving out to the war zones. The lessons learned at Laughlin were vital and proved to be important in air battles around the world.

As serious and as important as their training routine at the airfield was, the young pilots frequently found ways to relieve the pressure under which they worked. The fast and highly maneuverable Marauders became the aviators' favorite toy on occasion, frequently to the dismay of their commanders, local ranchers, and even distant military garrisons. According to Laughlin Field veteran Allard E. Stevens, one popular pastime involved the high-speed "buzzing" of ranch windmills in usually successful attempts to have the blades of the mill's fan fly off in the prop-wash of a low-flying, fast-moving B-26. Another intriguing target proved to be the long-suffering cavalry troops stationed at nearby Fort Clark. In this game, the pilots would roar over mule-riding troopers at a frighteningly low altitude "at full throttle," Stevens recalls, "scattering mules, GIs and artillery over the West Texas landscape."[50]

One pilot, Robert Ball, had flown with the Royal Canadian Air Force before being ignominiously discharged for flying his plane neatly through an open door on one side of a hangar and out the other. Despite this misadventure, the U. S. Army took Ball in and made him an instructor at Laughlin. Apparently still fun-loving and adventurous, Ball took a fiendish delight in making regular early morning flights to Fort Hood, located outside Killeen, Texas, for the sole purpose of seeing how rapidly he could disperse soldiers who had been marching in precise formation until his B-26 came hurtling overhead at barely flagpole topping altitude. Unfortunately for Ball, the Fort Hood commander did not appreciate this stunt. When his plane's tail number was spotted during one such prank, Ball was quickly dispatched to a combat zone.[52]

When they were not on duty, the pilots often crossed the Rio Grande to visit the Mexican village of Villa Acuña. Allard Stevens, who thought Del Rio looked like a set for a Hollywood Western, found the sun-baked Mexican town to be "usually hot and always dusty, dirty and very economically depressed." However, food and drink were extremely inexpensive on the Mexican side of the river, and cantinas and other even more unsavory establishments successfully catered to American servicemen.[53]

To its dubious credit, the Army was perhaps overly zealous in its attempts to protect the fun-seeking soldiers who crossed over the border. With total disregard for international courtesies, the military police routinely inspected Mexican places of business, checking for cleanliness, honest trade practices, and confirming the proprietor's reliability for selling the soldiers exactly what the soldiers thought they were buying. As a direct result of these inspections that more often than not resembled raids, many businesses catering to the servicemen were declared off-limits and sometimes ultimately forced to close. Military policemen also patrolled the streets of Villa Acuña on a regular nightly basis, arresting misbehaving soldiers and even shuttering offending dens of iniquity.

Despite such overt and probably illegal heavyhandedness by the U. S. military authorities, the relationship between Del Rio's airfield and the neighboring Mexican village seems to have been good-natured and amicable enough. After all, Americans had been visiting the little city for decades. A few pesky regulations and a handful of military police did not manage to change things to any lasting extent. In fact, the Army was often invited to cross the river to formally parade down village streets, much to the delight of the Mexican citizens.

On one occasion, Laughlin's 706th Army Band was asked to stage a concert in Villa Acuña's Plaza. Some four thousand locals attended the concert, reportedly cheering loudly as the band offered its renditions of such predictably thematic pieces as "Lady of Spain," "La Golondrina," and "Rio Rita." When the band concluded its performance with a particularly rousing version of the old Mexican Revolutionary hit "La Cucaracha," village Mayor Graciano Patino was moved to make a lengthy speech thanking the American soldiers for the performance.[54]

It can be argued that despite curfews, strict enforcement of customs regulations, and a strong American military police presence on Mexican soil, the war caused the two neighboring countries to grow closer together in terms of understanding and shared interests, at least at this point on the river. When Texas Governor Coke Stevenson came to Del Rio in 1945 to launch a bond drive, he was joined at a rally by his political counterpart from across the river, Benecio Lopez Padillo. The two officials stood side by side in the bed of a pickup truck to jointly promote War Bond sales.

Despite experiencing twenty-six major accidents and the loss of seventy-four flyers during the 962 days the training base was in operation, Laughlin Field proved to be a particularly vital training facility. However, when the war ended and the demand for B-26 pilots instantly disappeared, the airfield was declared surplus and closed on September 30, 1945.[55]

On May 1, 1952, however, the old field was reactivated as Laughlin Air Force Base, even though many of its World War II buildings had been razed and much of its vast acreage again put to use as grazing land. Initially a pilot training wing at the beginning of its reincarnation, Laughlin became a Strategic Air Command (SAC) facility in April 1957 and home to the U-2 reconnaissance aircraft before again serving as a combat pilot training center in 1962.[56]

Since then, nearly ten thousand graduates have earned their silver wings at Del Rio, in the process generating a major economic impact on the region. According to Air Force figures released in 1999, the base was annually responsible for a $156 million dollar contribution to the regional community. There can be little question that Laughlin Air Force Base, the direct successor to a once-vital World War II Army airfield, continues to be a key factor in both Del Rio's economy and in the nation's defense, just as it was sixty years ago.[57]

El Paso

Fort Bliss is unique among Army posts. It has been captured by Confederates, laughed at by bandits, been home to America's first military air combat operations, and is now El Paso's biggest employer and the Army's biggest installation.

Edward C. Hurley
El Paso, Texas

Located 425 miles up river from Del Rio, El Paso has a colorful military history that spans over four and a half centuries. As a result of that history, the city has earned its reputation as a first-class soldiers' town. Although conquistadors, Confederates, and cavalrymen have all enjoyed the scenery, climate, and hospitality to be found in Texas's westernmost city over the centuries, military aviation has been on the local scene only since 1916, when the activities of one Doroteo Arango, better known to history as Francisco "Pancho" Villa, forced the Army to experiment with airplanes temporarily based at El Paso's Fort Bliss.

As something of an offshoot to his main role as a major participant in revolutionary imbroglios south of the border, Villa often delighted in engaging in skirmishes across the Rio Grande and into the United States. As previously noted, Villa's killing raid at Columbus, New Mexico, in 1916 finally compelled America to retaliate. When Brig. Gen. John J. Pershing's cavalry could not find the wily and elusive Villa in his rugged northern Mexico haunts, the Army's First Aero Squadron was called upon to join in the search.

Although this action marked the first use of U.S. Army planes in anything resembling combat, the results were lamentable if not downright laughable. As an El Paso newspaper put it at the time, the entire undertaking was similar to "turning a jackrabbit loose in Oklahoma and sending the El Paso police to find him."[58]

Frustrated, Pershing finally declared the entire Mexican charade to have been a victory, sent what little remained of his feckless air force back to San Antonio, and soon marched into history as the supreme commander of the American Expeditionary Force in the First World War.[59]

Despite its lackluster debut, Army aviation activities at Fort Bliss continued to expand following the successes of American aviators in the skies over France. In 1919, the Army formally established a flying field on the gigantic fort and in 1925 named it Biggs Field in honor of Lt. James B. "Buster" Biggs, an El Pasoan who had died in a plane crash near Beltran, France, during the war.[60]

Even though the airfield now had a name and enjoyed an important strategic location on the Mexican border, the El Paso military air facility was in every sense highly subservient to the traditional ground-oriented Army hierarchy that ruled the fort. On those frequent occasions when blowing sand made landings on Biggs's tiny dirt strip all but impossible, for example, pilots were officially advised to bring their planes down on the less dusty drill field at the adjacent Fort Bliss. Stubborn ground commanders, however, steadfastly refused to order their drilling troops to yield to the approaching aircraft, forcing the pilots to face the dangers of a blind landing on the dirt strip.[61]

Despite such intra-service rivalry, Biggs Field continued to grow in importance in the late 1930s, as America's air power expanded. The runway was extended and even given a hard surface, new hangars were built, and, in time, the field's overall area was increased from 208 to 3,156 acres.[62]

With World War II came even greater expansion. By November 1942 there were eight thousand personnel assigned to Biggs Field compared to the thirteen men who had served there only three years earlier. Though located within the boundaries of Fort Bliss, the airfield was now under a separate command structure and happily operated as a wholly independent branch of the Army, free from the often-nettlesome supervision of cavalry and artillery commanders.[63]

During the war, the social and economic impact of Biggs Field and Fort Bliss on El Paso was immense. Alicia Gonzalez, a city resident during that time, remembers that "World War II changed our lives forever." Her neighborhood within the Hispanic barrio began to improve significantly when wartime conditions created new employment opportunities in the city. As El Paso's military establishments continued to grow, many Hispanics found good-paying jobs available to them for the first time. [64]

A particularly significant aspect of the plentiful new jobs was that nearly all of them required the successful applicant to be an American citizen. Ms. Gonzalez recalls that many Mexican nationals began studying English and attending citizenship classes. The greatly enhanced incomes derived from the newly acquired jobs caused her family's "standard of living to change dramatically," Ms. Gonzalez notes, "allowing the family to buy things unattainable by them just months earlier."[65]

Some of the new money went toward buying clothes, either in El Paso or across the Rio Grande in Ciudad Juarez, where rationing did not exist. Frequently, some of the older girls put on their new outfits and went to the railway station to watch troop trains pull in on their way to the West Coast. The more daring young ladies would give their names and addresses to soldiers in hopes of someday perhaps receiving correspondence from men fighting in the South Pacific. Ms. Gonzalez believes that the eventual exchange of letters must have led to some of the many weddings she attended at her church, where her older friends married soldiers back from the front lines, "looking so handsome in their uniforms."[66]

Another El Pasoan, Ysidro Cervantes, watched his brother and his cousins go off to serve in the Navy early in the war before later enlisting himself. Once in uniform, Mr. Cervantes was delighted to find doors that had long been closed to him as a Hispanic begin to swing open. He also discovered that a great sense of pride came from wearing his Navy uniform." "We were Americans first," he recalls, "and were now sharing in the civic culture through our participation in the war."[67]

Back home on leave, Seaman Cervantes discovered that the war had brought an almost instant prosperity to El Paso, which had grown steadily along with the expansion of Biggs Field and Fort Bliss. Perhaps the most telling and significant of all his memories is the realization that his hometown "came together as a united community during the war." In El Paso, as in other cities across the state, the national military emergency had helped blur many long-established barriers of racial misunderstanding and mistrust.[68]

By the time the war had ended, a large number of the previous residents of the economically restrictive barrio had been able to move to better neighborhoods in the city, and many of them had become new citizens of the United States. Returning veterans were able to take advantage of the GI Bill to enroll in colleges and universities that would have been too costly for them before the war. The conflict had also brought tragedy and loss to El Paso, of course, and many Gold Star flags signifying the home of a serviceman killed in action were too frequently seen in neighborhood windows. For Alicia Gonzalez and many other El Pasoans, however, as terrible as the war had been, it had also provided an open door to a better way of life and a brighter future for the Hispanic community.

When the war ended, El Paso was spared the social and economic trauma associated with the closing of surplus military bases. Both Biggs Field and Fort Bliss were considered to be exceptionally important to the nation's future defense, and as a consequence, the two facilities each experienced expansion in the years immediately following the war. Reflecting the still increasing importance of air power, Biggs Field was soon enlarged to include over four thousand acres while its runways were constantly being lengthened and reinforced to accommodate faster and heavier aircraft.[69]

In 1947, the U. S. Air Force became a totally independent service and Biggs Army Airfield became Biggs Air Force Base, although it was still located on the huge piece of real estate it had long shared with the Army. When SAC brought its long-range bombers to Biggs in the postwar years, an additional $8 million was expended to build even more buildings and longer runways. SAC's big bombers, including B-36s, B-47s, and B-52s, continued to take off from the nearly three-mile long runway at Biggs AFB until 1965 when, despite frequent promises to the contrary, the planes were transferred to Abilene's Dyess AFB and the venerable old El Paso military flying facility was closed.[70]

Once again, however, the city was spared the anguish that customarily accompanies the shuttering of such a major military installation. In a unique hand-off, the Air Force simply returned its base to Fort Bliss, the Army facility from which it had been initially acquired, and the historic name Biggs Army Airfield once again appeared at its main gate. Although no longer exclusively used for flying purposes, the field is still very much an integral part of Fort Bliss.

The military presence in El Paso continues to be an extraordinarily vital part of the community, just as it has been for centuries. At the end of the twentieth century, a full 25 percent of the city's permanent working population was employed at Fort Bliss/Biggs Field. One of every five dollars injected into the community's coffers was directly generated by the twin military installations. Further, thousands of veterans who once served either at the fort or on the base returned to the city as retirees at the end of their final tour of duty, pumping additional millions of dollars into the economy. In 1999, it was estimated by city officials that the overall annual financial impact of Fort Bliss/Biggs Field on the El Paso community exceeded $1.5 billion.[71]

Of the six World War II airfields that were located along the Texas-Mexico border, only two, Biggs and Laughlin, are still active military installations, yet it should be clear that even though more of the old fields are closed than remain open, the cumulative social and economic effects of the World War II Air Force experience along the Rio Grande have proved to be both significant and indelible.

[1] Vance Delone Raimond, *Transportation: Key to the Magic Valley*, 134.

[2] *Valley Morning Star*, February 1, 1941.

[3] Raimond, 135.

[4] *Valley Morning Star*, June 20, 1963.

[5] *Valley Morning Star*, July 30, 1944.

[6] *Valley Morning Star*, January 12, 1941.

[7] Raimond, 137.

[8] Doris Brinker Tanner, *Who Were the WASP?*, 101.

[9] Charlotte Meade Blankenship, interview with author, Brownsville, Texas, October 28, 1998.

[10] *New York Daily News*, June 25, 1943.

[11] *Chicago Tribune*, June 26, 1943.

[12] James Lydon, letter to the author, August 6, 1998.

[13] *Texas Almanac 1955-1956*, 171.

[14] *Valley Morning Star*, November 12, 1960.

[15] *Valley Morning Star*, July 30, 1964.

[16] *Valley Morning Star*, August 12, 1997.

[17] "Corps of Engineers Status Update: Formerly Used Defense Site Environmental Investigations at the Former Laredo Air Force Base," 1.

[18] *The Laredo Times*, February 16, 1943.

[19] Hermelinda Aguirre Murillo, "A History of Webb County," master's thesis, Southwest Texas State Teachers College, 1941.

[20] *The Laredo Times*, November 1, 1940.

[21] *The Laredo Times*, May 13, 1942.

[22] Ibid.

[23] *The Laredo Times*, May 14, 1942.

[24] *The Laredo Times*, May 31, 1942.

[25] Ibid.

[26] *The Laredo Times*, January 13, 1943.

[27] *San Antonio Evening News*, December 18, 1951.

[28] Ibid.

[29] *The Laredo Times*, January 24, 1943.

[30] *San Antonio Evening News*, December 18, 1951.

[31] *The Laredo Times*, February 16, 1943.

[32] *The Laredo Times*, January 20, 1943.

[33] *The Laredo Times*, January 21, 1943.

[34] *The Laredo Times*, February 3, 1943.

[35] "Corps of Engineers Report," 6.

[36] *San Antonio Evening News*, December 18, 1951.

[37] Ibid.

[38] *Laredo Times*, May 20, 1979.

[39] E. Roebuck Daughtery, *U. S. Air Force Activities In and Near Del Rio, Val Verde County, Texas*, 3.

[40] Ibid., 4.

[41] James H. Doolittle, *I Could Never Be So Lucky Again*, 63.

[42] Ibid., 64.

[43] *Del Rio News-Herald*, April 2, 1942.

[44] *Del Rio News-Herald*, April 18, 1942.

[45] *Del Rio News-Herald*, May 15, 1942.

[46] Daughtery, 9.

[47] Ibid., 10.

[48] *Tarfu*, March 12, 1943, 1.

[49] Gerald C. Brant, "Dedicatory Address at Laughlin Army Airfield," March 28, 1942.

[50] Paul O. Russell, letter to author, January 12, 2002.

[51] Allard E. Stevens, letter to Paul O. Russell, December 1, 1997.

[52] George M. Carnahan, letter to Paul O. Russell, April 13, 1997.

[53] Stevens to Russell

[54] *Tarfu*, September 12, 1944.

[55] *Del Rio News-Herald*, September 7, 1945.

[56] James S. Long, interview with author, Del Rio, Texas, October 4, 1999.

[57] "Report of the 47th Comptrollor Flight, Laughlin Air Force Base," 1999.

[58] *El Paso Times*, June 12, 1919.

[59] Maurer Maurer, *Aviation in the U. S. Army*, 1919-1939, 99.

[60] *El Paso Times*, October 28, 1956.

[61] "Biggs Field Fact Sheet," 10.

[62] *U. S. Army Air Forces Directory of Airports*, vol. III, 203.

[63] *History of Biggs Field*, 48.

[64] Alicia Gonzalez, "El Paso Public Libraries Oral History Project."

[65] Ibid.

[66] Ibid.

[67] Ysidro Cervantes, "El Paso Public Libraries Oral History Project."

[68] Ibid.

[69] *El Paso Times*, September 13, 1945.

[70] *El Paso Times*, November 24, 1964.

[71] "Economic Survey Bulletin," El Paso Convention and Visitors Bureau, 1.

Lt. Benjamin D. Foulois, the U.S. Army's first aviator and the man who made Texas the military aviation center of the United States, 1911.
Courtesy the UT Institute of Texan Cultures at San Antonio.

The headstone of Lt. George E.M. Kelly, the first Army pilot to lose his life in a military training flight. Kelly Field in San Antonio was named in his honor.
Courtesy the UT Institute of Texan Cultures at San Antonio.

Top: **This aerial view of San Antonio taken in 1931 shows the location of the city's Army airfields. Randolph Field was under construction at the time.**
Courtesy the UT Institute of Texan Cultures at San Antonio.

Left: **Mrs. Mary Edwards, a "Kelly Katie," works on an airplane engine during the war at Kelly Field, June 13, 1942.**
Courtesy the UT Institute of Texan Cultures at San Antonio.

Capt. Elliott Roosevelt, son of the president of the United States, receives his navigator wings at Kelly Field on December 20, 1941. Brig. Gen. Hubert R. Harmon does the honors.
Courtesy the UT Institute of Texan Cultures at San Antonio.

Top: **Aviation Cadets John B. Modica and Don Jones hear all about the early days from L.C. Whitsett and H.O. Campbell, members of the Old Trail Driver's Association. Taken at San Antonio's Gunter Hotel, October 9, 1942.**
Courtesy the UT Institute of Texan Cultures at San Antonio.

Bottom: **A view of Randolph Field's distinctive "Taj Mahal" administration building in July 1931, taken as construction work continued.**
Courtesy the UT Institute of Texan Cultures at San Antonio.

Top: **A custom-made double-decker bus transported soldiers to and from Hondo. The train station, now the Medina County Museum, is in the background.**
Courtesy Medina County Museum, Hondo, Texas.

Bottom: **Hondo Army Airfield's 743rd WAC Squadron passes in review, October 1943.**
Courtesy Medina County Museum, Hondo, Texas.

Top: **Greenville's widely publicized street sign, which adorned the city's main street from 1921 to 1968.**
Courtesy Photography by Narramore, Greenville, Texas.

Bottom: **A rare photograph of the 201st Mexican Fighter Squadron taken soon after its arrival in Texas in August 1944.**
Courtesy Air Education Training Command History Office, Randolph Field, Texas.

Top: Lt. Cmdr. Lyndon B. Johnson on his way to the South Pacific, early 1942. His wife ran his congressional office in his absence and helped bring Bergstrom Field to Austin.

Courtesy Admiral Nimitz Museum, Fredericksburg, Texas.

Bottom: The coffin of Lyndon B. Johnson, life-long champion of Austin's Bergstrom Field, returns to the base, January 1973.

Courtesy Bergstrom/Austin Community Council, Austin, Texas.

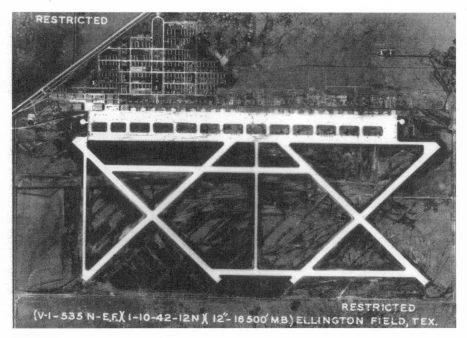

Top: An official USAAF photograph of Ellington Field, taken at high noon on January 12, 1942. The wide white strip visible at upper center was reportedly the world's largest single slab of concrete at the time.
Courtesy Texas Military Forces Museum, Austin, Texas.

Bottom: A group of Ellington Field cadets move toward their training aircraft.
Courtesy Texas Military Forces Museum, Austin, Texas.

Top: Dallas Love Field, 1944. The 5th Ferrying Group area is on the left with Bachman Lake shown at the top of the photograph.
Courtesy Frontiers of Flight Museum, Dallas Love Field, Dallas, Texas.

Right: A WASP and her Army escorts pose outside the main gate at Love Field, Dallas, during the war.
Courtesy Dallas Historical Society, Dallas, Texas.

Left: **A beaming Amon Carter, Sr., helps a rain-soaked Brig. Gen. Gerald C. Brant break ground for Consolidated Aircraft's new bomber plant in Fort Worth, 1941.**
Courtesy the University of Texas at Arlington Libraries, Special Collections Division.

Bottom: **Consolidated's mile-long assembly line produced thousands of B-24 Liberators for the Fort Worth Army Airfield located directly across the runway.**
Courtesy Tarrant County Historical Commission, Fort Worth, Texas.

Top: **Aircraft from Harlingen's Gunnery School fly over the field's main gate in 1942 for the benefit of Paramount Picture's movie cameras.**
Courtesy the Academy of Motion Picture Arts and Sciences.

Bottom: **Actor Jimmy Lydon (front row, fifth from right) leads fellow actors "Sgt. First Class" Richard Arlen and "Sgt. First Class" Chester Morris in an after-shooting sing-along with real gunners. The actors were at Harlingen's Airfield for location shooting for the 1942 motion picture "Aerial Gunner."**
Courtesy the Academy of Motion Picture Arts and Sciences.

Top: The building to the right was the headquarters of Laredo's Air Base.
Courtesy Webb County Heritage Foundation, Laredo, Texas.

Left: Texas Governor Coke Stevenson and Benicio Lopez Padilla, Governor of Coahuila, Mexico, share a truck bed platform during a wartime event in Del Rio.
Courtesy Whitehead Memorial Museum, Del Rio, Texas.

Right: Pancho Villa was the elusive prey of the Army's earliest air campaign and perhaps could be considered the godfather of modern American airpower, ca 1912.
Courtesy the UT Institute of Texan Cultures at San Antonio.

Bottom: After long years of service as a U. S. Air Force Base, Biggs Field rejoined the Army in 1965.
Author's photograph.

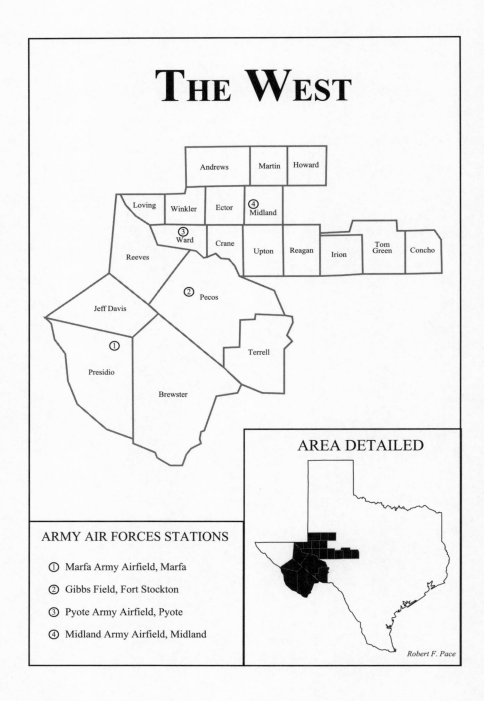

THE WEST

Andrews

Martin

Howard

Loving

Winkler

Ector

④ Midland

③ Ward

Crane

Upton

Reagan

Irion

Tom Green

Concho

Reeves

② Pecos

Jeff Davis

①

Terrell

Presidio

Brewster

AREA DETAILED

ARMY AIR FORCES STATIONS

① Marfa Army Airfield, Marfa

② Gibbs Field, Fort Stockton

③ Pyote Army Airfield, Pyote

④ Midland Army Airfield, Midland

Robert F. Pace

THE WEST

When West Texas made its bid for the many air bases located
there, that section's boast was, "three hundred and sixty-five
flying days a year!"

> Lucy Kuykendall
> *P.S. To Pecos*
> 1946

As Army wife Kuykendall learned firsthand during the war, both
the flying weather and the people of rugged West Texas were unique
and unpredictable. Of the five arbitrarily defined geographical
regions used in this text, however, "The West" affords perhaps the
best opportunity to fully appreciate the significant impact the Army
Air Force had on rural Texas.

Throughout those wartime years, the less densely populated part
of the state was dotted with communities that were smaller, fewer,
and farther between than cities located in Eastern Texas. Quite often
serving as relatively isolated supply centers for ranches and oil companies, the towns tended to be clannish, closed, and seemingly
impervious to change.

By 1941, in fact, little in the way of change had come to many of
the small towns since the railroads had first laid track from east to

west fifty years before. In more than a few of those communities, some old timers could actually still remember when the United States Army troopers had marched away in the late 1880s, leaving behind such colorfully named but suddenly abandoned historical installations as Fort Concho, Fort Stockton, and Fort D.A. Russell. By the late 1930s, just over a half-century since the days of boots and saddles, bugles and spurs, military forces were poised to return to West Texas on a very large scale.

In time, well over half of the sixty-five airfields that the Army operated throughout Texas during the war years can be categorized as being in the West, in that they were located west of the modern-day I-35 corridor that now perhaps too conveniently serves to separate West Texas from the eastern part of the state. Included in this section of the book are the stories of such diverse military installations as Midland's bombardier school, Marfa's pilot training field, the famous Rattlesnake Bomber Base at Pyote, and the small flight school that was located at Gibbs Field on the northwestern edge of Fort Stockton.

Fort Stockton

The Air Force changed Fort Stockton at least 100 percent.
A.E. Ivy
Fort Stockton, Texas
February 13, 2002

The city of Fort Stockton has been at the crossroads of West Texas military history for over a century and a half. A fort established there in 1859 near the then ever-flowing Comanche Springs also had the unique distinction of being one of the few Army installations, if not the only one, named for a commodore of the United States Navy.[1] As an important outpost on the Butterfield Overland Mail Route, as well as a safe haven for travelers seeking protection from Indian raiders, the fort remained operational until 1886 after being rebuilt in 1867 following the Civil War. The civilian frontier village that had grown up around the fort and its highly prized springs flourished primarily as an agricultural supply center until 1926 when the discovery of a major oilfield nearby gave Fort Stockton a more broadly based economy than many other small West Texas communities.

The increasing popularity of general aviation following World War I served to benefit the community as it had other towns located in the immense region west of the Pecos, where vast distances were the stuff of legend. Small airports, such as the one at Fort Stockton, often consisting of little more than a dirt runway and perhaps a rudimentary directional beacon light, began to dot the otherwise empty and barren terrain. Oil entrepreneurs and affluent ranchers, weary of driving hundreds of miles each day on business, soon began to acquire small aircraft in order to use their time more efficiently.

Even before America entered the war, the Army Air Force had determined that Fort Stockton was an ideal site for a pilot training facility. A headline in the July 25, 1941, edition of *The Fort Stockton Pioneer* clearly indicates that the Army had been in the vicinity as early as 1939 to inspect the town's airport and to begin preliminary negotiations for leasing the property. As a result of the earlier meetings with Army officers, the city had agreed to provide electricity, gas, water, and telephone service to the site should the War Department decide to assume control of the airport.[2]

By September 14, 1941, the negotiations were completed and the Army formally announced that it had signed a fifty-year lease on the city's airport at the standard rate of one dollar per year. According to a newspaper article on that date, no immediate improvements were planned for the facility and no date for the beginning of training was disclosed.[3]

In April 1942, it was announced that the Army, acting through one of its pilot training contractors, had totally revised its original plan and now intended to build a completely new airfield on another tract of land located on the northwest edge of Fort Stockton, with construction to begin immediately. Judging by the absence of any prior newspaper reference to this sudden change in plans, it would appear that the general public had not been advised that their county officials had already acquired the new twelve hundred-acre site and quietly closed a deal to provide the land to Pacific Air School, Ltd., the government-subsidized pilot training contractor. It was also announced that the federal government would build the facility on the newly acquired land at an estimated cost of $800,000.[4]

The news electrified Fort Stockton. The small town previously had been bypassed by two railroads but here at last was tangible evidence that the community's role in modern transportation was secure. Subsequent editions of the paper gave its readers an idea of the scope of the new project. There soon would be five hundred cadets on the field with plenty of civilians also present to provide the necessary services for the military personnel. Further, the plans called for a major influx of construction workers to build the hangars, barracks, ramps, and runways that would be vital to the airfield. Even better, the newspaper announced that the facility would generate an ongoing regular monthly payroll of from $50,000 to $75,000 plus an additional $37,500 per month for paying the cadets. This was indeed welcome news to a region that had seen the Great Depression severely diminish national demand for its agricultural and petroleum products.[5]

Within two weeks of the announcement of the flight school, construction on the facility was well under way. Four hangars, a ten-bed hospital, a mess hall, and a recreation center were built along with a dirt runway to accommodate the take-offs and landings of the projected 120 aircraft to be eventually assigned to the field. Further, fifty houses were authorized for construction in Fort Stockton proper to provide housing for incoming personnel. To provide the balance of what was correctly foreseen as a critical shortfall of accommodations, local residents were implored to make whatever space they had available to both military families and civilians working on the field.[6]

Work on the airfield continued virtually around the clock throughout late spring and into the summer of 1942, and on June 26 the base was considered sufficiently complete to receive its first class of student pilots. According to Lt. William Koontz who was stationed at the field, the rush to complete the facility did not impair the facility's attractiveness. "Gibbs Field," he wrote many years later, "was architecturally the most attractive field in the training command."[7]

Although Lieutenant Koontz was likely unaware of it, the buildings erected on the Fort Stockton site had in fact been designed for another Pacific Air School facility originally planned for Safford, Arizona. When the Texas land suddenly became available, its superior terrain and weather conditions caused the Arizona project to be cancelled and the building plans already approved by the government were simply transferred intact to Fort Stockton.[8]

With pre-construction planning and the need for federal approval of the building design removed from the schedule, Fort

Stockton once again found itself a full-fledged military town in record time. Local citizens joined business leaders in welcoming the first class of cadets to town, while newspaper ads admonished readers to "fix that spare bedroom" in anticipation of the shortage of living accommodations that was sure to escalate as additional military families moved to the city. "We have a large stock [of beds, mattresses, springs, dressers]," claimed the Clarke-Harwell-Owen, Inc., furniture store, "but we cannot guarantee that we can replace all items."[9] "Paint-up and fix-up for the air school" advised the local Western Auto Store, urging the good citizens of Fort Stockton to show the newly arriving military personnel that they were coming to a "warm and welcoming" community.[10]

Perhaps the most telling evidence of how important the coming of the air school was to the community can be found in the May 1, 1942, edition of *The Fort Stockton Pioneer*. In a front-page editorial remarkably free of the usual small town boosterism too frequently presented in local papers in those days, the editor wrote, "When we face the facts squarely and honestly, we realize that had it not been for the location of the Pacific Air School here at the time it was announced, Fort Stockton business would have suffered a serious setback...we were right on the verge of a severe slump."[11]

While rejoicing at the town's rescue from serious economic woes, *The Pioneer* also recorded the social events that welcomed the newcomers. On Friday, June 1, 1942, the paper noted that personnel from the nearly completed airfield, and their wives, were feted at a picnic in James Rooney Park. The article also added the somewhat cryptic line that "nine dozen scientifically barbecued chickens provided the repast." No clue was provided, however, as to what was required to scientifically barbecue a chicken.[12]

On October 9, 1942, the name of the Fort Stockton training facility was changed from Miller Field to Gibbs Field. The new name honored local resident Maj. David R. Gibbs, who had been killed in action in the Philippines.[13]

The first class of cadets at Gibbs Field arrived before either their mess hall or their barracks were ready. The group of thirty-two pilots-to-be were housed in the Community Recreation Building located in the city's Rooney Park and fed at the nearby Stockton Hotel until the base facilities were complete. Both buildings remained standing into the twenty-first century, although the dilapidated old hotel building appeared ready to collapse momentarily.

As the second cadet class arrived, life on the base had begun to settle into a routine that would continue for the short two-year existence of the flight school. During the nine week course of primary flying instruction, the cadets would complete ground school, dual instruction, and then fly their first solo mission. Upon completion of the initial solo flight, the young pilot was required to kiss the field mascot, a miniature mule appropriately named "Solo." The mule mascot proved to be so popular its image was included in the field's logo, which was designed by Cecil Lang Casebier in 1942. A replica of the original logo was painted on what had been the Gibbs Field Operations Building in 1988 to welcome veterans who were returning for the base's first reunion.[14]

A.E. Ivy, who was a flight dispatcher at the school, remembered that the availability of funds often determined how lenient the instructors were in grading their pupils. "If the government was on time with its payments to the school," Ivy said, "more cadets passed, but if the money was late, the requirements for becoming a pilot mysteriously became much tougher and a greater number of cadets were washed out." Regardless of how many cadets graduated from the school, each instructor was paid $500 per month for working five four-hour days per week, according to Ivy.[15]

The former flight dispatcher agreed with Gene Riggs and Albert Bean, who were also familiar with both Gibbs Field and Fort Stockton, that the relationship between the field and the town during the war years was always friendly. None of these men could recall a single conflict between base personnel and the local citizens, although Ivy did remember a local deputy sheriff who on at least one occasion attempted to show some military men that the local constabulary was very much on the job. The deputy, whom Ivy recalls as fancying himself a West Texas version of the legendary cowboy star Tom Mix, stopped a car full of Army aviators who had driven to Fort Stockton from Pyote. "Where are you-all from?" inquired deputy "Mix." "We're from Chicago," replied the driver. "Oh, yeah," snapped the no-nonsense deputy reaching for his six-shooter, "then what are you-all doing with them Illinois license plates on your car?" One thing then led to another, apparently, but in time the deputy's geographical confusion was resolved through the use of a road map. The aviators, perhaps shaking their heads in wonderment, were soon on their way out of town.[16]

During the time the field was operational, many marriages took place between military personnel and Fort Stockton's small legion of eligible young ladies. Among those who married a local girl was dispatcher Ivy himself. Many other longtime residents of the town fondly recall the excitement and new ways of thinking the military personnel brought to the town, yet how well they deported themselves.[17]

In late February 1944, not quite two years after it had opened, it was announced that Gibbs Field was soon to be closed as a contract flight training school. Over five thousand young men had completed the primary phase of their pilot training while assigned to the field and had gone on to basic training elsewhere. The town had embraced each one with a genuine warmth and hospitality, mourning the deaths of the only two aviators who had died during training and rejoicing at the dozens of marriages that had taken place. The population of the town had grown by nearly a thousand in the two years the field had been in operation, mostly either civilians employed on the base or dependents of military personnel. By all accounts, Fort Stockton had benefited immensely from the coming of Gibbs Field.[18]

There can be little question that the student pilots who had been sent to Fort Stockton had learned to love their civilian neighbors. As evidence of that affection, the following almost rhapsodic dedication appeared in "Solo," the yearbook for Cadet Class 43-A.

> We swung off the train under loaded barracks bags that warm June day—wondering what phantom fingers might have fashioned this community on the skirts of the desert, vast and tawny, where the crow routes and the doggie trails lead but to more vastness and where every breeze was like the business end of a blowtorch.
>
> [The people of Fort Stockton] listened and talked with us enthusiastically. They renewed invitations and always found room for one more. They planned the good times, the good meals, the good fellowship, and what man of us will forget the day they saluted us with applause as we marched from the depot!
>
> Lacking the cosmopolitan aspect of larger centers with their thousand and one attendant diversions, Fort Stockton's people manufactured pleasure and entertainment from no other materials than sincerity and abundantly fresh personalities.[19]

By early 1944, it was clear that the demand for even such erudite pilots would soon diminish, yet the people of Fort Stockton did not want to see their airfield go away. Committees traveled to various Army headquarters in an effort to find some other use for the attractive facility, but to no avail. On March 3, 1944, the newspaper announced that Class 44-G would be the final group of cadets to graduate.[20]

For a time, the all but deserted airfield served as a storage site for surplus military aircraft being prepared for sale to outside interests. On April 21, 1944, just two years and four days from the official announcement of its opening, a newspaper advertisement made it painfully clear that Gibbs Field was going to be permanently closed. "Pacific Air School Clearance Sale," proclaimed the ad, "Equipment and supplies, blankets and bed pads, kitchen equipment, stoves, tools and gift shop merchandise" were all to be offered for sale at promised bargain prices. Sales hours were announced to be from 9 A.M. to 4 P.M., on April 22 and the public was invited to inspect and buy these once-in-a-lifetime bargains. According to contemporary accounts, the local citizens put all sentiment aside to flock to the old base early and often on the day of the clearance sale. Soon, the surplus merchandise had all been sold, and Gibbs Field's once exciting military days faded to only fond memories.[21]

To one man, however, the field was too precious to be allowed to die. Bill Hargus, who had flown P-47 Thunderbolts over Europe and on D-Day, came back from the war as a seasoned combat pilot with a love for aviation and a strong belief that West Texas in general and Fort Stockton in particular had much to gain by maintaining old Gibbs Field as a county aviation center. When he became manager of what had become the Pecos County Airport in the mid-1950s, the buildings that remained from Gibbs's military days were in a sorry state. Ceilings had fallen, walls had crumbled and hangar doors had buckled, yet, surprisingly, much of the old base was still intact. All four of the original hangars were standing, as were the operations building, some barracks, and a mess hall. Hargus slowly began to rebuild and repair the buildings and their furnishings so Pecos County and Fort Stockton could claim a presence in the aviation era that surely lay just ahead. Largely through his efforts, much of what was once Gibbs Field remains intact. [22]

Having logged more than thirty thousand flying hours in his over sixty years as a pilot, Bill Hargus is still at the controls of his

Cessna on a regular basis. As he approaches the historic airport that he continues to manage, he can easily spot the dirt runways used by the aviation cadets of 1942-1944 as well as the original tetrahedron that so long ago told the fledgling aviators which way the capricious winds of West Texas might be blowing at any given moment. The old field is in all likelihood now the best preserved of all the historic World War II bases in West Texas.[23]

As final proof of the continuing economic legacy of Gibbs Field, Hargus can recount an unusual stipulation in the federal government's agreement to surrender the airfield to county administrators after the war. Although there was no current petroleum activity on the 1,320-acre airport site when the county bought it from the federal government for $40,000 in 1947, it was stated that any royalty income from oil or gas production flowing from future wells on the property was to be invested in airport improvements. When several significant producing gas wells were in fact soon discovered on the huge tract of land, the terms of the lease agreement were honored, at least technically. While most of the funds gained from the petroleum royalties have indeed gone to pay for improvements on airport property, only some of the money has gone to improve the airport facility itself. Thus, a convention center, a golf course, school buildings, etc., have been constructed on airport lands over the past decades, with money generated by the royalties. As Bill Hargus somewhat ruefully observes, "Not all of those funds have gone into keeping the airport itself up with the times."[24] Even so, it is clear that old Gibbs Field, though created for a war, still continues to directly benefit the good people of Fort Stockton and Pecos County who so warmly embraced it over sixty years ago.

Marfa

A large portion of the success of this field may be attributed to the fine helpful spirit of the residents of the Big Bend area.
                    Maj. Gen. Ralph P. Cousins
                    U. S. Army Air Forces
                    The Big Bend Sentinel
                    May 13, 1945

While Gibbs Field at Fort Stockton is quite likely the best preserved of the many World War II airfields that once flourished in West

Texas, Marfa's Army air base is without doubt the least preserved. All evidence of it is, in fact, mostly gone, save for two concrete entrance gate walls. Where tourists now gather nightly to search the horizon for the famous "Marfa Mystery Lights," an Army flying field that was once home to as many as six thousand airmen hummed with activity twenty-four hours each day. The roadside park that attracts those who hope to see nature's light show is actually located on what was the northern edge of the giant wartime base.

Marfa was chosen as the site for a World War II airfield largely as a direct result of military experience in the region that dated back to 1911, some thirty years before Marfa Army Airfield became operational. Continuing disturbances along the Mexican border during that neighboring country's revolution had created the need for a series of cavalry outposts near the Rio Grande. One of these, Camp Marfa, took its name from the tiny town that lay just a few miles to the north. Soon, in addition to mounted cavalry patrols, aerial reconnaissance flights were being staged from the camp.

By 1930, Camp Marfa had grown in importance and had acquired the name Fort D.A. Russell befitting its status as a permanent Army installation. As it developed, the initial permanency of the fort had lasted a scant three years when it was abandoned in 1933. However, in 1935 the Army decided that the facility had permanent value after all, and D.A. Russell became active once again.[25]

When World War II started, it became apparent to Army officials that in addition to its fort, the Marfa vicinity would also be an excellent location for an airfield. Many of the older aviators who were now senior officers had flown reconnaissance missions out of the old fort and they recalled the excellent flying conditions in the region, as well as the exceptionally warm welcome extended to them by the citizens of Marfa. As a direct result of those two factors, the decision was made to acquire land in the immediate area to build a major flight-training center.[26]

On March 27, 1942, Maj. Norman L. Callish of the Army Air Force arrived in Marfa to inspect various sites that had been identified as likely locations for the field. The major left after a few days but returned ten days later and soon found what he had been seeking, namely a 2,750-acre site near town and on the railway. The owner agreed to sell the land for $6.50 per acre and the War Department quickly agreed to the purchase. Soon the coming of another military installation was officially announced in the Marfa newspaper.[27]

Marfans and their neighbors throughout the entire region were elated at the news. The community launched a major effort to locate suitable housing for those who would be building the base and for those military families who, in time, would be coming to Marfa. Despite this unified effort, housing shortages would present a continuing and serious problem during the airfield's entire existence.[28]

Perhaps because of its long and pleasant relationship with Marfa, the Army seems to have taken special pains to prepare the local citizenry for the social and economic shockwave due to hit the town when the airfield opened. On August 3, 1942, a crowd of Marfans gathered to hear from speakers who had experienced something of those same upheavals when the Air Force had opened facilities in Austin, Odessa, and Midland. The audience learned that traffic and utility overloads should be expected, along with crowded schoolrooms, and, mostly, the already foreseen shortage of housing.

Somehow, all of these potential problems seemed to become more bearable when considered in light of the positive side of the matter. Mr. Paul Nelson, who was manager of the J.C. Penney store in Midland, told a group of area retailers that his store had experienced sales increases of from 50 to 100 percent each month in the first year after Midland Army Airfield's huge bombardier school opened. According to the local *Big Bend Sentinel*, Mr. Nelson's report brought forth enthusiastic cheers from his fellow retailers.[29]

One month later, it was announced that the first aircraft and the initial class of cadets would be arriving in less than thirty days, along with the first of the permanent support personnel who would stay at the base when the newly-trained pilots moved on to their combat assignments. When the airfield was at the peak of its operation, over five thousand such support personnel were assigned to the base.[30] As the civilian population of Marfa had been only 3,805 in 1940, the new airfield obviously had a significant impact on the community.[31]

In late November 1942, the base was declared operational by the War Department and the first of the five hundred aircraft that would eventually be assigned to the airfield began to arrive. Although the construction time required to complete the facility to its operational level had been relatively short, it was announced that over $6 million had been expended in the process. This published amount was roughly twice what the initial estimate of construction costs had been, and even more work on the facility continued from the day it opened until it closed in 1945.[32]

The massive and ongoing construction, the crowds of newcomers, the stunning increase in vehicular traffic, and the constant roaring of five hundred airplanes did not seem to overly concern the patriotic Marfans. As C.M. "Fritz" Kahl, a onetime flight instructor and later Marfa's mayor put it in 1999, "They took us in and assimilated us into their society. We were foreigners in a vague sense, and they accepted us fully."[33]

The local newspaper and the Marfa Chamber of Commerce joined forces to make certain that newcomers such as Fritz Kahl were indeed warmly welcomed. A front-page editorial admonished the paper's readers that "the general reputation of the community was at stake" when it came to being courteous and fair to the newly arriving servicemen. The editor went on to point out that "no undesirable advantage" should be taken of the airmen, even though the War Department had already imposed rent and price ceilings to ensure that at least no economic advantage could easily be taken by civilian landlords and shopkeepers.[34]

It is clear that, for the most part, Marfans heeded the message delivered to them by their newspaper. Servicemen were invited into churches and private homes. On Christmas Day, 1942, Molly Atwell's parents invited a group of airmen into their home to celebrate the holiday. She remembers, "We sat around and talked, sharing memories of past Christmases and hearing how the holiday was celebrated in other states." Miss Atwell also recalled how the revelers "laughed at each other's funny sounding accents."[35]

After weeks of preparation and the inspection of aircraft, flight training officially got underway on the huge base on December 7, 1942, the first anniversary of the Japanese attack on Pearl Harbor. One hundred eighty cadets made up Class 43-B, the initial group of advanced pilot candidates. This first class graduated on February 6, 1943. After receiving their silver wings, the new pilots and their families were treated to "a sumptuous banquet" at the First Christian Church of Marfa.[36]

The next class, 43-C, graduated exactly one month after its predecessor. Each month thereafter, a newly winged group of pilots would celebrate its success with a banquet and usually a dance following the ceremonies. In its three and a half years of pilot training, the Marfa program produced nearly eight thousand new aviators.[37]

Records indicate the town's population grew by nearly 50 percent during the war years. This growth was reflected in a 47 percent increase in the number of telephones in use and a 92 percent increase in the volume of mail handled by the Marfa Post Office. The latter figure, as remarkable as it was, did not include the estimated three thousand free letters sent daily by the servicemen on the air base.[38]

Among the soldiers stationed at the field was a singing military policeman who would later gain fame in Hollywood. According to Fritz Kahl, the base chaplain opened his chapel each day at noon for servicemen to enjoy the remarkable voice of the singularly overweight police sergeant named Alfred Arnold Coccozza. As word of the Air Force tenor's extraordinary talent spread throughout the region, he was asked to sing at other churches, women's clubs, schools, and virtually any other place where people gathered. "That guy," Kahl remembers with a laugh, "would sing anywhere at the drop of a hat." Long after the war, Kahl went into a motion picture theater and instantly recognized the face on the film and the voice on the soundtrack as being those of his old friend Alfred Arnold Coccozza, who by then was better known to his countless fans as Mario Lanza.[39]

While the pilot training program at Marfa Army Airfield continued at an ever-accelerating pace, activities at old Fort D. A. Russell remained fairly static. The pace at the fort quickened somewhat early in 1944 when 195 German prisoners-of-war arrived shortly after being captured in North Africa. The men were veterans of Field Marshal Erwin Rommel's recently defeated *Afrika Korps*, and according to several contemporary accounts, each was "good-looking and blond and very well-behaved." Myrtle Shepherd remembered that her "YWCA and Baptist Women's Group would bake cookies" for the prisoners, while the local schoolchildren would wave at them as they were transported off the fort to perform menial duties in town each day.[40] In one of the few violent incidents recorded during the war years in Marfa, an ill-advised route of march had a group of prisoners pass by a local saloon. One of the patrons, whose son had been killed in action in the European Theater, became enraged upon seeing the marching Germans and ran outside to throw a beer bottle at them.[41]

A small group of prisoners escaped from the fort on April 2, 1944, and remained on the move for several days. The leader of the group, Raymond Moler, stated after his capture that he and his comrades had planned to travel the sixty-odd miles to Mexico, cross the border, and move farther into Latin America in hopes of finding a way to get back to Germany. As it turned out, the escapees, apparently lacking either a compass or a reliable sense of direction, were apprehended some 130 miles northwest of Marfa near the small town of Sierra Blanca, Texas. Had they headed south toward Mexico as planned and traveled the same distance in the same number of days, the men would have been seventy miles south of the Rio Grande with at least a very remote chance of returning to German soil.[42]

Meanwhile, the tide of war was rapidly turning against other Germans soldiers and their allies. By spring 1945, with the end of the war in sight, it was announced that with the graduation of Class 45-C on May 23, all flight training at Marfa Army Airfield would come to a halt. In a short time, only a skeleton force remained to close down what only weeks before had been a thriving military city with nearly 250 buildings and some 5,200 residents. Despite some preliminary indications that the base might get a reprieve and be allowed to stay open with another mission, it soon became apparent that there would be no future for the Marfa base.[43]

By all accounts, the impact of the closing was overwhelming. "The town fell on its face," remembers Fritz Kahl.[44] Civic spirit plummeted, businesses closed, the population rapidly began to shrink. As local historian Cecilia Thompson was to write years later, "The glory days of military activity were over. Marfa would never be the same again."[45]

At the beginning of the twenty-first century, the population of Marfa was estimated to be just over twenty-five hundred and no longer troubled by a shortage of housing. The once-whitewashed gateway into what had been the little city's vital Army airfield slips into further decay less than twenty yards east of the Marfa Lights viewing area. As eager viewers gaze southeasterly in an often vain attempt to see the mysterious lights dance and dart as advertised, few are aware that they are looking across a vast area where, long ago, a great military community once thrived. Again a desert of sage and creosote bush, it has been for six decades the home of nothing but jackrabbits, rattlesnakes, and a galaxy of ghostly memories.

Midland/Odessa

The bombardier was a child of World War II . . . his specialty
was born, flourished and died all within one decade."
              Bruce Callender
              Air Force Times
              April 1984

Although what was destined to become the world's largest bombardier school was officially known as Midland Army Airfield, it was in fact located halfway between Midland and its longtime arch rival, the city of Odessa. Even though the latter community was every bit as proud of the important military installation as was its namesake town, the *Odessa American* could never quite bring itself to refer to the base by its official name. In one edition, the paper might use the phrase "our field," or in another edition, the term "the big bombardier school" might be suggested, but the name "Midland" was only rarely employed to accurately identify what had become one of the most important training schools in the nation.[46]

Regardless of what the *Odessa American* chose to call the facility, the simple truth was that both of the airfield's host cities were delighted with the economic boom that occurred when it opened in early 1942. Unlike most Texas cities at the time, however, neither Odessa nor Midland was suffering any particular hardship because of the Great Depression. To be sure, times had been tough in both of the petroleum-oriented communities during the early 1930s, but a federal tariff on foreign oil and a new state-ordered regulation on production had brought both stability and new exploration to the oil-rich Permian Basin.

Even as the oil continued to flow, efforts to obtain a military air base for the region had started well before World War II. As early as 1939, Congressman R. Ewing Thomason had been at work in Washington trying to convince War Department officials that Midland's Municipal Airport was an ideal spot for a major military air installation. Later records indicate that although Congressman Thomason apparently was sincere in his convictions that the region was worthy of a military airfield, he was also simultaneously lobbying the Army to establish a cavalry remount station near Midland. It seems that his efforts to gain favor with the U.S. Cavalry were in fact initially successful, as a team of equine experts visited the region and acquired twenty-two horses before abandoning the project in late 1940.[47]

By June of the next year, Thomason was able to report to his constituents that the Army was giving "careful consideration to the possibility of establishing an air training school at Midland."[48] Exactly one year later, the possibility of a bombardier training facility became a reality. A *Midland Reporter-Telegram* headline on June 13 proudly proclaimed, "Midland Gets Air School."[49]

The first class of bombardier trainees arrived on the nearly completed base on February 6, 1942. After swearing a solemn oath to protect the top secret Norden bombsight with their lives if need be, the cadets settled into a twelve-week course of instruction that included, among other subjects, how to use the closely guarded sighting instrument effectively against enemy targets.[50]

Art Cole, who served as a public information officer on the wartime base, recalls that at any given time, there were approximately five thousand men and women assigned to it.[51] As the combined population of Midland and Odessa was just under nineteen thousand in 1940, it is safe to assume that an almost instantaneous population increase of 25 percent had a significant positive economic impact on the entire region. The civilian population also increased dramatically, as military families and workers flooded into the towns. According to the *Texas Almanac and State Industrial Guide, 1943-1944,* Midland's civilian population grew by over 33 percent in the first year the base was open.[52] As might be expected, housing quickly became a critical issue. In both Odessa and Midland, as Cole remembers, many family garages were converted into "minimal living quarters," but even then, the shortage continued.

Art Cole also recalls that most G.I.'s assigned to the base used their first off-base pass to go into Midland, "if for no other reason" to see an impressive eleven-story building they had observed as their troop train passed slowly through town on its way westward to the airfield. Quickly satisfying their curiosity about a rarely seen Texas skyscraper, many of the soldiers caught the first bus west to Odessa after realizing the "awful truth" that Midland had no bars. Apparently, the fact that Odessa had something in profusion that Midland sadly lacked gave the town an early reputation as the place to go for a good time. "There were plenty of bars [in Odessa]," states Cole, "where the 'dollar a day, once a month' guy could hock his watch and buy a bottle of whiskey."[53]

One observer also notes that the girls of Odessa were keen to entertain any and all airmen who found their way to what was known as Oil Patch City. "With their eyelashes curled upward and the latest New York fashion fads on their minds," wrote historian Irene Paulette, "the gals set out to entertain the soldiers and make them feel at home."[54]

Most people in the bombardier school's two host cities clearly went out of their way to welcome the base personnel. Barbecue dinners for the cadets were regular occurrences at churches, country clubs, and private homes. Graduating classes were feted en masse at rodeos, banquets, and dances held in both towns. The war years' editions of the *Odessa American* and the *Midland Reporter-Telegram* also frequently contained accounts of marriages of local girls to servicemen from the airfield.

Corporal Sam McClelland, for example, remembers going to a USO dance at Odessa's American Legion Hall on the Fourth of July 1942. When he saw a particularly attractive girl dancing with a fellow soldier, McClelland cut in and boldly invited himself to come to the girl's home for dinner the very next Sunday. Perhaps understandably taken aback by his direct approach, she agreed, and exactly one year later the two were married. As was frequently the case in such marriages, the McClellands joined countless other couples across Texas in returning to the bride's home after the war was over in 1945 rather than locating in the veteran's hometown.[55]

Even though the war was far from over in late 1943, the demand for highly trained bombardiers slackened when the Air Force adopted a novel lead crew concept for its bombing missions. As a result, bombardier training at other Texas bases such as Big Spring and Childress was discontinued and consolidated at the "Mother School" at Midland. Although Air Force officials persisted in declaring that the facility was a permanent one, announcement of its closing was made public in June 1946. In the four years of its operation, the school had trained and graduated 6,627 bombardiers, more than any other Army airfield in the nation.[56]

The impact of the base on Midland and Odessa undeniably had been significant, yielding as it did additional economic prosperity, broadening social viewpoints, and, perhaps almost as important, creating the infrastructure for the building of a regional airport on the site of the old bombardier school facility. In the end, however, it was Midland which got the lasting credit when the Federal Aviation

Administration chose the letters "MAF" as the designation symbol for the new civil air facility. Those letters, insist veteran pilots, stand for Midland Army Field, thus preserving the colorful legacy of "The World's Largest Bombardier School."

As Art Cole, now a well-known Santa Fe artist sees it, however, the most vital legacy of the old airfield stems from the people who were assigned to it during the war years. "They brought an awareness of a larger world," noted Cole. Further, he believes a more lasting effect of the base "came from the men who were stationed there and, when the war was over, returned to make their home in West Texas." These former airmen, remembering the "welcoming semi-frontier atmosphere" they had enjoyed during their assignment at Midland/Odessa, brought with them, as Cole terms it, "new energy, new ideas, and new demands." These newcomers, originally from all parts of the nation, carried with them the seeds of change that became perhaps the most durable heritage of the World War II experience in Midland, Odessa, and, indeed, throughout the state of Texas.[57]

Pyote

I don't know why we even bothered to take that place away from them damned snakes. Since they liked it so much, I think we should have let them keep it all to themselves.
> Art Pringle
> Racine, Wisconsin
> June 1944

Of all the historic Army airfields located in West Texas during the war, none seems more fascinating or more symbolic of the entire wartime Air Force experience than the present-day ruin that was once the Rattlesnake Bomber Base at Pyote.

Whenever veterans, historians, and even the most casual students of the war years gather to speak of those glorious times now shrouded by six decades of smoke and dust churned by more recent history, a discussion of this ghostly old base is quite likely to be included. And why not? All of the elements for good storytelling are there, just a short distance from the town that enjoyed a providential rebirth when the base opened in 1942 and all but died when it closed a quarter of a century later.

The colorful Pyote drama includes such diverse elements as the conversion of thousands of acres of harsh desert land into a thriving military city, the presence of one of the Army's most highly decorated combat units, the emergence of a boomtown of almost fictional proportions, and the arrival of what was arguably the war's single most famous aircraft. With its many colorful aspects, the story of Pyote is *the* classic tale of wartime Texas on a grand scale.

That story began in early January 1942 when Ward County Commissioner Ted Thomas traveled to the headquarters of the Army Engineers in Roswell, New Mexico, to persuade officials to consider the building of an air base in his county. Apparently, Commissioner Thomas presented his case extremely well, as rumors began to circulate that a major Army airfield was indeed soon to be announced for Pyote. When fences began to be erected around a 2,745-acre site belonging to the University of Texas and located on the very edge of the tiny town, the rumors appeared to be valid.

Before any official announcement was made, however, huge quantities of lumber and other building materials began to arrive on railroad cars shunted onto spur tracks that had been hastily laid through a heavily guarded gate in the new fence. One of the war's most poorly kept secrets was finally made officially public on July 31, 1942, when the *Monahans News* confirmed that the University's land had indeed been leased to the War Department which planned to immediately build a $12 million airfield on the site.[58] As the value of the entire county had been appraised at only $41 million a short time earlier, it was apparent to the excited local residents that big things were about to happen in their neighborhood.[59]

Unlike most other wartime air facility projects, the announced field at Pyote had no existing foundation upon which to be built. There were no civilian runways to thicken and extend, no utility services of any kind to expand to accommodate the expected ten thousand military personnel, and there were no roads to resurface to handle an almost unbelievable flow of vehicular traffic to and from the base. At Pyote, there was nothing, save for a good rail line, a highway, and a town of 250 West Texans who found it hard to believe that their county commissioner had turned out to be such a remarkable salesman.[60]

There were, however, some things included in the four sections of University land that the persuasive Commissioner Thomas had in all likelihood neglected to tell the Army Engineers. As soon as construction on the facility began on September 5, 1942, it swiftly came to the attention of workers that the terrain was home to thousands of particularly ill-tempered rattlesnakes who deeply resented being dispossessed from their dens, war or no war. At the end of each shift, the bulldozers would push the remains of dead rattlers dispatched in the course of the day's grading activity into large piles. Once liberally soaked with a combination of diesel and gasoline, the piles would be ignited. One veteran of the early days of construction on the field recalled that the dead snakes seemed to writhe and coil even as the blazing funeral pyre consumed their bodies. The impression made by the rattlesnakes, perhaps those still living more than the ones so recently dead, was profound enough in 1942 to give the field the nickname of the Rattlesnake Bomber Base. A sign on what was once part of the airfield's main gate still bears this very appropriate nomenclature.[61]

With most of the angry snakes eventually either permanently subdued or voluntarily relocated, work on the airfield continued night and day. Within a month after construction had started, Army personnel began to move into still incomplete facilities. Five hangars were built to support aircraft that would soon fly from the three, eighty four hundred foot long runways that stretched across the harsh landscape. There were enough barracks, gymnasiums, offices, service clubs, and mess halls to accommodate the nearly ten thousand military and civilian personnel who would soon be working and living on the field.[62]

In the village of Pyote proper, just yards away from the airfield's main gate, an unprecedented boom was taking place. As was the case in other oil towns, Pyote was accustomed to the legendary boom-to-bust-to-boom cycle of the petroleum business, but even the most seasoned roughneck had never seen anything like the boom that came with the airfield. From its 1939 population of just over two hundred hardy souls, Pyote grew almost overnight to become a city of nearly four thousand, including construction workers, military families, and civilians employed by the base. As additional families arrived daily, the demand for housing was always increasing and, as was true in other military towns, almost any structure was considered a viable accommodation, be it a barn, a chicken house, or a garage.[63]

By most contemporary accounts, the social relationship between military personnel and the local residents was cordial. Civilians were frequently invited to receptions and dances on the base, at either the officers' club or the non-commissioned officers' service club. Photographs of some of these events indicate that the ladies often wore long gowns with corsages and appropriate full-length gloves as accessories. Their officer-escorts traditionally wore their dress uniforms, most of which were ablaze with colorful medals and battle ribbons.

Although there are few indications that any serious altercations took place off the base between the servicemen and local citizens, there is proof that at least one nearby community took steps to lessen the potential for trouble. In 1943, the city council of Monahans, a town some fifteen miles east of the airfield, passed an ordinance that made it illegal for women to wear either shorts or swimsuits on public streets, regardless of the heat to be expected on a summer day in West Texas. In reporting this unusual civic action, the *San Antonio Express* noted that "any cocky young officer with an Errol Flynn mustache and a new convertible had it made," at least presumably until the so-called cover-up rule went into effect. Unfortunately, no record has survived to indicate if the ordinance served in any way to dampen the ardor of visiting pilots. Not surprisingly, however, the new law did win the unanimous support of local church officials.[64]

On January 1, 1943, the primary mission of the Rattlesnake Bomber Base was launched with the arrival of the famed 19th Bombardment Group from active duty in the South Pacific. The B-17s of the unit had participated in air battles over the Philippines and New Guinea, earning distinction and acclaim as the most highly decorated combat unit in the Army. Because of its many presidential citations for both valor and efficiency, the 19th was chosen to come to the Pyote facility to instruct flight crews slated for duty in the combat zones. As the official base records for 1944 put it, "The main objective of a place such as Pyote is to turn out the crews to man the bombers—it is the reason for our existence and Pyote can say without boasting or bragging that it is doing its share and often more."[65]

Evelyn Blair, who worked in the airfield's maintenance office during the war, remembers that the planes were being serviced around the clock to ensure that they could withstand the grueling flight scheduling of the training crews. In one outstanding month of flying, the 19th mounted fifty eight-hour missions each and every day. The rigorous schedule took a heavy toll of men and machines, however. In one week during June 1943, nineteen aviators were killed in two separate incidents.[66]

When the war ended in 1945, Pyote's airfield was not immediately closed as were a majority of the Army's air facilities in Texas. After being transferred from the Second Air Force to San Antonio's Air Technical Command headquartered at Kelly Field in November 1945, Pyote became a storage and dismantling center for combat aircraft. According to historian Jim Marks, as many as two thousand battle-weary planes were flown to West Texas to be either sold to civilian interests or dismantled and smelted into base aluminum.[67]

When the smelting project first began, bulldozers pushed whole sections of airplanes into a white-hot furnace. When the aluminum melted, it was formed into eight-foot-long bricks weighing five hundred pounds. Jack Coursey, who worked at the smelter, found the process almost disrespectful. "I didn't much like to watch it," he recalled, "[but] maybe it was the way they ought to go."[68]

Glen Garland of Pyote remembers that his father, Hank, also played a major role in a different smelting process that reduced the once gallant war birds into even smaller metal ingots. "My dad rigged up this furnace on wheels," said the younger Garland, "so that he could take it to where pieces of planes sat on the field." A small scrap of a wing or a rudder flap or other airplane part was placed into the moveable furnace and molten aluminum would quickly begin to flow into a conduit that fed the liquid metal into forms placed on a circular rack. "The ingots came out of those forms," said Garland "weighing around ten or twelve pounds." The conversion of complete aircraft into a pile of metal ingots could be completed in a matter of minutes.[69]

Among the planes flown to Pyote after the war for storage was the famous "Enola Gay," the B-29 flown by Col. Paul Tibbett on the atomic bomb mission over Hiroshima. Never intended to be a victim of the smelting furnace, the aircraft was eventually flow to Washington, D.C., to be prepared for exhibit by the Smithsonian Institution. Joining the "Enola Gay" in storage at Pyote was "The Swoose," the B-17 in which Lt. Cmdr. Lyndon B. Johnson made a forced landing during his tour of the South Pacific early in the war.[70]

With no war to fight and no more aircraft to melt, there were no further missions for the Rattlesnake Bomber Base. As the official history of Ward County puts it, "By 1966, time, weather, and vandals had taken their toll, and the Defense Department found it no longer economical to maintain such a remote facility."[71] As a result, the land upon which the now ghostly base had been built reverted back to the University of Texas Lands System and most of the buildings were either moved off the base or sold as scrap. The wells dug by government contractors for the airfield now supply the town of Pyote with its water, but the demand upon that supply is not great. As of 1990, the town contained only some four hundred residents, some of whom fondly remember the roar of B-17 and B-29 engines that echoed throughout the West Texas night.

Although a few ghostly old buildings still dot the twenty-seven hundred acres that comprised the once vital base, the only residents occupying it now are multitudes of jackrabbits, small packs of coyotes, and, of course, the innumerable diamondback rattlers, who have at last reclaimed their ancestral domain.

[1] Robert Field Stockton (1795-1866) was an American naval officer and an ardent champion of the annexation of Texas by the United States in 1845. President James A. Polk sent him to Texas with the federal resolution formally offering statehood to the Republic.

[2] *The Fort Stockton Pioneer*, July 25, 1941.

[3] *The Fort Stockton Pioneer*, September 14, 1941.

[4] *The Fort Stockton Pioneer*, April 7, 1942.

[5] Ibid.

[6] *The Fort Stockton Pioneer*, May 6, 1942.

[7] William Koontz, "Gibbs Field 1988 Reunion Questionnaire."

[8] *The Fort Stockton Pioneer*, April 17, 1942.

[9] Ibid.

[10] Ibid.

[11] *The Fort Stockton Pioneer*, May 1, 1942.

[12] *The Fort Stockton Pioneer*, June 1, 1942.

[13] Nila Luce and Bob Luce, "Gibbs Field," *Pecos County History*, 208.

[14] Ibid.

[15] A. E. Ivy, interview with author, Fort Stockton, Texas, February 12, 2002.

[16] Gene Riggs, interview with author, Fort Stockton, Texas, February 12, 2002.

[17] Nila Luce and Bob Luce, 208.

[18] *The Fort Stockton Pioneer*, February 25, 1944.

[19] *Solo, the Yearbook of Cadet Class 43-A*, Gibbs Field, Texas, 7.

[20] *The Fort Stockton Pioneer*, March 3, 1944.

[21] *The Fort Stockton Pioneer*, April 21, 1944.

[22] William Hargus, interview with author, Fort Stockton, Texas, April 11, 2001.

[23] William Hargus, interview with author, Fort Stockton, Texas, February 12, 2002.

[24] Hargus interview, April 11, 2001.

[25] Susanne Grube, "A Brief History of Camp Marfa and Fort D.A. Russell," 1.

[26] *The Big Bend Sentinel*, November 6, 1942.

[27] Cecilia Thompson, *History of Marfa and Presidio County, Texas 1535-1946*, vol. 2, 493.

[28] *The Big Bend Sentinel*, May 29, 1942.

[29] *The Big Bend Sentinel*, August 8, 1942.

[30] Ron Tyler, ed., *The New Handbook of Texas*, vol. 4, 504.

[31] *Texas Almanac and State Industrial Guide, 1943-44*, 79.

[32] Kirby F. Warnock, "Wings West of the Pecos," *Big Bend Quarterly*, Summer, 1999, 14.

[33] C.M. Kahl, interview with author, Marfa, Texas, October 11, 1999.

[34] *The Big Bend Sentinel*, November 20, 1942.

[35] *The Big Bend Sentinel*, December 28, 1942.

[36] *The Big Bend Sentinel*, December 14, 1942.

[37] Tyler, ed., 504.

[38] *Texas Almanac and State Industrial Guide, 1949-1950*, 107.

[39] Kahl interview.

[40] Thompson, 515.

[41] Ibid., 517.

[42] Ibid.

[43] *The Big Bend Sentinel*, May 8, 1945.

[44] Kahl interview.

[45] Thompson, 531.

[46] James L. Colwell, "Hell From Heaven, Midland Army Airfield in World War II," *The Permian Historical Annual XXVI*, 68.

[47] *Midland Reporter-Telegram*, November 19, 1940.

[48] *Midland Reporter-Telegram*, June 13, 1940.

[49] *Midland Reporter-Telegram*, June 13, 1941.

[50] *Life Magazine*, May 18, 1942, 64.

[51] Art Cole, e-mail to author, February 6, 2002.

[52] *Texas Almanac, 1943-1944*, 79.

[53] Cole e-mail.

[54] Irene Paulette, "Odessa During the War Years," *The Permian Historical Annual, XXI*, 22.

[55] *Odessa American*, March 20, 1988.

[56] Walter Prescott Webb, ed., *The Handbook of Texas*, vol. II, 187.

[57] Cole e-mail.

[58] *Monahans News*, July 31, 1942.

[59] *Texas Almanac, 1939-40*, 460.

[60] Elizabeth Heath, comp., *Ward County, 1887-1977*, 222.

[61] *Rattlesnake Bomber Base Museum Dedication Program*, April 22, 1978, 2.

[62] *United States Army Air Forces Directory of Airports*, vol. 3, 202.

[63] Heath, comp., 235.

[64] *San Antonio Express*, July 29, 1976.

[65] *Museum Dedication Program*, inside front cover.

[66] *Monahans News*, June 19, 1943.

[67] *Museum Dedication Program*, 35.

[68] W.E. Syers, "Death of the Aluminum Warriors," *Texas Parade*, vol. xxii, no. 5, (October 1961), 21.

[69] Glen Garland, interview with author, Pyote, Texas, February 14, 2002.

[70] *Museum Dedication Program*, 35.

[71] Heath, comp., 235.

PANHANDLE/PLAINS

Dallam ①	Sherman	Hansford	Ochiltree	Lipscomb
Hartley	Moore	Hutchinson	Roberts	Hemphill
Oldham	Potter ②	Carson	Gray ③	Wheeler
Deaf Smith	Randall	Armstrong	Donley	Collings-worth
Parmer	Castro	Swisher	Briscoe	Hall	Child-ress
Bailey	Lamb	Hale	Floyd	Motley	Cottle
Cochran	Hockley	Lubbock ④	Crosby	Dickens	King
Yoakum	Terry	Lynn	Garza	Kent	Stone-wall
			Scurry	Fisher
			Mitchell	Nolan ⑤

AREA DETAILED

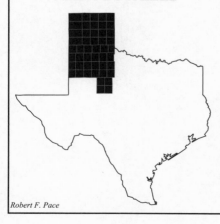

Robert F. Pace

ARMY AIR FORCES STATIONS

① Dalhart Army Airfield, Dalhart

② Amarillo Army Airfield, Amarillo

③ Pampa Army Airfield, Pampa

④ Lubbock Army Airfield, Lubbock

⑤ Avenger Field, Sweetwater

CHAPTER SIX

PANHANDLE/PLAINS

It may be the intensity of light and the immensity of space that
makes this region seem universal.
                        Mondel Rogers
                        Old Ranches of the Texas Plains
                        ©1976

The vast cattle rangeland of Texas that sweeps north from Sweetwater to the Oklahoma Panhandle, sharing its long western border
with New Mexico before stopping just short of touching Colorado,
might have been created as much for flying airplanes as for raising
cattle or growing wheat. The towering skies of the region are even
more endless than the unbroken stretches of relatively flat terrain,
where potentially hazardous promontories are even more rare than
trees. Given these natural advantages, the Army chose the Panhan-
dle/Plains to be home to thirteen of its wartime airfields. Some were
smaller contract flying fields such as those located at Coleman and
Stamford, but most were enormous facilities such as Lubbock,
Amarillo, Pampa, and Dalhart, each with several thousand personnel and hundreds of aircraft assigned to it.

While the region's legendary wide-open spaces and magnificent light-filled skies made it apparently ideal for training aviators, the notoriously capricious weather often made flying challenging if not downright impossible. It is tempting to speculate exactly what might have prompted the Army to place a major airfield at Dalhart, where extreme seasonal temperatures can range from twenty degrees below zero to a torrid hundred and seven above. In Lubbock, which hosted two wartime airfields, dust and blowing sand are regular springtime occurrences not at all conducive to safe flight operations. Yet, despite such harsh climatic conditions that often took their toll on both men and machines, the airfields managed to accomplish their missions, and in doing so, left an indelible mark upon the storied land of the Panhandle and on its hardy people.

Sweetwater

The use of women pilots serves no military purpose.
                                        Gen. Henry H. (Hap) Arnold
                                        July 1942

According to some accounts, the publicly affable and seemingly cherubic General Arnold was, in private, occasionally quite volatile to the point of being downright choleric. The mere thought of female pilots at the controls of any of his hard won Army airplanes was, at least early in the war, enough to launch the Air Force chief into one of his legendary tirades.[1]

However, as the war progressed through the dark days of 1942, it became apparent even to Arnold, and most surely to his staff, that the nation was facing an alarming shortage of pilots. No matter how fast the many training bases in Texas and elsewhere could churn out qualified male aviators, deadly demands of combat attrition were nearly outstripping his traditional sources of supply. During this vexing time, General Arnold was also being strongly urged by famed aviatrix Jacqueline Cochran to give women pilots a chance. She argued that if women could be trained to ferry aircraft to the edges of battle zones, but no farther, to tow targets for aerial gunners, and to fly myriad other non-combat missions, the men whom they would thus replace could then move on to the cockpits of fighters and bombers. The persuasive Miss Cochran, abetted by a continuing loss of manpower in combat, eventually won out. Under her guidance, the now legendary Women Airforce Service Pilots organization (WASP) was formed. The WASP won instant favor among the nation's many women flyers when Cochran's first call for volunteers to join the organization was made public. Her office was swamped by twenty-five thousand applications, and of that number, 1,830 women were eventually selected for training.[2]

To become a WASP, a female was required to hold a private pilot's license, have logged thirty-five hours of solo flight time, and be willing to provide her own transportation to her first training assignment. Further, she had to be willing to serve in only a quasi-military status, receiving none of the benefits offered to her male counterparts who, as military officers, wore the uniform of the United States Army Air Force. If a WASP were to die while on active duty, for example, her family was required to pay all of her funeral and burial expenses.[3]

Despite the absence of benefits, women from all walks of life volunteered to serve as WASPs. One was an heiress to the Florsheim shoe fortune while another, Helen Richey, had once flown as co-pilot with Amelia Earhart. Mary Wiggins had been a stunt pilot in Hollywood before volunteering for duty, and the wife of author Damon Runyan had traded an active social life to become a WASP. Mothers, ski-instructors, a biologist, and several models were also among those who came to Texas to learn to fly the Army way under the watchful eye of Jacqueline Cochran.[4]

At first WASP training took place in Houston, but it quickly became apparent that temptations to sample the many off-duty social delights offered by such a big city were too distracting for this high-spirited group of women. As a result, the decision was made in early 1943 to transfer the WASP training school to Sweetwater's Avenger Field, located some four hundred miles northwest of Houston. Sweetwater, with its population of ten thousand and a well-earned reputation as being one of the brighter buckles on the Texas Bible belt, seemed a likely place to avoid anything remotely resembling the glittering lure of the big city.

The region's official history notes, with perhaps some degree of understatement, that indeed "the advent of the girls to Avenger Field was received with mixed emotions by the citizens and field personnel alike."[5] The reception of the WASPs was in part less than enthusiastic because their planned arrival at the airfield had made it necessary to transfer an all-male Army flight school to another distant base. One writer notes that "now the town swarmed with pretty, self-assured girls on Saturday night, not handsome young fellows." According to this account, "Sweetwater families with marriageable daughters weren't happy about the situation." It would seem that the city's initial coolness toward the WASPs was not caused by their arrival at Avenger Field but rather by the departure of "the handsome young fellows" from it. [6]

It took time for Sweetwater to accept the fact that it was going to be the wartime host to a contingent of very lively young ladies. An editorial in an early issue of the WASP newspaper, *The Avenger,* clearly indicates that the community had not eagerly received the female newcomers. As the editor saw it:

> They [the townspeople] didn't understand us.
> In the first place, we came here with two strikes
> against us. We were women pilots – a profession
> which, until recently, has carried the stigma
> attached to the girls who rode "astride" in the days
> of the sidesaddle skirt. We were supposed to be
> rough and uncouth and not quite right in the head.

The editor might have made her point a bit more effectively had she not gone on to indicate that perhaps some of the WASPs might have indeed contributed to the town's misunderstanding of them. "When a few of us let our hair down and broke the tension," she lamented, "we acquired the titles of 'drunks and roughnecks,' an unfair and not very far seeing conclusion."[7]

If some of the citizens of the town were unhappy and not farseeing about the presence of the women pilots and their perceived antics, there were others in the vicinity who were overjoyed to learn that Avenger Field had become the Army's first all-female training facility. Male cadets flying from their nearby training bases often found it necessary to declare an in-flight emergency to gain a clearance to land at Avenger Field in hopes of seeing the attractive WASPs at work or play. In one seven-day period in mid-1943, over one hundred "emergencies" were declared by eager cadets, which compelled the field's commanding officer eventually to close the field to all but his own training aircraft.[8]

One young WASP experienced a genuine in-flight emergency of her own that was not resolved after she successfully made a forced landing in a farmer's field in West Texas. The pilot, Ayang Lee, was the Chinese-American wife of a general in the Chinese Army, a citizen of the United States, and a well-qualified aviator. As she pushed back the canopy on her only slightly damaged plane, she saw a burly pitchfork-bearing farmhand running toward her. The hand, not knowing one airplane from another nor anything whatever about aircraft insignia, knew only that he had seen an Asian pilot crash land in his field. Despite WASP Lee's explanations delivered in perfect English, the young Texan was convinced that he had captured a Japanese pilot. Using the business end of his pitchfork, the youth escorted Lee into a nearby small town. There, a deputy sheriff quickly accepted the pilot's credentials and called Avenger Field to report her situation. The disappointed would-be hero of the day slunk back to his hayfield, with his trusty pitchfork in hand.[9]

Although the initial impact of the WASPs on Sweetwater society was stunning, the community eventually came to accept them. Churches invited the women to attend services and local families adopted whole groups of the trainees, sharing their hopes and sorrows while taking them in as parts of a newly extended Texas family.

The community even sponsored a service club for the women to use when they came into town. Called the Avengerette Club, the facility provided an off-base haven to listen to music, play games, and drink a Coca-Cola or two before catching the last bus to the airfield. Although the selling of any alcoholic beverage that might be used to enhance the Cokes was illegal in Sweetwater, some of the WASPs managed to find a grandmotherly gift shop owner who thought it her patriotic duty to sell bottles of "fairly good bourbon" to the women for a mere two dollars. It is reported that business at the gift shop was brisk on occasion.[10]

There is much evidence that the dashing women pilots became idols to many local teenage girls. Watching from a respectful distance as the tanned and physically fit young women laughed and smoked at Sweetwater's municipal swimming pool which was reserved for their exclusive use on certain days of the week, one of the town's teenagers was awestruck. "I'll never forget them," she wrote many years later, "they were so independent and so self-assured. To me, they symbolized what I had suspected for some time, there truly could be a bright future for us girls beyond the city limits of Sweetwater if we wanted to seek it."[11]

During the two years the WASP training program was at Avenger Field, 1,074 candidates successfully completed their training and received their wings. From Sweetwater, the women pilots went to other airfields to take on the flying assignments just recently filled by males who were now freed to move on to combat units. By early 1944, even General Arnold was noticeably impressed with the professionalism and piloting skills being demonstrated by the women pilots whose use in military aviation he had earlier so publicly deplored. "I am looking forward to the day," said Arnold, "when Women Airforce Service Pilots take the place of practically all AAF [Army Air Force] pilots in the United States for the duration."[12]

The general, by then an obviously true convert to the concept of women flying airplanes, made a valiant effort in mid-1944 to get each WASP a commission as an Air Force officer, but to no avail. Instead, it was determined by Congress that the Army in fact had too many male pilots, making the WASP program unnecessary.[13]

This controversial congressional decision triggered a full-scale campaign on the part of Sweetwater's townsfolk to save the once unwelcome but now beloved WASP organization from extinction. A front-page story in *The Avenger* of July 14, 1944, declared, "Congressmen, senators, and women's clubs throughout the United States have been contacted by Sweetwater's citizens and asked to aid in saving the WASP program."[14]

In the end, the concentrated effort proved to be in vain, and soon the entire WASP organization was disbanded. Years later, in 1977, it was General Arnold's son, Col. W. Bruce Arnold, who, in conjunction with Senator Barry Goldwater, helped gain official Army veterans' status for the surviving WASPs.[15]

In 1993, on the fiftieth anniversary of their arrival in Sweetwater, 250 veterans of the wartime WASPs came back to Sweetwater for a reunion. As the women proudly marched down the main street, the townspeople cheered them more loudly than ever, perhaps realizing at last how truly important it had been when the WASPs had first come to their West Texas town so many years before. The success of the WASPs, to put it in the perspective of the 1940s, was the fact that they *did not fail* as the vanguard of females at the controls of military aircraft, thus permanently opening the doors for future generations of women pilots.

Lubbock

Even from the beginning, the people of Lubbock were most
supportive of the military and Lubbock Army Airfield.
Gordon Treadaway
Lubbock, Texas

While the Army airfield in Fort Worth was largely the creation of one very powerful and politically well-connected newspaper publisher named Amon Carter, the coming of a military air base to Lubbock was for the most part a direct result of the efforts of a single-minded, grassroots executive of the local chamber of commerce. Although he lacked Carter's direct access to the president of the United States and any close comradeship with vast numbers of senators and congressmen, Lubbock's A.B. Davis was every bit as persistent in his quest for an airfield as was Carter, and quite possibly even more prescient when it came to foretelling the coming of World War II.

Beginning as early as 1936, probably well before Carter had launched his campaign for a Fort Worth airfield, Davis apparently envisioned that the Army would soon be seeking West Texas locations as sites for air training facilities. It is highly doubtful that he was privy to any inside information about the Army's plan to expand its air arm in preparation for war, but judging by his correspondence, Davis sensed intuitively that military airfields would someday be coming to West Texas. As a good chamber of commerce man, he fully intended to get one of those airfields for Lubbock.[16]

Davis's plan to accomplish this was deceptively simple. To obtain an air base for his city, he would single out those Army officers who might someday be involved in deciding where airfields would be placed, and he would cultivate their friendship. Clearly embracing the longstanding West Texas tradition that real men, while hunting and fishing together, formed long-enduring bonding relationships, Davis used his position as manager of the chamber of commerce to extend invitations to military officers to come hunt and fish in the Lubbock area. Once they accepted—and many of them did—he would arrange for each guest to receive free annual fishing passes at Buffalo Lake State Park. Around the lakeside campfire at night, he would extol the virtues of Lubbock as a potential military town. When the seasons changed, hunting for birds or game on private ranches gave Davis another opportunity to know his new Army friends even better and to let them, in turn, learn more about his beloved Lubbock and its potential as the site of a military airfield.

Elaborate sojourns to the city for the officers were frequently arranged throughout the late 1930s, and the visitors received all of the attention and entertainment that Lubbock could offer. As a result of his tireless and dedicated efforts, Davis was eventually on a casual first name basis with many key colonels who were soon to become generals, and as such, empowered with the ability to influence the airfield site-selection process. There was no dishonesty or skullduggery in any of this. It was clearly Davis's job to bring good things to Lubbock, and since he had somehow correctly divined that getting an Army airfield would indeed be a good thing, the man simply set about making it happen in the way he knew best.[17]

Sometimes, his tactics failed, but rarely if ever his strategy. When one officer declined an invitation from Davis to visit Lubbock to go hunting on the grounds that "he didn't have a gun," the chamber manager then politely suggested they might go fishing together in the springtime. When the officer again refused, adding "I only rarely fish," Davis exploded, in private of course, and fumed, "Well, he's the damndest officer I've ever heard of."[18]

After nearly five years of letter writing and countless hunting and fishing excursions with officers who had become his personal friends, but with no tangible indications that he was making any progress in his airfield campaign, Davis began to show uncharacteristic signs of discouragement. In a letter dated May 31, 1940, he wrote, "I am very, very doubtful that there will be an air base established at Lubbock or anywhere in this vicinity."[19] Perhaps one reason for Davis's temporarily bleak outlook was a published policy statement issued by a senior Army officer that declared, "Primary training centers in areas in excess of 2,000 feet [in elevation] were not acceptable."[20] If this criterion were indeed true, Lubbock's elevation of 3,256-feet above sea level would automatically disqualify it as an airfield site, regardless of how many bass had been caught or how many deer had been taken by visiting officers over the years.

When Davis learned that Amarillo, located at least by West Texas standards a short 120 miles to the north, was also actively pursuing an airfield, he renewed his campaign with vigor. He sent a wire to R.D. Shinkle, his lobbyist in Washington, urging him to strongly reiterate to Army officials that the terrain around Lubbock was in every way superior to Amarillo's for flight training purposes. Davis also urged Shinkle to "work like hell" for a Lubbock base, just as he himself had been doing for nearly a decade.[21]

While the chamber manager was clearly the point man in the long campaign for a Lubbock airfield, he did not rely solely on the wooing of military hunters and fishermen to accomplish his goal. In addition to the lobbying efforts of Shinkle, Davis also had a strong ally in U.S. Representative Charles Mahon, who aggressively pursued the airfield quest in the nation's capital.

When the federal government soon unveiled its plan to order fifty thousand new aircraft in 1939, it suddenly became clear that Davis's speculation about the Army's eventual need for a great many additional airfields had been uncannily well founded. Realizing that the successful end of his campaign was finally in sight, he stepped up the intensity of his efforts, which were now directed at the commanding officer of the Gulf Coast Air Training Center, Brig. Gen. Gerald C. Brant. The general and his staff were inundated with hunting and fishing invitations and letters full of praise for Lubbock, all penned of course by A.B. Davis, the city's greatest champion. One of Brant's staff officers, Maj. T.W. Spurgin, apparently found the endless flood of mail from the chamber offices to be just too much to handle. In a curt, one sentence letter to Davis, Spurgin stated, "pls omit my name from your mailing list." The major, it seems, had heard more than enough about Lubbock, Texas, and its qualifications as an airfield location.[22]

By April 15, 1941, there was even greater proof that Davis's long-running campaign on behalf of his city was about to bear rich economic fruit. On that date, his fishing comrade, General Brant, led a delegation of officers back to Lubbock to inspect a potential airfield site of some fourteen hundred acres located ten miles west of town. Obviously anticipating Davis's ultimate success, the city had already purchased the land from its owner, Mrs. J.H. Lindsey, for $35 per acre and it was now being offered, at no cost, to the War Department.[23]

Just two weeks after Brant's visit, Army engineers had been to the site and had completed their testing of the soil and surveying the boundaries. Upon receipt of the engineers' positive report, General Brant quickly endorsed it and sent it on to his superiors in Washington.

On June 21, 1941, just sixty days after General Brant had inspected the suggested airfield site, Davis received the message he had been awaiting for over five years. "I am authorized to announce," wired his ally, Congressman George Mahon, "that a flying school for Lubbock has been approved here [Washington, D. C.]."[24]

Official plans called for the new airfield to be constructed at a cost of $3.2 million, but the *Lubbock Avalanche-Journal* reported the cost was actually estimated to be around $5.2 million. By the time World War II ended four years later, it was revealed that the government had in fact spent almost $6 million to complete just the initial building phase of the field.[25]

The construction contract called for the field's completion date to be only 120 days from the August 21, 1941, starting date. The government now viewed the Lubbock project with obvious urgency. It had taken Davis five years of intensive lobbying to get the base, and now, even though there was not quite yet a shooting war for which to prepare, the Army wanted its new airfield to be operational in a mere four months.[26]

In order to meet the daunting construction deadline, over eight hundred workers began preparing the site even before the binding contract with the government had been signed. A barbed-wire fence was erected around the perimeter of the field to keep curious onlookers from interfering. At the peak of the construction period, over sixteen hundred workers labored to complete the base on time.[27]

Even though the coming of war in December 1941 quickly thrust the project onto a twenty-four hour-a-day, seven day-a-week schedule, Lubbock's flying school did not become fully operational until February 25, 1942, some sixty days later than originally projected. Still, it was an amazing accomplishment that had seen the construction of 215 buildings and the completion of four miles of concrete runways in six months time, despite some of the worst winter weather in Lubbock's legendary history of unexpected and often severe sleet and snowstorms. It was reported that the quantity of paving materials used on the base was sufficient to "replace approximately two-thirds of all the pavement that has ever been laid in the city of Lubbock."[28]

It took an additional four months for the contractors and the Army to add the final touches to the facility, even though flight training was already being conducted on a full schedule. On June 21, 1942, with the base still incomplete, officials invited the public to visit Lubbock Army Airfield for the first time. According to Gordon

Treadaway, who was stationed on the base, nearly thirty thousand people accepted the invitation to swarm over the newly completed facility. As the population of the immediate Lubbock vicinity was fifty thousand at the time, it is apparent that the open house was highly successful.[29]

In time, some four thousand military and civilian personnel worked on the base, which was continuously expanded as the war went on. New construction projects were seemingly endless and the need for workers attracted newcomers to the community. Because of this constant growth, plus the arrival of additional military personnel, Lubbock reportedly was, as a percentage, the second-fastest-growing metropolitan area in the entire United States during the war years.[30]

The citizens of Lubbock were delighted with their airfield. With the city growing and its economy rising almost daily to record levels, the people warmly embraced the military personnel who had made it all happen. When the national United Service Organization (USO) rejected the city's request to establish a local facility to entertain the soldiers, the community promptly created the Lubbock Service Organization (LSO) to serve the men and women stationed at the field. The LSO operated day and night, offering its visiting patrons a variety of social and recreational activities that included dances, games, a library, and indoor sports. As Lubbock was legally dry and otherwise noticeably lacking in the traditional off-duty opportunities that usually appealed to servicemen, the LSO quickly proved to be a popular center for social activity in town.[31]

Of particular interest to a great many soldiers were the regular weekly dances held at the club. The hostesses at these events were known as the Hub-ettes, a group of single young Lubbock women who took their title from the community's nickname "The Hub City." According to those who belonged to the group, the men from the airfield far outnumbered the Hub-ettes at the earlier dances, but as word spread to co-eds attending nearby Texas Tech University that hundreds of young and attractive men were always in attendance at these functions, the ratio of men to women quickly came into balance.[32]

The dances were heavily chaperoned and off-premises dating between the Hub-ettes and the airmen was strictly forbidden. However, as might be expected, this rule was frequently broken and many visiting soldiers found their future brides among the hostesses. Izora Edwards, who was one of the first Hub-ettes, met a young soldier named Harlan Fisk at the LSO and eventually became his wife. "Oh, I dated a lot of [soldiers]," she admitted many years later, adding that both she and Fisk were each seriously involved with someone else they had already met at the LSO at the time they were first introduced.[33]

Although African-American military personnel were not admitted to the LSO, they did have a service club of their own at 21st Street and East Avenue C. The World War II era clearly had rules of racial segregation that were stringent, and by today's standards both unacceptable and illegal. However, at least some of the black soldiers who served at the Lubbock field during the early 1940s appear to have retained relatively pleasant memories of their tour of duty there. Even though Rudolph Delvan, a private in 1943, was compelled to live off base in substandard housing and eat in segregated areas, he summed up his time spent at Lubbock by saying long after the war, "I wouldn't change the experience for nothing [sic]."[34]

As the war neared its conclusion, the lessening demand for pilots was reflected in the arrival of fewer aviation cadets. By January 1, 1946, the last class of pilots had graduated and the base was closed. During its four-year existence, Lubbock Army Airfield had seen exactly 7,008 aviators receive their silver wings.[35]

Through the immediate postwar efforts of the redoubtable A.B. Davis and his colleagues in the nation's capital, the old airfield did not remain closed for long. Fortunately for Lubbock, the wartime field had not reverted to either private or municipal ownership in the years immediately following the war. In an unusual move, the federal government had retained title to the property and had simply closed and padlocked the gate when the war ended.

As a consequence, on August 1, 1949, less than four years after closing, the padlock was removed and the main gate at Lubbock's airfield swung open again. The completely renovated airfield was now to be known as Reese Air Force Base in honor of a local pilot who had been killed in action during the war. It is easy to accept that the seeds of goodwill sown by A.B. Davis many years earlier were still fertile enough to put Lubbock high on the list for consideration when the need for additional air bases arose.

The coming of the Cold War had indeed created such a need, and the reactivated facility was soon back in full operation as a pilot-training school. Within a short time, there were two thousand personnel assigned to the base with an annual payroll of $11 million. In late 1949, it was announced that Reese AFB had been designated a permanent installation, and for the next half-century it appeared that Lubbock was going to have an air base as its welcome neighbor forever, just as the Department of Defense had promised.[36]

In 1991, six years before government promises about the permanence of the base would prove to be hollow, it was reported that the annual payroll at Reese had risen to an astounding $61 million. Further, off-base services generated by the facility also figured significantly in the region's financial well-being. When the chamber of commerce duly evaluated all of these statistics, it was revealed that Reese AFB was fueling a full one-third of Lubbock's total economy.[37]

In view of this stunning disclosure, it seemed all but impossible that the 3,954-acre facility, with its 1,200,000 square feet of occupied building space valued at over $90 million could ever possibly be closed again. Yet, in mid-1997, the governmental axe once again fell on Lubbock's military air base. This time, the cut of the axe was permanent.[38] However, just as it had at the end of World War II, Lubbock managed to survive the full brunt of the closure, and the old airfield was in time transformed into a world-class research training and business center.

A good share of Lubbock's present and future fiscal success is clearly built on the solid legacy put in place during the city's long years as an important military aviation installation. The architect of that legacy, A.B. Davis, died on November 5, 1967. In his obituary that appeared in the *Lubbock Avalanche-Journal* the next day, the editors finally gave him long-overdue credit for his tireless efforts to twice bring a military airfield to his beloved city. "A.B. Davis," declared the newspaper, "was known throughout the U.S. Air Force as 'Mr. Lubbock.'" It was an epitaph he richly deserved.[39]

Amarillo

The United States Army survey party here last night brought to Amarillo the most thrilling news it has had in years.
Amarillo Globe-Times
September 10, 1941

In its announcement that the Army Air Force was coming to Amarillo to construct a heavy bombardment air base, the *Globe-*

Times gave partial credit to Brig. Gen. Billy Mitchell, who, according to the newspaper, had long before recommended the Panhandle city as the future center of a vast air combat training area. Although the United States was still over a year away from actual involvement in any war, a site survey team headed by Col. W.T. Blackburn had studied Amarillo and its environs thoroughly before ultimately deciding that Mitchell had been right in his earlier assessment.[40]

The scale of the proposed base as outlined by Colonel Blackburn stunned even Amarilloans who were accustomed to thinking and acting in Texas-sized terms of immense proportions. According to the colonel, the airfield was to cost at least $10 million and be the home of over six thousand officers and men when completed. Precisely thirty-two hundred acres of land would be required to build a base large enough to accommodate so many personnel. When Blackburn went on to casually remark that the Army fully expected Amarillo to give the land for the base and build a three lane highway to it, no one at city hall appears to have so much as flinched. As Colonel Blackburn saw it, these voluntary if expensive prerequisites were "only reasonable contributions by Amarillo to the cause of victory," although at this point it would be a victory in a war not yet declared.[41]

The Army's preliminary plans for the airfield it intended to build and operate on the land provided by the city were truly impressive. Sixty-nine B-17 bombers would be assigned to the base, utilizing a bombardment practice range of many additional thousands of acres to be leased from area ranchers. To allay any fears of accidents on the range, it was pointed out that all bombs used in such target practice would be [intentional] duds - sacks of flour, sand and sawdust."[42]

As it developed, however, the Army's initial plans were destined by unforeseen international events to be drastically changed. On November 29, 1941, a mere eight days before America's sudden entry into the war, a local newspaper ran a startlingly accurate prophetic story that foretold much of what was soon to occur." "If Moscow were to fall to the invading German Army and if Japan and America go to war," speculated the *Amarillo Daily News*, it would be highly likely that all tactical air bases currently being planned for the continental United States "will have to wait development of bases which the Army will be compelled to establish quickly in the Philippines and the Aleutians." Having no earthly way of knowing that at least half of their military prophecy would come to pass in about a week, the paper hastened to reassure its readers that the approved list of new airfield sites would be made public almost immediately, and that "the chances are ten to one that Amarillo will be on that list."[43]

Following the momentous events that began on December 7, 1941, the Army finally moved forward with plans for an Amarillo airfield that had been languishing for several months. The city, however, had lived up to its end of the bargain almost immediately following Colonel Blackburn's visit on September 9, 1941. The agreed upon amount of land had been acquired, an additional eight hundred-acre tract had been placed under option, and a bond election had overwhelmingly approved the funding for the required highway to the site.[44]

On April 1, 1942, the Army sent Col. Edward C. "Red" Black to Amarillo to supervise the construction on what was now planned to be an aircraft mechanics school rather than a heavy bombardment base. Black enjoyed a reputation for both building airfields in record time and for being a colorful character of the old Army. Upon seeing the site of his newest project, the colonel proclaimed to the *Amarillo Globe-Times*, "When we get finished building this thing, it'll be bigger than Lubbock." His well-crafted remark made him an instant celebrity throughout the Panhandle, if not on the South Plains.[45]

To some onlookers it might have appeared that Black's remark was not merely an idle boast intended to gain instant community support. When the construction workers departed and the dust settled just five months after the site had been cleared, eight hundred buildings stood where cattle had only recently grazed. Twenty-seven miles of pavement ran past six hundred barracks, in front of a seven hundred-bed hospital, and on to five hangars, twenty warehouses, sixty tennis courts and fifty-four softball diamonds. While it was not larger than Lubbock, as Colonel Black had jested, it was surely one of the larger Army airfields in Texas.[46]

When it came time to assign personnel to the sprawling new aviation mechanics school, the Army displayed an unusual if not downright curious amount of sensitivity. Perhaps having concerns that the residents of the remote Panhandle might not readily embrace soldiers from all parts of the nation, Colonel Black, as base commander as well as construction supervisor, made a unique public announcement. According to the colonel, most of the enlisted men ordered to report to the Amarillo facility for training as mechanics would be from Texas, Oklahoma, and neighboring New Mexico, with only a few from Arizona and California. Further, Black assured the community, all students bound for the new facility would definitely not be "of the underprivileged and illiterate section of humanity."[47]

Colonel Black invited all Panhandle residents to be his guests on the field on Armistice Day 1942. A reported forty thousand people accepted his invitation to both tour the facility, albeit under relatively tight security restrictions, and to extend a personal welcome to over five thousand soldiers who had already begun learning how to maintain the B-17s that now, because of the fickle fortunes of war, would never be coming to Amarillo.

There is, however, nothing to indicate that the revised mission of their airfield, from bombardment to aircraft maintenance, was at all disheartening to the Amarilloans who flocked onto the base to meet their new military neighbors. During the three-year period that Amarillo Army Airfield served as a technical training school, roughly eleven hundred mechanics and other ground crew personnel were trained on the base. Over two thousand WACs were also assigned to the facility.[48]

In August 1945, with the war soon to end, the Army once again invited the citizens of the Panhandle to visit the airfield that had proved to be such a good neighbor to them. This time the visitors were permitted to actually inspect the flight decks and bomb bays of the giant B-29 bombers that were now the major focus of the base's mechanics school curriculum. The famous Tony Pastor Orchestra played at a dance attended by soldiers and civilians alike and a formal military review staged in the blowing dust of a Panhandle afternoon provided what soon proved to be the final curtain for the World War II airfield.[49]

When the war concluded just a few days later, it was soon announced that the base was to be closed within a matter of months. By the summer of 1946 many of the buildings had been destroyed or moved off the base and, to most observers, it seemed that Amarillo's days as the military air center envisioned by Billy Mitchell were to be merely a short but memorable chapter in the history of the Panhandle.

However, Mitchell's prediction enjoyed a second chance to come to fruition in 1951 when the Korean War created a renewed need for military aviation training centers. As a result, a new, multi-million dollar Amarillo Air Force Base soon emerged phoenix-like from the ruins of the old Army airfield.

Over the next seventeen years, the Air Force invested nearly $80 million on the facility in building new structures, expanding the size to encompass nearly five thousand acres and to lengthen the main runway to an impressive 13,500 feet. During its second lifetime, Amarillo's military air installation was home to flight engineer and aviation mechanic training schools, radar and missile units, and an operational wing of SAC. It was during the SAC era that the runway was enlarged to accommodate the Command's huge B-47, B-52, and KC-135 aircraft that constantly roared aloft into the bright Panhandle skies.[50]

At its peak, the Air Force base employed nearly seventeen thousand military and civilian personnel while another estimated thirty thousand individuals provided off-base support to those stationed at the field. In an apparent confirmation of the combined military and economic importance of the facility, Air Force Chief of Staff Nathan F. Twining announced during a 1954 visit that Amarillo AFB was to be a permanent installation.[51]

Naturally enough, the entire Panhandle region was stunned to learn in 1964, contrary to Twining's pledge, that the base was to be closed within four years. Despite the efforts of local and national politicians, the facility was indeed decommissioned and all but abandoned in mid-1968.

Even though the actual closing had been anticipated for four years, the brutal reality of it sent economic shockwaves throughout the entire Panhandle and well beyond. According to the *New Handbook of Texas*, "The closing damaged the economy of Amarillo," but some who lived in the region at the time believe that the *Handbook's* assessment is more than just an understatement.[52] "It was a catastrophe," recalls Ron Russell, who had trained as a mechanic at the SAC base before becoming a civilian. "Real estate values collapsed, people lost their jobs and left town, and many businesses closed."[53]

There was, however, something of a silver lining in the dark economic cloud that hovered over Amarillo for many years following the field's closing. In 1971, capitalizing on the remarkably long runway that SAC had built at a cost of $17 million almost twenty years previously, the city used some of the former Air Force base land to establish a modern air terminal designed to serve as a regional hub for commercial and passenger traffic. Many buildings on the old base were leased to aviation-related industries, and a city-operated technical instruction facility was established to utilize long-vacant classrooms.

The old field's twin water towers still stand as looming reminders of Amarillo's colorful military aviation history. The city itself has slowly recovered from the economic woes that stemmed from the closing of the base over thirty years ago, and while the recovery has often been difficult, many old-timers fondly remember the days when America's mighty war birds brought a new excitement to the limitless Panhandle skies.

Pampa

I asked a guy in town once why they called this place Pampa and he said it was because it looked something like Argentina around here. I told him if that was so, I didn't think I ever wanted to go to Argentina.

S/Sgt. Ernest Hewlett
Pampa, Texas
July 14, 1944

The soldier who apparently had some serious doubts about the landscape around Pampa was stationed there during much of the summer of 1943 as one of over four thousand personnel then assigned to the Army airfield located twelve miles east of town. According to another veteran who was stationed there, the citizens of the small Panhandle town took such ribbing from its Army guests good-naturedly and made every effort to make them feel welcome.[54]

Unlike many Texas communities that had actively been seeking an Army airfield for several years before the war started, it would appear that Pampa only entered the search in the spring of 1942. Economic conditions in the immediate vicinity had not been as dire as in most other parts of Depression-ridden Texas, so perhaps local leaders had not felt compelled to make the obligatory air base-seeking trek to Washington until the nation had actually entered the war. According to the *Pampa News*, the city's mayor, Fred Thompson, led a delegation to the nation's capital on March 14, 1942, to make contact with "unidentified governmental officials," ostensibly "to find some ways in which the Pampa area's extremely low-cost natural gas might be employed in the war effort."[55]

It is likely that either the mayor and his committee were particularly persuasive or behind-the-scenes negotiations with the War Department had been going on much longer than the *Pampa News* article might have indicated. Just two months after Thompson's visit to Washington, the newspaper's front page carried three-inch headlines announcing the Army's decision to open an airfield nearby "within the next nine months."[56]

It was estimated that the cost of the base would exceed $5 million, with the overall construction project to be supervised by the Army Corps of Engineers. The 2,544-acre site located twelve miles east of Pampa had already been quietly acquired by the War Department and work was expected to start immediately.[57]

The reasons given by the government for its selection of Pampa as a flight school location included the city's "excellent location, its housing facilities, its water supply, and its schools and churches."[58] Presumably the low cost of the region's natural gas was also a factor in the favorable decision, but no matter what the major determinant, it was clear that Mayor Thompson and his retinue had definitely impressed the War Department with the Pampa site proposal as presented.

By mid-July, all excavating, fence building, and pipe laying work had been completed. Over 540,000 yards of dirt had been removed to make room for runways and foundations, while 26,000 feet of water pipe and eight miles of fence had been installed. Contractors routinely issued urgent pleas for additional workers. The community's housing situation, which the government had initially described as being excellent, rapidly deteriorated and soon became woefully inadequate.[59]

The base became operational on November 22, 1942, but a dedication ceremony to officially open the new sixty-five hundred foot concrete runway went awry because of some bad flying weather many miles away. The celebration called for Lt. Col. Daniel S. Campbell, the field's newly appointed base commander, to be the first pilot to land his airplane on the runway. However, inclement weather at an airfield near Chickasha, Oklahoma, had forced a pilot attempting to land there to urgently seek another and more welcoming runway. Most likely unaware that he was ruining Colonel Campbell's well-planned moment of glory, the diverted pilot brought his aircraft down onto Pampa's pristine runway just three minutes before the base commander was scheduled to touch down.[60]

Despite this somewhat awkward beginning, flight training at the new field was soon in full operation. The aviation cadets' day started at sunup and continued for seventeen hours until taps sounded an hour and a half before midnight. The mornings were filled with classroom sessions or time in the link trainer, with seven hours of actual flying rounding out the day following a noontime lunch. Studying and a quick leisure hour completed the schedule after dinner. This routine was observed five days a week, but following a formal review on Saturday morning, the cadets were given time off until Sunday evening. On Monday morning, the intensive training resumed.[61]

When they were not flying or going to ground school, the cadets soon discovered that although Pampa's landscape did not really look anything at all like the verdant grasslands of Argentina, its people nonetheless were friendly, helpful, and hospitable. Vernon Baumgarten, a cadet in Class 43-B, later declared, "I have always been proud to have been a pioneer at Pampa [Army Airfield] in those memorable years. We never forgot the friendliness and hospitality we encountered from everyone we encountered in Pampa."[62] According to an article in the February 23, 1943, edition of the *Pampa News*, one class of cadets grew so fond of the community and its citizens that it formally expressed a desire to be adopted, in total, by the city.[63]

Despite the cordial reception they received, military personnel were faced with a serious shortage of suitable housing. Jamie Gough, an instructor pilot who went on to become an Air Force major general, recalls that the only accommodation he could find for his family was a former funeral home. To their dismay, the Goughs found "discarded caskets in the basement plus a long, slanting metal counter and sink in the kitchen."[64]

On February 28, 1943, only ninety days after the first training flights had taken off from the field, its commander released a letter of invitation to all Pampans to visit the base during an open house. According to the local newspaper, Colonel Campbell's invitation proved to be effective. Over ten thousand Panhandle citizens toured the field on March 7, 1943. Since all of surrounding Gray County could claim only twenty thousand residents at the time, it is clear that the event was a popular success. Due to the unexpectedly large response, the traffic congestion was massive, resulting in a great number of overheated automobiles and a booming business for local tow trucks.[65]

Mayor Fred Thompson, who had been so remarkably successful in quickly convincing the Army to establish an airfield at Pampa, was gracious in thanking Colonel Campbell for the open house event. "We cannot offer you the entertainment facilities or other attractions you might find in other cities," Thompson noted, "but we do offer you our hospitality and 'what we have' for your entertainment in our homes, our business houses, or churches—anywhere in our city, we hope to make you feel that you are a citizen of Pampa."[66]

The temporary but highly welcome citizens of the city came from all walks of life. Included in the cadet companies were former drugstore clerks, farmers, salesmen, mechanics, and, of course, many students. George R. Montgomery had been a dance instructor before the war, while George H. Brown had earned a living as a glasscutter. John R. Steward built elevators, and Raymond A. Duran had served as a page for a New York City radio broadcasting company. Kenneth E. Proctor of Evanston, Illinois, had given up a promising career as a licensed mortician to learn to fly Pampa's advanced training aircraft.

Throughout the war years, the *Pampa News* proved to be a dedicated reporter of the daily activities of cadets such as these. Almost every daily edition carried the results of intra-base athletic events, promotion lists, news of reassignments, and accounts of the exploits of the many flight school graduates who had gone from Pampa directly into combat. Unfortunately, the news from the airfield was not always good. During one month-long period when ten pilots were killed in training accidents, the *News* grimly reported the details of each tragic crash.

Advertisements carried by the newspaper also reflected the town's interest in the airfield and its personnel. Banks, grocery stores, dry cleaners, as well as G.S. Shirley's combination liquor store and filling station, all invited the patronage of the cadets as well as the field's permanent assignees. Many of the ads carried patriotic messages urging the flyers to get ready to fight on to the ultimate victory, but in the meantime while learning to do so, the cadets were encouraged to do all of their shopping in Pampa.[67]

During its almost three years of flight training operations, the Pampa field graduated 6,292 advanced multi-engine pilots. Among the graduates were future movie actor Jack Palance and future senator and presidential candidate George McGovern. During the war, ninety-two of the Pampa trained pilots were killed in action, sixty-two were listed as missing in action, and another eighty-one were prisoners of war.[68]

Just before the field was closed on September 30, 1945, the base commander stated, "I am sincere when I say that no community in the United States could be more patriotic, public spirited, and downright American than this." The Army Air Force and Pampa clearly parted company on a cordial basis.[69]

Only a few buildings remain on the site of the once-busy airfield. A water tower and guardhouse can be seen, along with a solitary hangar and a few concrete foundations. One of the taxiways, however, still serves a useful, if vastly different, purpose as a relatively mud-free surface for thousands of feedlot cattle. One returning veteran of the airfield's glory days was bemused at the sight of thousands of cattle standing where sixty years before hundreds of B-25s had taxied into position for take-off and as many as fourteen thousand smartly uniformed cadets had once marched to the beat of Army drums. "It was the best example I have ever seen," commented "Doc" Savage of Class 44-K, "of beating swords into plowshares."[70]

Dalhart

We got exposed to a little couth.

> Doyle Hanbury
> Dalhart, Texas
> April 16, 2002

Doyle Hanbury, a native of Dalhart, was ten years old when Japanese aircraft attacked Pearl Harbor. After the Army opened an airfield just west of town not quite a year later, the son of one of the colonels assigned to the new base soon came to be one of his closest friends. Hanbury remembers that when he was invited to a Sunday dinner at the Bostonian colonel's home, he suddenly feared that his new friendship with the younger Brahmin was very likely doomed. Although his mother had long labored to teach her young Texan proper table manners, Hanbury found himself totally unprepared to eat his fried chicken with a knife and fork as his hosts were soon doing with great aplomb. A life-long practitioner of the fine Texas art of eating fried chicken without benefit of any utensils, Hanbury nevertheless gamely attempted to emulate the dining skills of the newly arrived Easterners. However, things by no means went smoothly for him. "I was so embarrassed," he recalled sixty years later, "and I still think it was the longest meal in my entire life."[71]

It was not just the eating techniques of Texans that were challenged when Dalhart Army Airfield was introduced to the Panhandle in late September 1942. Located at the very top of the state, the city of Dalhart boasted a population of 4,682 hardy souls in the year before the war, some of them related to the cowboys who had long worked the three million acres of the fabled XIT Ranch that surrounded the city.[72]

As headquarters of the XIT, Dalhart served as the railway shipping point for the thousands of cattle being sent to markets throughout the nation. The two railroads that had come to Dalhart to carry away the XIT cattle were in fact responsible for the little city's very existence. Originally a scattered collection of rail workers' tents that had first been known as Twist Junction, the tiny community initially had been incorporated as a village in 1900 and then as a city in 1906.[73]

Although hard hit by the combined one-two punch of the Depression and the Dust Bowl of the early 1930s, Dalhart survived to become the principal agribusiness center of the vast northernmost Panhandle region. However, a visit by Army Air Force officials soon after World War II had begun set in motion a series of events that swiftly transformed the small city into a bustling boomtown and brought thousands of strangers into what had been an isolated rural community.

The Army Air Force, it developed, was seeking an ideal location to construct a base to teach its personnel how to operate the still-experimental CG4A glider. It was envisioned that the engine-less, and therefore silent, aircraft would become a vital element in the multiple invasions of enemy territories likely to occur if the war went the way senior military planners hoped it would.

The single most important factor in selecting a site for glider flight training was an abundance of flat terrain. Although lacking many other things in 1942, the Dalhart area unquestionably offered a virtually limitless expanse of nearly table-flat Texas landscape. While the visiting Army officials were clearly impressed with the highly desirable terrain and the region's convenient railroad facilities, they believed the city of Dalhart should donate the 3,040 acres of flat land needed for glider training. Fortunately, the citizens of the town concurred and quickly passed a $60,000 bond package to secure funds to buy the vast acreage rather arbitrarily demanded by the Air Force.[74]

As soon as the land was deeded to it, the government began construction on what in time would become a military city consisting of nearly seven hundred buildings and home to an estimated ten thousand Army personnel, more than double the population of the town. On May 22, 1942, while the construction process was under way, the temporary headquarters for the Army Air Forces Glider School was established in tents located some eighty-five miles south in Amarillo. Exactly 121 days later, the school's headquarters were moved to the completed glider facility at Dalhart.[75]

The CG4A glider itself, the prime and in fact the only aircraft in the school's armada, was an ungainly looking fabric-covered conveyance capable of carrying a payload even greater than its own weight of 3,750 pounds. Such a payload might consist of a platoon of infantrymen, or a jeep or possibly a 75-millimeter cannon or even specially designed bulldozers and road graders. During the war, 13,909 CG4As were built, and the site initially chosen to teach men how to handle the frequently challenging aircraft was Dalhart Army Airfield.[76]

Those who remember the opening of the glider school in September 1942 also remember the impact the airfield had on the small community. In addition to such highly irregular behavior as using a knife and fork on a fried chicken drumstick, the Army also brought with it an insatiable demand for housing that instantly outstripped Dalhart's meager supply. As had been true in countless other Texas cities, nearly every building with four walls and a roof became a home to a soldier's family. Sheds, barns, warehouses, and, of course, chicken coops were brought up to barely minimum standards to serve as bedrooms for civilian workers and military dependents.[77] One can only wonder what the rudely dispossessed chickens of Texas used for shelter during the early 1940s.

One veteran recalled that the rent being demanded for even the poorest of accommodations was unreasonably high due to the dire shortage of living space of any sort. People often found themselves residing in cold basements or unheated garages in a region where wintertime temperatures often plummet to the sub-zero range, with seventeen degrees below zero being the dubious record claimed by Dalhart during one particularly bleak January.[78]

As might be imagined, bathroom facilities were also at a premium and often sorely limited. The wife of one officer shared an outside privy with several other individuals, and although she usually waited for everyone else to be on their way to the airfield, work, or school, she had another formidable obstacle to overcome before gaining access to the outhouse. Like many of their neighbors, the owners of the home with the one outside facility also kept a horse in the backyard. An Easterner, the officer's wife had never seen a horse before coming to Dalhart with her husband, and upon seeing the horse that lived in what was temporarily her backyard, she formed an instant fear of it. The animal, with a typically fiendish equine sense of humor, apparently sensed her fear and delighted in making himself a general nuisance every time the young woman attempted to make her way to the privy. Finally, after days of fearful anguish, the renter learned to wait until her landlord fed his horse in the morning before dashing to the facility as the distracted steed concentrated on his early ration of oats.[79]

Aside from such misadventures with fun-loving livestock and the ongoing fierce competition for housing, Dalhart afforded its many new residents a warm welcome. According to one veteran of the war years, the only real problem was that off-duty military personnel had absolutely nothing to do during their leisure hours. Those with automobiles frequently drove to Amarillo on weekends, but most others stayed on the base or came into Dalhart to go to the movies.

Doyle Hanbury remembers that lines would begin to form outside the movie houses for at least an hour before the films started to roll. He and his friends would eye the long queue of soldiers often stretching around two blocks to calculate if there was any chance they might squeeze into the next showing. On one occasion, Hanbury found a seat next to a large black sergeant from the airfield. He was the first black man the boy had ever seen.[80]

Unlike certain other Texas cities during the war, the arrival at the base of what was then termed a "colored squadron" did not trigger any large-scale practice of segregation in Dalhart. The black troops were allowed to sit wherever they chose in the movie theaters and their movements about town were not nearly as restricted as had often been the case elsewhere. The black troops did have a service club of their own in town where over one hundred men often visited on a regular basis.[81]

The glider training at the airfield continued until February 1943 even though a tragic accident at the end of January that same year nearly brought all glider flight training to an abrupt halt. The memories of that dark and horrible night are still vivid in the minds of some. Billie Brown, who was a high school student and a part-time funeral home employee, arrived early at the accident scene about a mile and a half northwest of the airfield. He learned that a CG4A had experienced an unintended cutoff from its tow plane on a moonless night mission and in attempting a gliding landing had struck a vacant thirty-three year old cement block house, killing all six of the Army men on board.

A report of the incident not only gave details of the tragedy, but also served to underscore the often-dark whimsy of fate. According to the report, what the glider hit "was the only obstruction within miles. A slight deviation in heading and there would have been nothing for the glider to strike for countless miles. It happened to hit the only solid object possible."[82] Today, the old base is only a memory, the gliders are all destroyed, but the sturdy cement house remains, standing alone on the north bank of Rita Blanca Creek about a mile outside of town.

Twelve days after the nighttime crash, the glider school was transferred from the Gulf Coast Training Center to the Second Air Force. As the motorless and silent CG4As were phased out, the multi-engine and unquestionably noisy B-17 Flying Fortresses began arriving at the airfield. It had become the base's new mission to train heavy bombardment crews just prior to their assignment to combat zones located around the world.

When the B-17s arrived at Dalhart, many bombing ranges were established in the more remote areas of Texas and in nearby Oklahoma. Some of the bombing targets were lighted to give flight crews a realistic impression of nighttime missions. At one of the lighted sites, the level of illumination far exceeded that of a nearby city, thus causing an incident that still remains a popular topic of conversation throughout the entire Panhandle region and beyond.

On July 4, 1943, most of the citizens of Boise City, Oklahoma, had gone to bed well before midnight, blissfully unaware that their little town located some fifty miles north of Dalhart, was poised to go into the history books. Boise City, it developed, was about to be bombed by an American Air Force B-17!

The Dalhart-based pilot had flown his giant bomber northward from the airfield to make a practice run on the illuminated target located near Conlen, Texas, not far from the sleeping Oklahoma town. When he saw the brightly lit target area at Conlen, the pilot mistakenly assumed he was seeing a well-illuminated city rather than a remote bombing range. Unfortunately, when he spotted another dimly lit area nearby with but a few pinpoints of light, he jumped to the dangerous conclusion that he was at last on his way to the assigned target zone. The B-17 was now in fact winging toward a darkened Boise City with its bomb bay doors swinging open.[83]

On the ground below, seven oil company truck drivers were enjoying a late night hamburger at the city's Library Café when they heard the drone of the bomber's four big 1,200 horsepower Cyclone engines. As B-17s frequently flew over the Oklahoma Panhandle, the sound of the aircraft's motors did not alarm anyone, but the sudden and unmistakable whistle of falling bombs quickly turned the sleeping town into a scene of alarm and panic.[84]

The first bomb, containing four pounds of gunpowder and ninety-six pounds of sand, crashed through the roof of F. F. Bourke's garage, creating a hole some four feet wide and four feet deep. The garage was about ten yards from the city's post office and an equal distance from the S.E. Ferguson home where eight people had just been very rudely awakened. Having no way of knowing that he was attacking Boise City rather than a vacant target zone, the pilot confidently nosed his plane around for a second drop, with this bomb hitting the wall of a Baptist church. Obviously dedicated to his mission, the errant pilot had his bombardier release four more missiles, one of which narrowly missed the courthouse and another blasted a crater in Lee Wright's front yard.[85]

As the plane banked to complete yet another run, a quick-thinking power company employee hit the city's master electrical switch, plunging the entire city into total darkness. An article in the July 6, 1943, *Daily Oklahoman* noted, "That act apparently was the first intimation to the pilot that he was not scoring 100% in his lessons, as the bombing stopped after that."[86]

A *Time* magazine article observed that the citizens of the first U.S. city to ever experience an actual bombing attack had reacted the way people might well be expected to, despite several previous mock air raid drills. "Most of them ran like hell," wrote the magazine's editor, "and in no particular direction."[87]

After the shock of their historic attack had subsided, the town's residents took the event in stride and with amazingly good humor. The minister of the slightly damaged Baptist church rather wistfully remarked that he wished at least a quarter of the people who came to look at the hole in the church wall would also come to Sunday services. Deputy Sheriff C.S. Ricks proclaimed the bombing event had created "the most darned excitement in Boise City in years."[88]

Back at the Dalhart base, the error was treated with far more gravity, of course, yet one wag saw fit to place a notice on the squadron operation's bulletin board that read: "Remember Pearl Harbor! Remember the Alamo! And for God's sake, don't forget Boise City!"[89] Suffice it to say, Oklahoma was not bombed again during the war by either friend or foe.

In February 1945, the first contingent of WACS arrived at the Dalhart installation. Sergeant Gertrude McCarthy was transferred from wintry Spokane, Washington, to what she somehow had envisioned would be an ideal climate in Texas. "Dalhart indeed!" she later wrote, "When we heard we would soon be traipsing the plains of Texas, our hearts were gay. We would soon be turning a golden brown in the enchantingly mild and syrupy climate." Sadly, McCarthy was disillusioned after only a few days at Dalhart. "So far, wind burned faces, two quarts of sand in eyes, noses, and ears," she reported, "plus hacking coughs that reign supreme. War is hell."[90]

The dire effects of the hellish war were felt throughout the city as well as on the airfield. For example, Doyle Hanbury remembers that his family took in a total of seven Air Force wives during the time their husbands were training for combat in the B-17s at the base. Each of those husbands was later killed in action.[91]

On a brighter note, Hanbury recalls that his mother joined hundreds of other Panhandle women in working at the airfield. As a result of these new employment opportunities, the economic situation in the region improved tremendously during the war years, reaching a peak that has not been matched since.

The military importance of the Dalhart training facility was underscored in 1943 when two additional satellite fields were constructed, and again in July 1944, when the Air Force's new B-29s flew to the Panhandle base to replace the aging B-17s. Later in the war, one of the satellite fields was used as a German prisoner-of-war camp.

On Wednesday, August 1, 1945, the main field was opened to the public in celebration of the thirty-eighth anniversary of the creation of the Army Air Service. Within a few days, the war that had catapulted Dalhart from an historic ranch headquarters into a major military facility was essentially over. Without doubt, the airmen who had trained at the Panhandle base had clearly played a key role in the winning of that war.

In saluting those airmen and the Air Force that had sent them to Dalhart, the editor of the local paper penned a short article that says much even now. "The Dalhart airfield has meant a lot to Dalhart," wrote the newspaperman, "and we hope that Dalhart and this territory have meant a lot to it." After candidly acknowledging that "perhaps the field has not always found things in Dalhart as it wished," the editor went on to record that, "on the whole relations have been cordial, friendly, helpful, [and] laid on a broad basis of mutual willingness to understand." Then after making the not unexpected nor unusual plea that the base become a permanent installation, the writer closed by accurately predicting that the "importance of air power, in war and in peace, would reach unbelievable levels in the years yet to come."[92]

Although the Dalhart *Daily Texan's* editor was absolutely correct in his prediction about air power, he failed to convince the War Department that his city's airfield should become a permanent military base. After becoming inactive in late 1945, the entire airfield was given to the city of Dalhart by the federal government. The exceptionally long runways are now part of the town's municipal airport, while another section of the base has become a state prison unit and the city's largest employer.[93]

Little remains to reflect what important and deadly business once took place on this flat, glider-perfect acreage. A few hangars stand silent and empty, one with the distinctive "rudder-notch" cut over its massive doors to accommodate the B-29's nearly thirty-foot-tall vertical stabilizer. Elsewhere, small concrete piers mark the sites where barracks, service clubs, and offices once stood. The effect is eerily reminiscent of a military cemetery, with literally hundreds upon hundreds of uniformly arranged short concrete pillars stretching almost as far as the eye can see. It is the sheer magnitude of the place that makes it so hauntingly memorable, even though there is no historical marker nearby to tell the story of what happened on this sprawling site. Only the tombstone-like piers remain to reflect the swiftly fading memories of a mighty air base and the proud people of a small Texas Panhandle city who welcomed and nourished all who served upon it. Together they helped win the twentieth century's most terrible war.

[1] Sally Van Wagenen Keil, *Those Wonderful Women In Their Flying Machines*, 109.

[2] Mary Beth Rogers, Sherry A. Smith and Janelle D. Scott, *We Can Fly: Stories of Katherine Stinson and Other Gutsy Texas Women Pilots*, 149.

[3] Sheilah Henderson, "Zoot Suits, Parachutes, and Wings of Silver, Too," *Texas Highways*, September 1987, 10.

[4] Ibid.

[5] E.L. Yeats and Hooper Shelton, *History of Nolan County, Texas*, 106.

[6] Jean Hascall Cole, *Women Pilots of World War II*, 3.

[7] *Avenger*, May 11, 1943, 3.

[8] Keil, 163.

[9] Rosa Lee (Fullwood) Meek Dickerson, interview with author, March 18, 2002.

[10] Keil, 277.

[11] Doris Brinker Tanner, comp., *Who Were the Wasp?*, 42.

[12] *Avenger*, March 17, 1944.

[13] Jacqueline Cochran, *The Stars at Noon*, 197.

[14] *Avenger*, July 14, 1944.

[15] Keil, 340.

[16] A.B. Davis to George B. Mahon, letter dated January 9, 1936.

[17] Davis to Gerald C. Brant, letter dated September 8, 1936.

[18] Davis notation dated June 29, 1941.

[19] Davis to T.L. Patterson, letter dated May 31, 1940.

[20] Ibid.

[21] Davis to R.D. Shinkle, telegram dated May 26, 1940.

[22] W.T. Spurgin to A.B. Davis, letter dated April 9, 1941.

[23] *Lubbock Avalanche-Journal*, April 16, 1941.

[24] *Avalanche-Journal*, June 21, 1941.

[25] *Avalanche-Journal*, June 22, 1941.

[26] Ibid.

[27] "Department of Defense Legacy Resource Management" film, 1997.

[28] Ibid.

[29] Ibid.

[30] Ron Tyler, ed., *The New Handbook of Texas*, vol. 4, 321.

[31] "The Hub," vol. 4, no. 1, 6.

[32] *Avalanche-Journal*, March 15, 1992.

[33] Ibid.

[34] DOD "Legacy" film.

[35] *History of Reese Air Force Base and 64th Flying Training Wing*, 9.

[36] *Avalanche-Journal*, November 12, 1949.

[37] *Avalanche-Journal*, June 4, 1991.

[38] *History of Reese Air Force Base*, 28.

[39] *Avalanche-Journal*, November 6, 1967.

[40] *Amarillo Globe-Times*, September 10, 1941.

[41] Ibid.

[42] Ibid.

[43] *Amarillo Daily News*, November 29, 1941.

[44] *Amarillo Globe-Times*, October 11, 1941.

[45] Ibid., April 1, 1942.

[46] *Amarillo Daily News*, September 27, 1942.

[47] Ibid., May 27, 1942.

[48] Wesley W. Jones and Joe D. LaCrone, "History of Amarillo Air Force Base," 8.

[49] *Amarillo Globe-Times*, August 4, 1945.

[50] Jones and LaCrone, 12.

[51] *Amarillo Globe-Times*, October 25, 1967.

[52] Ron Tyler, ed., *The New Handbook of Texas*, vol. 1, 142.

[53] Ron Russell, interview with author, Amarillo, Texas, October 8, 1998.

[54] Mike Porter, interview with author, Pampa, Texas, August 17, 2001.

[55] *Pampa News,* March 14, 1942.

[56] *Pampa News*, May 15, 1942.

[57] Pampa News, May 23, 1942.

[58] Ibid.

[59] *Pampa News*, July 23, 1942.

[60] *Pampa News*, November 22, 1942.

[61] *Pampa News*, December 15, 1942.

[62] Vernon Baumgarten, *Who's Who: Pampa Army Airfield Reunion Directory*, 3.

[63] *Pampa News*, February 23, 1943.

[64] Jamie Gough, *Pampa Reunion Directory*, 35.

[65] *Pampa News*, February 28, 1943.

[66] *Pampa News,* March 7, 1943.

[67] *Pampa News,* February 21, 1943.

[68] *Pampa News,* January 5, 1944.

[69] *Pampa News*, September 23, 1945.

[70] Rod "Doc" Savage, *Pampa Reunion Directory*, 82.

[71] Doyle Hanbury, interview with author, April 17, 2002.

[72] *Texas Almanac and State Industrial Guide, 1943-1944*, 74.

[73] *The New Handbook of Texas*, vol. 2, 475.

[74] *The Dalhart Bomber*, vol. 2, no. 40, 1.

[75] *The Daily Texan*, July 31, 1945

[76] *National World War II Glider Pilots Association Fact Booklet*, 2.

[77] Hanbury interview.

[78] Letter in Dalhart Army Airfield vertical file, XIT Museum, Dalhart, Texas.

[79] Hanbury interview.

[80] Ibid.

[81] F.E. Thomas, Jr., interview with author, Fredericksburg, Texas, January 31, 2002.

[82] *Silent Wings*, 13.

[83] John Davis, "Boise City Bombed," *Grain Producers Magazine*, February 1980, 12.

[84] Ibid.

[85] Kay Peck, "The Night They (Whoops!) Bombed Boise City," *Ford Times*, July 1983, 47.

[86] Davis, 12.

88 Ibid, 12.
89 Peck, 47.
90 *The Dalhart Bomber*, February 9, 1944, 3.
91 Hanbury interview.
92 *The Daily Texan*, July 31, 1945.
93 "Community Fact Sheet," Dalhart, Texas, 1998, 5.

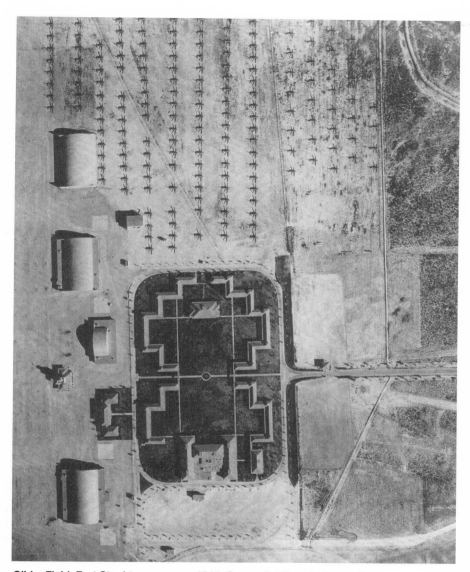

Gibbs Field, Fort Stockton, summer 1944. One cadet thought it was the most architecturally pleasing of all Army airfields. The planes are in storage awaiting sale by the government. Courtesy A.E. Ivy, Fort Stockton, Texas.

Top: Pecos County Airport, Fort Stockton, formerly Gibbs Field. The original stone gateway pillars flank the roadway with the control tower in the distant center of the photo. Author's photograph.

Bottom: Cadets on parade at Fort Stockton's Gibbs Field. Note "Solo," the field's mascot, in the line of march.
Courtesy Annie Riggs Hotel Museum, Fort Stockton, Texas.

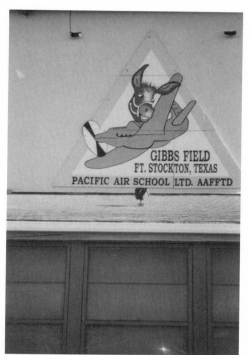

Left: A replica of the wartime insignia of Gibbs Field, featuring "Solo" in flight. Recreated on the original control tower for a 1988 reunion of former cadets.
Author's photograph.

Bottom: The Stockton Hotel, 2002. Here, the first class of Gibbs Field cadets dined in 1942, awaiting completion of the mess hall on the base.
Author's photograph.

Top: **The main gate of Marfa Army Airfield, winter 1943.**
Courtesy Museum of the Big Bend Archives, Sul Ross State University, Alpine, Texas.

Bottom: **Absolutely all that remains standing of Marfa Army Airfield, 1999.**
Author's photograph.

Left: Known as Alfred Arnold Coccozza when he was stationed at Marfa during World War II, this singer became better known as Mario Lanza.
Courtesy Metro Goldwyn Mayer Studios.

Bottom: Midland Mayor M.C. Ulmer welcomes Lt. Col. Isaiah Davies to his new command at Midland Army Airfield in 1942.
Courtesy Midland County Historical Museum, Midland, Texas.

Right: **Newly arrived cadets take the solemn Bombardier's Oath at Midland. The top secret Norden bombsight is hidden from prying eyes and protected by armed guards.**
Courtesy Permian Historical Society Archival Collection, the University of Texas of the Permian Basin, Odessa, Texas.

Bottom: **Officers from Midland Army Airfield are the guests at a backyard barbecue, 1944. Odessa's "Chuck Wagon Gang" frequently catered such events.**
Courtesy Midland County Historical Museum, Midland, Texas.

Top: Pyote's Main Street did not offer much in the way of shade or, in fact, anything else in 1943.
Courtesy Ward County Historical Commission, Monahans, Texas.

Bottom: Pyote Army Airfield while still under construction, 1942. At its peak, the base would be home to nearly ten thousand personnel.
Courtesy Ward County Historical Commission, Monahans, Texas.

Top: **There was probably little other than this to do at Pyote's Airfield on Christmas Day, 1942. Note the two-handed beer aficionados.**
Courtesy Ward County Historical Commission, Monahans, Texas.

Bottom: **After the war, Pyote's hangars rapidly fell into great disrepair.**
Courtesy Ward County Historical Commission, Monahans, Texas.

Top: **These bank-like vaults once housed the top-secret Norden bombsights at Pyote.** Author's photograph.

Bottom: **No longer needed, these Boeing B-29s joined two thousand other aircraft to be dismantled and smelted at Pyote after the war.**
Courtesy Ward County Historical Commission, Monahans, Texas.

Top: **The famous "Enola Gay" came to Pyote after the war but was spared destruction in the smelting furnace.**
Courtesy Ward County Historical Commission, Monanhans, Texas.

Bottom: **This roaring furnace transformed giant airplanes into small ingots of aluminum.**
Courtesy Ward County Historical Commission, Monahans, Texas.

Left: **Glen Garland, son of the smelting chief, holds one of the ingots that was the end product of the aircraft smelting process.**
Courtesy Steve Nixon, Ward County Historical Commission, Monahans, Texas.

Bottom: **The WASPs pass in review at Sweetwater's Avenger Field, ca 1944.**
Courtesy Pioneer Museum, Sweetwater, Texas.

Top: **The WASPs returned to parade in downtown Sweetwater in 1972.**
Courtesy Texas Woman's University, Women's Collection, Denton, Texas.

Right: **A.B. Davis, aka "Mr. Lubbock," vigorously pursued his dream of an Army airfield in his city for many years prior to World War II.**
Courtesy *Fort Worth Star-Telegram* Collection, Special Collections Division, the University of Texas at Arlington Libraries.

Top: **Mr. Davis's dream at last came true on June 21, 1942, when Lubbock Army Airfield was officially opened.**
Courtesy Texas Tech University Special Collections Library/Southwest Collection, Lubbock, Texas.

Bottom: **A very dusty parade and an impressive fly-over were highlights of a 1942 Open House at Amarillo Army Airfield.**
Courtesy English Field Air and Space Museum, Amarillo, Texas.

Top: **Two young Texans study a huge Superfortress during the August 1945 Open House at the Amarillo field.**
Courtesy English Field Air and Space Museum, Amarillo, Texas.

Bottom: **Saluting the colors at Pampa Army Airfield, 1944.**
Courtesy Freedom Museum USA, Pampa, Texas.

Top: **An estimated fourteen thousand men participated in this formal review at Pampa Army Airfield in 1943. The population of the city of Pampa was slightly less at the time.**
Courtesy Freedom Museum USA, Pampa, Texas.

Bottom: **Some of the more recent occupants of the ramps and runways of what was once Pampa Army Airfield.**
Author's photograph.

Top: One of the few remaining vestiges of Dalhart Army Airfield. Note the notch created over the hangar door late in the war to accommodate the towering tail fins of B-29s. They were nearly nine feet taller than those of the B-17.

Author's photograph.

Bottom: These tombstone-like concrete foundation pilings, along with thousands more still visible at Dalhart, once supported the nearly seven hundred buildings that stood on the airfield.

Author's photograph.

CHAPTER SEVEN

ON MEMORY'S WINGS

*I guess the Army boys liked our Texas gals, because when I got
back here [from the South Pacific], almost all the good ones had
married soldiers and moved away.*

> Bill Davenport
> Pecos, Texas
> October 3, 1998

What the dismayed Navy veteran Davenport discovered when he
came back after the war was not unique to his hometown of Pecos.
All across Texas, women had been frequently wooed and often won
by the soldiers who served at nearby airfields during the wartime
years.

The brides' absences from their Texas homes often proved to be
only temporary. When their husbands were discharged from the service at war's end, the still-new families frequently returned to the
cities and towns where the couples first had met.

Mike Porter was among the many new veterans who returned to
the Lone Star State after the war, bringing his wife back to live in
Pampa where she had been born. "We came back mainly because of

the welcome I had received when I came here the first time as a cadet," the former bomber pilot recalls. Porter became a permanent Pampan and led a successful effort to create a local museum to honor his fellow pilots who served with him at the city's Army airfield.[1]

Fritz Kahl made Marfa his permanent home after serving as an instructor at the airfield and marrying a local rancher's daughter. "I had a lot of places I could have gone after the war ended," he declares, "but I liked it here and I am glad that this is where we settled." Kahl served his postwar hometown as its mayor for many years.[2]

Porter and Kahl and their fellow aviators joined the many native Texans who came home when the war was over. The state had sent approximately 750,000 of its sons and daughters to serve in military units from 1941 through 1945, and 23,022 of them lost their lives while on active duty. Thirty-six Texans received the Medal of Honor for exemplary valor under fire.[3]

Those who came back to Texas caused the state's population to expand by nearly 15 percent in the five years immediately following the war.[4] While impressive in its own right, this significant surge in population represented far more than just a statistical headcount. Each returning veteran, either native born or a newly minted Texan, having been afforded a rare if often dangerous opportunity to view the exciting world that existed beyond the borders of Texas, brought with him new perspectives and contemporary attitudes that would have been denied him without the wartime experience. These broader and modern viewpoints, when superimposed upon the state's long-established social traditions, continued the process of cultural evolution that had begun the day the very first Army airman had arrived at his newly built wartime base in Texas.

Some of the changes had become immediately apparent. The women of San Antonio, for example, had left their kitchens or their afternoon tea parties to learn how to repair B-17 engines at Kelly Field, gaining for the first time an independence and self-reliance denied them under traditional social customs. Other women such as WASPs Florene Miller and Rosa Lea Fullwood took to the skies as pilots of the Army's most challenging aircraft. Their steadfast refusal to ask for any special considerations or to settle for attaining anything less than the highest of performance standards set the pace for generations of women who were to follow. They also became attractive and influential role models for countless younger Texas women who admired their courage and self-assurance.

Kelly Field also opened doors for others who had long been barred from an equal opportunity to learn and to earn. Many of the airfield's wartime employees were drawn from San Antonio's large Hispanic community, establishing a trend that greatly expanded after the war. Proof of the Hispanic workers' ability to perform, once afforded the opportunity to do so, can readily be found in the numerous accounts of what came to be known as "Kelly Families." Comprising several successive generations of usually Hispanic workers, each family group enjoyed ever improving levels of economic accomplishment that likely would have been unimaginable and perhaps even impossible had it not been for the Kelly Field wartime opportunity.

In El Paso, the Hispanic community also took giant strides forward during the 1940s, when Biggs Field and Fort Bliss were at their highest level of activity. When many war-generated jobs were made available only to American citizens, Hispanics flocked to English language and citizenship classes to become qualified for employment. Once hired, the new citizens were often able to earn more than enough money to break the traditional chain of barrio existence.

Many young Hispanic men who were already citizens volunteered for military service and immediately found to their delight that entrenched racial barriers were dissolved through the wearing of their uniforms. Once the war ended, these proud ex-servicemen were not willing to accept the racial discrimination they had all too often encountered throughout Texas before the conflict began. As Robert A. Caro has noted, the Hispanic soldiers had served in combat alongside their white counterparts, "and they returned home in a different frame of mind."[5] In their new resolve to gain racial equality, the Hispanic veterans took advantage of government programs to gain a college education or to start a business of their own.

Sometimes, the curious fortunes of war caused Hispanics to blur century-old lines of separation between blacks and whites. The temporary insertion of a Mexican military unit into Greenville's tightly structured racial division created an unknown element into the mix and in the process at least helped fray the bonds that had defined the social order since the Civil War.

In other parts of Texas, the war and the coming of hundreds of thousands of uniformed aliens brought about, in four short years, more social changes than might have been expected in countless decades. These changes were not wrought through an invasion of arrogant Yankee evil-doers and mischief-makers, but simply through the insertion of huge numbers of ordinary, well-intentioned if sometimes high-spirited men and women. They were, for the most part, no more pleased to find themselves in Pyote or Marfa or Pecos than the lifelong residents of those frontier communities were to suddenly find them on their doorsteps.

As Lucy Rountree Kuykendall wrote in her appropriately entitled *P.S. to Pecos*, "What occurred at Pecos was no different than what happened in many towns throughout the nation. The small communities were simply unprepared for the great Army influx, but this fact was overlooked in the furor of the Battle of Pecos!"[6]

Mrs. Kuykendall was by birth a Texan and by choice the wife of an Army Air Force officer. Even being a Texan in no way protected her from the "social unpleasantries," as she termed them, that came her way as an Army wife. "What an absurd tempest in a teapot!" she declared. The Pecosites called the Army "an aggregation of hard-to-please snobs," who did nothing but "sit and moan of their life in the sticks." The Army personnel, however, were not without their often loudly outspoken opinions. "The civilians," Kuykendall reported, were seen as being "a bunch of bloodsucking dumbclucks — and Texas dumbclucks at that."[7]

It would seem likely that in Pecos and elsewhere, something of a cautious barrier between old timers and newcomers remained in place throughout the war. To be sure, the relationship between the military and the civilians was for the most part cordial. Odessa's Chuck Wagon Gang, for example, catered memorable barbecues for the men at the airfield located east of town, and Texas Tech coeds turned out in droves to dance with the cadets from Lubbock's pilot school, but many accounts seem to reflect evidence of at least some forgivable hesitation in accepting all of these new neighbors with arms open wide.

How could it possibly have been otherwise? It is difficult to imagine, even with the advantage of six decades of perfect hindsight, how a community such as Marfa, for instance, with a population of 3,805 when its airfield opened in 1942 could embrace without at least some reservation a new and totally unknown social element over twice as large as the town itself. Even more challenging, tiny Pyote and its 201 inhabitants became host virtually overnight to a military city at least forty times more populous. The patriotic Texans and the nearly one million military strangers who experienced what obviously was an unprecedented, traumatic and upsetting period of cultural upheaval clearly displayed uncommon patience and limitless forbearance. That the entire social infrastructure of the state did not simply buckle under the weight of such a vast number of instant newcomers is in itself a lasting tribute to all who survived it.

On the other hand, the short and long term economic changes caused by the coming of the Air Force were understandably far more welcome throughout the state than were the social and cultural shocks and after-shocks. In literally browbeating the president of the United States while successfully lobbying for a bomber plant and an airfield, for example, Amon Carter gave his beloved city of Fort Worth an economic foundation that sustained it through postwar downturns and recessions and initially providing wartime employment to over thirty thousand workers. A.B. Davis's equally important contribution to Lubbock's future was the creation of a long-serving military air facility, which evolved into a future-seeking civilian technological research center. Both accomplishments reflect the dedication of two tireless Texas promoters who believed in the potential of their cities and did whatever was required to make those cities better, bigger, and stronger.

Many other parts of Texas also had leaders as far-sighted and dedicated as Carter and Davis. Lyndon B. Johnson pressed the flesh and pulled the lapels of official Washington on behalf of Austin's efforts to get a big Army airfield. When he was away from his congressional office on temporary naval duty, it was his Lady Bird who closed the deal and ensured Austin's future in bringing Bergstrom Field, a future international airport, to the state's capital city.

Chambers of commerce, Rotary clubs, and elected officials all across Texas saw the economic potential in acquiring an Army airfield for their region, in anticipation of that field becoming a civilian airport when peace replaced war. In Amarillo, a massive sized runway constructed by the Air Force did eventually become the focal point for the region's only major peacetime air facility, while in Greenville, much of what was built by the Army during the war became the very key to the city's future. As one local historian describes it, Greenville's Majors Field "provided the threshold from an agrarian economy to an industrial one."[8]

Moreover, as the authors of *Aviation In Texas* observed, the towering presence of the Army Air Force in Texas during the war years also proved to be the threshold for the state's wholehearted acceptance of the modern air age. "Largely as a result of the wartime air bases dotting the state. . .," the book points out, "Texas had become unusually air-minded."[9]

Along the Rio Grande, the coming of six major wartime Army airfields brought about significant and positive economic change. Harlingen benefited from the flow of construction dollars on its World War II airfield and then enjoyed a military payroll that continued for many years with but a short interruption between a hot war and a cold one. Laredo saw its 1940s air base re-emerge as a Cold War facility, with both incarnations pumping huge amounts of federal dollars into the regional economy. Much of what were military airfields in the two cities during the war eventually became civilian aviation centers of great importance to the communities.

It can, of course, be argued persuasively that many of the social, cultural, and economic changes that took place when the Army Air Force came to Texas during the war would have occurred anyway, at least in due time. To be sure, sweeping postwar advances in technology, communication, education, and transportation would have eventually brought about change and modernization to even the most isolated of Texas communities. Further, the latter twentieth-century decentralization of industry, coupled with the popular flight from urban chaos to the often illusory calm of the countryside, would surely have provided countless outsiders with powerful motivation to breach the long-standing barriers of rural Texas. Even though such assumptions might be safely taken, it should nonetheless remain clear that the war-generated avalanche of Air Force men and women without question greatly accelerated the key elements which otherwise would have taken several decades to become manifest.

Of those sixty-five Army airfields that were in operation during World War II, only six—Randolph, Sheppard, Laughlin, Lackland, Brooks, and Abilene's Dyess—continued to function as active Air Force installations at the beginning of the twenty-first century. Biggs Field, in El Paso, had again become part of the Army that had spawned it just after the dawn of the last century.

The ongoing economic impact of these hardy survivors of the war is immense. It is amusing to consider how Benjamin Foulois might react were he around today to ponder what Randolph Field means to San Antonio. After the dismal and indeed fatal beginnings of his little Army aero squadron at Fort Sam Houston, Foulois was asked to speak at a farewell banquet arranged in his honor on July 7,

1911. Given the dire circumstances of his forced recall to an infantry assignment at an Army post in Maryland, Foulois must have summoned nearly all of his legendary resources of bravery to attend the banquet, let alone agree to be the evening's featured speaker. Yet, speak he did, uttering what stands today as a line both humorous and prophetic. Even as the Army's sole aeroplane was being crated for shipment by rail back to the east coast, the diminutive but fearless Foulois rose to address his listeners. "I am going east tomorrow," he stated, as if his audience didn't know it, "but I am confident that someday, another aviator with another aeroplane will come to San Antonio to take my place."[10]

He was so right. Not one aviator, but thousands of aviators, with thousands more airplanes did return to San Antonio over the years and have continued to do so for almost a century since Foulois took the morning train to Maryland. In 1997 alone, the overall Air Force payroll in San Antonio exceeded a billion dollars. Born of declared war and sustained by needs drawn from countless wars undeclared, the Air Force clearly remains a vitally important part of the Alamo City.

Other Texas towns and their wartime airfields have fared less well. Fort Stockton's old Gibbs Field is very likely the best preserved of the former military fields, at least in terms of original buildings that remain standing. Although now a county airport, it seems to exude that peculiar, almost ghostly, sensation that seems to hover over a handful of these once bustling military installations. It is as if all the vast energy that existed here long ago was just too intense to dissipate, even after sixty years of the relentless desert sun and the hot and sandy Sonoran winds. Only a few of these old airfields seem to have this inexplicable aura about them. Do some seem to be vaguely haunted only because, as is usually the case, so little physical evidence remains to remind us of what went on there during those terribly years of war? Or is it only a nostalgia-fueled imagination that conjures up this fleeting but no less eerie sensation?

Pyote is another deserted base with ghostly overtones. It seems to most of its very few visitors to be at once the most forlorn and yet the most evocative of the immense power that once dwelled upon it. Walls of only one of its giant hangars remain standing, its roof and all of the other hangars that once loomed nearby have become the victims of harsh years of raging winds, pounding hailstones and the acts of mindless vandals. Curiously, the thin blacktopped ramps where war-weary B-17s and B-29s once awaited postwar destruction have survived almost fully intact, while the thicker concrete runways that stretch for nearly two miles across the desert have been overtaken by the ubiquitous Texas mesquite trees that in their never-ceasing and ferocious quest for survival have not the slightest respect for the puny creations of man.

Still impressive bank-like vaults remain standing, thus far impervious to the most damaging forces of the wild West Texas weather. Within these vaults, behind massive steel doors, were stored the legendary Norden bombsights, America's most secret of weapons in the early years of the war. A good distance to the east of the derelict hangar, a perfectly preserved concrete swimming pool, lacking only a small amount of repair but a very great amount of filtered water, is all that marks the one time location of the officers' club.

In short, all is in ruin. To use the darkly descriptive vernacular of the vast oil patch that surrounds the deserted old airfield, Pyote's Rattlesnake Bomber Base has been plugged and abandoned, yet to some, the spirit of it lingers still.

Evelyn Blair, who worked at Pyote during the war, does not much care to talk about what life was like back then, when the place teemed with almost ten thousand men and women and later when long rows of fabled heroic airplanes awaited destruction in a white-hot furnace. Although she will speak of her wartime experiences only sparingly, she once found the courage to record her sentiments about the old airfield in a poem written in 1972, when even then only her memories were about all that remained of the old field. Perhaps it is fitting that someone who actually experienced life on the once vital base should have the final word in this text. Here then, in part, is Evelyn Blair's previously unpublished tribute to a vanished but no less immortal monument of Texas military history.

Aircraft Graveyard: West Texas

I walked the ramp beneath the planes assembled row on row;
The giants covered the desert lands
Where vultures soar, and hell-winds blow.

Great warrior eagles, as far as eye could span,
Reached the horizon and bent beyond,
Like ships upon a quiet sea after the battle fury is spent.

Dwarfed to ant-size among bald eagles
I heard the battle roll on the wind
Sinking down with eyes hard-closed,
I pressed each ear with a trembling hand.

The clamor ceased; I raised my head
And cried in anger, "Why must it be?"
Through the metal canyons the echo came
"That man, from bondage, might be free."[11]

[1] Mike Porter, interview with author, Pampa, Texas, August 17, 2001.

[2] C.M. Kahl, interview with author, Marfa, Texas, October 11, 1999.

[3] Ron Tyler, ed., *The New Handbook of Texas*, vol.6, 1079.

[4] *Texas Almanac and State Industrial Guide*, 1949-1950.

[5] Robert A. Caro, "The Compassion of Lyndon Johnson," *The New Yorker*, April 1, 2002, 65.

[6] Lucy Rountree Kuykendahl, *P.S. to Pecos*, 249.

[7] Ibid.

[8] Vincent Leibowitz, interview with author, October 15, 1998.

[9] Roger Bilstein and Jay Miller, *Aviation In Texas*, 131.

[10] *San Antonio Light*, July 8, 1911.

[11] Evelyn Blair, "Aircraft Graveyard: West Texas."

BIBLIOGRAPHY

Allison, Fred H. "The Fighting Eagles: Mexico's Squadron 201 in World War II Texas." Paper presented at the annual meeting of the Texas State Historical Association, Austin, Texas, March 3, 1998.

Amarillo Daily News: November 29, 1941, May 27, 1942.

Amarillo Globe-Times: September 10, 1941; October 11, 1941; April 1, 1942; September 27, 1942; August 4, 1945; October 25, 1967.

The Austin Statesman: May 27, 1941; March 14, 1942.

Avenger: May 11, 1943; March 17, 1944; July 14, 1944.

Baumgarten, Vernon. *Who's Who: Pampa Army Airfield Association Reunion Directory*. Pampa (TX): The Pampa Army Airfield Association, 1988.

Blair, Evelyn. "Aircraft Graveyard: West Texas." Pyote, Texas, 1972.

Blankenship, Charlotte Meade. Interview with author. Brownsville, Texas, October 28, 1998.

"Bergstrom Field History." Austin: Bergstrom Field Publication, n.d.

The Big Bend Sentinel: May 29, 1942; August 8, 1942; November 6, 1942; November 20, 1942; December 14, 1942; December 28, 1942; May 8, 1945.

"Biggs Field Fact Sheet." El Paso: Fort Bliss History Office, n.d.

Bilstein, Roger and Jay Miller. *Aviation in Texas*. Austin: Texas Monthly Press, Inc., 1985.

Boyne, Walter J. *Beyond the Wild Blue Yonder: A History of the U. S. Air Force*. New York: St. Martin's Press, 1997.

Brant, Gerald C. "Dedicatory Speech at Laughlin Army Airfield." March 28, 1942. Laughlin Heritage Foundation Files. Del Rio, Texas.

Brown, Jerold E. *Where Eagles Land: Planning and Development of U.S. Army Airfields, 1910-1941*. New York: Greenwood Press, 1990.

Byars, Napoleon B. "Kelly Air Force Base and the Hispanic Contribution." n.d. Kelly Field Vertical Files. Lackland Air Force Base Archival Collection. San Antonio, Texas.

Cagle, Eldon, Jr. *Quadrangle: The History of Fort Sam Houston*. Austin: Eakin Press, 1985.

Caplinger, W. A. Interview with author. Greenville, Texas, October 15, 1998.

_____. and Jim Conrad. "A History of Majors Airfield, Greenville, Texas." Greenville: Hunt County Historical Commission, 1994.

Carlson, Erik. *Ellington Field: A Short History, 1917-1963*. Houston: National Aeronautics and Space Administration, 1999.

Caro, Robert A. "The Compassion of Lyndon Johnson." *The New Yorker*. April 1, 2002.

Cervantes, Ysidro. "Transcript from an Oral History Project." El Paso: El Paso Public Libraries, n.d.

Chicago Tribune. June 26, 1943.

Cochran, Jacqueline. *The Stars at Noon*. Boston: Little, Brown and Company, 1954.

Cole, Art. E-mail to author. February 6, 2002.

Cole, Jean Hascall. *Women Pilots of World War II*. Salt Lake City: University of Utah Press, 1971.

Colwell, James L. "Hell from Heaven, Midland Army Airfield in World War II." *The Permian Historical Annual XXVI*. Odessa (TX): The Permian Basin Historical Commission, 1987.

The Dalhart Bomber, Vol. 2, No. 40. July 15, 1943. Dalhart: Office of Public Information. February 9, 1944.

The Daily Texan, July 31, 1945.

The Dallas Morning News: June 20, 1943; September 30, 1962.

Dallas Times-Herald. April 19, 1942.

Daughtery, E. Roebuck. "U.S. Air Force Activities In and Near Del Rio, Val Verde County, Texas." Del Rio (TX): Val Verde County Historical Commission, n.d.

Davis, A.B. to George B. Mahon. January 8, 1936. A.B. Davis File 15-8 C. Southwest Collection/Special Collections Library. Texas Tech University, Lubbock, Texas.

_____. to Gerald C. Brant. September 8, 1936, Davis File 15-8 C.

_____. notation, June 29, 1941. Davis File 15-8 C.

_____. to T.L. Patterson. May 31, 1940. Davis File 15-8 C.

_____. To R.D. Shinkle. May 26, 1940. Davis File 15-8C.

Davis, J. Frank. *Randolph Field: A History and Guide*. New York: The Devin-Adair Company, 1942.

Davis, John. "Boise City Bombed." *Grain Producers Magazine*, February 1980.

Del Rio News-Herald: April 2, 1942; April 24, 1942; May 15, 1942; September 7, 1945.

"Department of Defense Legacy Resource Management." Film, 1997.

Dickerson, Rosa Lea (Fullwood) Meek. Interview with author. Kerrville, Texas, March 18, 2002.

Doolittle, James H. *I Could Never Be So Lucky Again*. New York: Bantam Books, 1991.

"Economic Survey Bulletin." El Paso: El Paso Convention and Visitors Bureau, 1999.

El Paso Times: June 12, 1916; September 13, 1945; October 28, 1956; November 24, 1964.

Ellington Field Yearbook, 1943. Baton Rouge (LA): Army and Navy Publishing Company of Louisiana, 1944.

Fauver, Sherri. "Henrietta Lopez Rivas - Kelly Air Force Base: Her Proving Ground." U.S. Latinos and Latinas WWII Oral History." Austin: University of Texas, 2000.

Ferguson, W.C., Jr. *Who's Who: Pampa Army Airfield Association Reunion Directory*. Pampa (TX): The Pampa Army Airfield Association, 1988.

Flemmons, Jerry. *Amon: The Life of Amon Carter, Sr., of Texas*. Austin: Jenkins Publishing Company, 1978.

The Flying Times: February 5, 1944; March 18, 1944. San Antonio: Kelly Field Public Information Office, 1944.

The Flying "V." September 15, 1944; September 22, 1944; September 29, 1944; May 7, 1946. Dallas: Love Field Public Affairs Office.

The Fort Stockton Pioneer: July 25, 1941; September 14, 1941; April 7, 1942; April 17, 1942; May 1, 1942; May 6, 1942; June 1, 1942; March 3, 1944; April 21, 1944.

Fort Worth Star-Telegram: January 4, 1941; October 12, 1942; October 25, 1942; December 10, 1942; February 8, 1943; October 3, 1943; February 20, 1944; October 14, 1945; December 8, 1945; June 8, 1991.

Garland, Glen. Interview with author. Pyote, Texas. February 14, 2002.

Gonzalez, Alicia. "Transcript from an Oral History Project." El Paso: El Paso Public Libraries, n.d.

Gough, Jamie. *Who's Who: Pampa Army Airfield Association Reunion Directory*. Pampa (TX): The Pampa Army Airfield Association, 1988.

Greenville Evening Banner. January 6, 1942.

Grube, Susanne. "A Brief History of Camp Marfa and Fort D.A. Russell." Chinati Foundation Fact Sheet. n.d.

Guerra, Mary Ann Noonan. *The Gunter Hotel in San Antonio's History*. San Antonio: The Gunter Hotel, 1985.

Hanbury, Doyle. Interview with author. Dalhart, Texas, April 17, 2002.

Hargus, William. Interview with author. Fort Stockton, Texas, April 11, 2001; February 11, 2002; February 12, 2002.

Harrison, W. Walworth. *History of Greenville and Hunt County*. Waco: Texian Press, 1977.

Heath, Elizabeth. Comp. *Ward County, 1887-1977*. Monahans (TX): Ward County Historical Commission, 1977.

Henderson, Sheilah. "Zoot Suits, Parachutes, and Wings of Silver, Too." *Texas Highways*. Vol. 34. No. 9. (September 1987).

History of Biggs Field. El Paso: Fort Bliss History Office, 1945.

"History of Fort Worth Army Airfield." *Lone Star Scanner.* February 16, 1946.

History of Reese Air Force Base and 64th Flying Training Wing. Lubbock: Office of 64th Flying Training Wing Historian, Reese Air Force Base, 1993.

Hondo Anvil Herald: January 23, 1942; April 3, 1942; April 19, 1942; August 14, 1942; September 30, 1999.

Houston Chronicle: December 3, 1917; June 6, 1940; October 26, 1941; March 18, 1945; July 27, 1948; July 28, 1948.

The Houston Post. December 31, 1942.

The Houston Press. May 28, 1941.

"The Hub," Vol. 4, No. 5. Lubbock: The Lubbock Chamber of Commerce, 1944.

Hughes, L. Patrick. "To Meet Fire with Fire: Lyndon Johnson, Tom Miller, and Home-Front Politics." *Southwestern Historical Quarterly.* Vol. C, No. 4.

Hussey, Ann Krueger and Robert S. Browning III. *A Heritage of Service: Seventy-five Years of Military Aviation at Kelly Air Force Base, 1916-1991.* San Antonio: Office of History, San Antonio Air Logistics Center, Kelly Air Force Base, 1991.

Hussey, Ann and Robert Browning. *A History of Military Aviation in San Antonio.* San Antonio: San Antonio Air Logistics Center History Office, 1996.

Ivy, A.E. Interview with author. Fort Stockton, Texas, February 12, 2002.

Johnson, Mrs. Lyndon. Oral history interview XVI. Interviewed by Michael Gillette. Casa Lenore, Acapulco, Mexico. February 1, 1980.

Jones, Wesley W. and Joe D. LaCrone. "History of Amarillo Air Force Base." Unpublished essay, 1968.

Kahl, C.M. Interview with author. Marfa, Texas, October 11, 1999.

Keil, Sally Van Wagenen. *Those Wonderful Women in their Flying Machines.* New York; Four Directions Press, 1999.

"Kelly Field Vertical File." Institute of Texan Cultures, San Antonio, Texas.

Knight, Oliver. *Fort Worth: Outpost on the Trinity.* Fort Worth: TCU Press, 1989.

Koontz, William. "Gibbs Field 1988 Reunion Questionnaire," 1988.

Kuykendall, Lucy Roundtree. *P.S. to Pecos.* Houston: The Anson Jones Press, 1946.

The Laredo Times: November 1, 1940; May 13, 1942; May 14, 1942; May 31, 1942; January 13, 1943; January 20, 1943; January 21, 1943; January 24, 1943; February 3, 1943; February 16, 1943; May 20, 1979.

Leibowitz, Vincent. Interview with author. Greenville, Texas, October 15, 1998.

Letter from Ben [no last name given] to David Hutchinson, April 3, 2000. Vertical Files, XIT Museum. Dalhart, Texas.

Life Magazine. May 18, 1942.

Long, James S. Interview with author. Del Rio, Texas, October 4, 1999.

"Love Field Overview." Dallas Municipal Archives and Record Center. (File #87-3931) Dallas: Office of the City Secretary, 1992.

Lubbock Avalanche-Journal: April 16, 1941; June 21, 1941; June 22, 1941; November 12, 1949; November 6, 1967; June 4, 1991; March 15, 1992.

Luce, Nila and Bob Luce. "Gibbs Field." *Pecos County History*. Canyon (TX): Staked Plains Press, 1984.

Lydon, James. Letter to author. August 6, 1998.

Manning, Thomas, Pat Parrish, and Dick Emmons. "Randolph Field." *A History of Military Aviation in San Antonio*. San Antonio: History Office, Air Education and Training Command, 1996.

Maurer, Maurer. *Aviation in the U. S. Army, 1919-1939*. Washington, D.C.: U.S. Government Printing Office, 1986.

Midland Reporter-Telegram: June 13, 1940; November 19, 1940; June 13, 1941.

Miller, Tom. Letter to Lyndon Johnson, April 9, 1941. Letter Box 27, Lyndon B. Johnson Library, Austin, Texas.

Monahans News. July 31, 1942.

Murillo, Hermelina Aguirre. "A History of Webb County." Master's thesis, Southwest Texas State Teachers College, 1941.

National World War II Glider Pilots Association Fact Book. Oshkosh (WI) Experimental Aircraft Association, July 1992.

New York Daily News. June 25, 1943.

Odessa American. March 20, 1988.

Office of History, San Antonio Air Logistics Center, Kelly Air Force Base, Texas. *A Pictorial History of Kelly Air Force Base, 1917-1980*. San Antonio. n.d.

The Official World War II Guide to the Army Air Forces: A Directory, Almanac and Chronicle of Achievement, 1944. (Reprint). New York: Bonanza Books, 1988.

Pampa News: March 14, 1942; May 15, 1942; May 23, 1942; July 23, 1942; November 22, 1942; December 15, 1942; February 21, 1943; February 23, 1943; February 28, 1943; March 7, 1943; January 5, 1944; September 23, 1945.

Pate, J'Nell. "Impact of the Military Base Called Carswell." Paper given at the annual meeting of the Texas State Historical Association. Dallas, Texas, March 3, 1999.

Paulette, Irene. "Odessa During the War Years." *The Permian Historical Annual, XVI*. Odessa (TX): The Permian Historical Commission, 1981.

Peck, Kay. "The Night They (Whoops!) Bombed Boise City." *Ford Times*, July 1983. Dearborn (MI): The Ford Motor Company.

Porter, Mike. Interview with author. Pampa, Texas. August 17, 2001.

Raimond, Vance Delone. *Transportation: Key to the Magic Valley*. Edinburg (TX): Santander Press, 1996.

"Rattlesnake Bomber Base Museum Dedication Program." April 22, 1978.

Rehnquist, William H. Letter to author. June 11, 1999.

"Report of the 47th Comptrollor Flight." Laughlin Air Force Base, 1999.

Riggs, Gene. Interview with author. Fort Stockton, Texas, February 12, 2002.

Rogers, Mary Beth, Sherry A. Smith and Janelle D. Scott. *We Can Fly: Stories of Katherine Stinson and Other Gutsy Texas Women Pilots*. Austin: Ellen C. Temple, Publisher, 1983.

Russell, Paul O. Letter to author. January 12, 2002.

Russell, Ron. Interview with author. Amarillo, Texas. October 8, 1998.

San Antonio Evening News. December 18, 1951.

San Antonio Express: June 20, 1930; July 29, 1976.

San Antonio Light: July 8, 1911; June 20, 1930.

Savage, Rod. *Who's Who: Pampa Army Airfield Association Reunion Directory*. Pampa (TX): The Pampa Army Airfield Association, 1988.

Selvagi, Rossi L. "A History of Randolph Air Force Base." Master's thesis, University of Texas, 1958.

Silent Wings. National World War II Glider Pilots Association. March 1994.

Sligh, Robert. *Bergstrom AFB: A History*. Austin: Bergstrom/Austin Community Council, 1993.

Smith, Thomas T. *The U. S. Army & the Texas Frontier Economy, 1845-1900*. College Station: Texas A&M University Press, 1999.

Socioeconomic Impact Analysis Study of Disposal and Reuse of Carswell AFB, Washington, D.C.: Department of Defense, 1985.

Solo, The Yearbook of Cadet Class 43-A, Gibbs Field, Texas. Fort Stockton: Gibbs Field Public Information Office. 1943.

Spurgin, W.T. to A.B. Davis. April 9, 1941. A.B. Davis File 15-8 C. Southwest Collection/Special Collections Library. Texas Tech University, Lubbock, Texas.

State Superintendent of Public Instruction Annual Report, 1940. Austin: Department of Education, 1940.

"Status Update: Formerly Used Defense Site Environmental Investigations at the Former Laredo Air Force Base." Tulsa: U.S. Army Corps of Engineers. 1997. Vertical Files. Laredo Public Library Historical Collection.

Stephens, A. Ray and William M. Holmes. *Historical Atlas of Texas.* Norman: University of Oklahoma Press, 1989.

Stevens, Allard E. Letter to Paul O. Russell, December 1, 1997. Laughlin Heritage Foundation Files, Del Rio, Texas.

Syers, W.E. "Death of the Aluminum Warrior." *Texas Parade.* Vol. XXII, No. 5, (October 1961).

Tanner, Doris Brinker. Comp. *Who Were the WASP?* Sweetwater (TX): *The Sweetwater Daily Reporter*, 101.

Tarfu: March 12, 1943; September 12, 1944.

Texas Almanac, 1955-1956. Dallas: A.H. Belo Corporation, 1955.

Texas Almanac and State Industrial Guide, 1939-1940. Dallas: A.H. Belo Corporation, 1939.

Texas Almanac and State Industrial Guide, 1943-1944. Dallas: A.H. Belo Corporation, 1943.

Texas Almanac and State Industrial Guide, 1949-1950. Dallas: A.H. Belo Corporation, 1949.

Thomas, F.E., Jr. Interview with author. Fredericksburg, Texas, January 31, 2002.

Thompson, Cecilia. *History of Marfa and Presidio County, Texas 1535-1946.* Austin: Nortex Press, 1986.

Thompson, Robert D. *We'll Find the Way: The History of Hondo Army Air Field During World War II.* Austin: Eakin Press, 1992.

Tudor, William G. "Flight of Eagles: The Mexican Expeditionary Air Force 'Escuadron' 201 in World War II." PhD. diss., Texas Christian University, 1997.

Tyler, Ron. Ed. *The New Handbook of Texas*, 6 Vols. Austin: The Texas State Historical Association, 1996.

United States Army Air Forces Directory of Airports, Vol. 3. Washington, D.C.: War Department, 1945.

"USAF Almanac, 1998." *Air Force Magazine.* 81, No. 5. (May 1998).

U.S. Army Air Forces Directory of Airports, Vol. III, Washington, D.C.: War Department, 1944.

Valley Morning Star. January 12, 1941; February 1, 1941; July 30, 1944; November 12, 1960; June 20, 1963; July 30, 1964; August 12, 1997.

Wagner, Ray. *American Combat Planes.* Garden City (NY): Doubleday Company, 1981.

Watson, Florene (Miller). Telephone interview with author, March 8, 2002.

Warnock, Kirby F. "Wings West of the Pecos." *Big Bend Quarterly.* Summer, 1999.

Webb, Walter Prescott, Ed. *The Handbook of Texas, Vol. II.* Austin: The Texas Historical Association. 1952.

Webster's American Military Biographies. Springfield (Mass): G. & C. Merriam Company, 1978.

Welles, Marie Tanner. Interview with author. San Antonio, Texas, July 13, 2000.

Wentz, John. Inteview with author. Hondo, Texas, September 13, 1999.

Yeats, E.L. and Hooper Shelton. *History of Nolan County, Texas.* Sweetwater (TX): Shelton Press, 1975.

A P P E N D I X

United States Army Airfields Located In Texas During World War II

Abilene Army Airfield (AAF) Also known as Tye Field	Abilene	Became Dyess Air Force Base. (AFB). Still active (2002).
Aloe AAF	Victoria	Now a private facility.
Amarillo AAF	Amarillo	Became Amarillo AFB. Deactivated 1968. Now Amarillo's Airport.
Arledge Field	Stamford	Now a municipal airport.
Bergstrom Field	Austin	Became Bergstrom AFB. Deactivated. Now Austin Bergstrom International Airport.
Big Spring AAF	Big Spring	Became Webb AFB. Deactivated 1977. Now a municipal airport, prison, and Hanger 25 Air Museum.
Biggs Field	El Paso	Became Biggs AFB. Deactivated 1966. Now Army facility on Fort Bliss.
Blackland AAF	Waco	Now Waco Field
Bonham Municipal Airport	Bonham	Now a municipal airport.
Brooks Field	San Antonio	Became Brooks AFB. Deactivated 2002.
Brownwood AAF	Brownwood	Now a municipal airport.
Brownsville Municipal Airport	Brownsville	Now a municipal airport.
Bruce Field	Ballinger	Now a municipal airport.
Bryan AAF	Bryan	Became Bryan AFB. Deactivated 1961. Now part of Texas A&M University.
Childress AAF	Childress	Now a prison.
Coleman Flying School	Coleman	Now a municipal airport.
Corsicana Field	Corsicana	Now a municipal airport.
Cox Field	Paris	Now a municipal airport.
Cuero Municipal Airport	Cuero	Now a municipal airport.
Curtis Field	Brady	Now Brady municipal airport.
Dalhart AAF	Dalhart	Now a municipal airport.
Eagle Pass AAF	Eagle Pass	Now a county housing project.
Ellington Field	Houston	Became Ellington AFB. Deactivated 1976. Now the city airport.
Fort Worth AAF	Fort Worth	Became Carswell AFB. Deactivated 1992. Now a joint reserve base.
Foster Field	Victoria	Now a municipal airport.
Gainesville AAF	Gainesville	Now a municipal airport.
Galveston AAF	Galveston	Now a municipal airport.
Gibbs Field	Fort Stockton	Now a county airport.
Goodfellow Field	San Angelo	Became Goodfellow AFB. Still Active (2002).
Harlingen AAF	Harlingen	Became Harlingen AFB. Deactivated 1962. Now a regional airport.
Hicks Field	Fort Worth	Now a privately owned airport.
Hondo AAF	Hondo	Became Hondo AFB. Deactivated 1958. Now a municipal airport.
Kelly Field	San Antonio	Became Kelly AFB. Deactivated 1998. Now an industrial park.
Lamesa Field	Lamesa	Now a municipal airport.

Laredo AAF	Laredo	Became Laredo AFB. Deactivated 1973. Part is now city airport.
Laughlin Field	Del Rio	Became Laughlin AFB. Still Active (2002).
Love Field	Dallas	Now a city airport.
Lubbock AAF	Lubbock	Became Reese AFB. Deactivated 1997. Now a technological center.
Majors Field	Greenville	Now a Raytheon facility and a municipal airport.
Marfa AAF	Marfa	Vanished.
Midland AAF	Midland	Now the Midland Airport and the Commemorative Air Force Museum.
Moore Field	Mission	Became Moore AFB. Deactivated 1960. Now a Department of Agriculture facility.
Pampa AAF	Pampa	Now a feedlot.
Pecos AAF	Pecos	Now the municipal airport.
Perrin Field	Sherman	Became Perrin AFB. Deactivated 1970. Now a county facility.
Pounds Field	Tyler	Now the municipal airport.
Pyote AAF	Pyote	Vanished
Randolph Field	San Antonio	Became Randolph AFB. Still active (2002)
San Marcos AAF	San Marcos	Now an airport.
Sheppard Field	Wichita Falls	Became Sheppard AFB. Still active (2002).
South Plains AAF	Lubbock	Became Lubbock's airport.
Sweetwater Municipal Airport (Avenger Field)	Sweetwater	Now a municipal airport and a Texas State Technical College Campus.
Victory Field	Vernon	Now a state hospital unit.
Waco AAF	Waco	Became James Connally AFB. Deactivated 1966. Now a Texas State Technical College Campus.
Wink Auxiliary Field	Wink	Now Winkler County Airport

Note: Other auxiliary fields, gunnery and bombing practice facilities, and emergency landing fields were located throughout the state of Texas from 1940 through mid-1945.

I N D E X